# Protect your people – and your business

Bryan Toone BSc (Eng) CEng MICE CFIOSH

## What the experts say

"People responsible for managing small or medium-sized enterprises, and middle managers in larger companies, are often confused and feel threatened by the complexities of health and safety in the workplace. This book provides comprehensive information on what needs to be done, and how to do it. By applying the clear and simply expressed guidance in this book, managers can expect to establish sensible standards of health and safety at work."

Tony Linehan FIOSH
Former HM Chief Inspector of Factories
and Director of Field Operations, Health and Safety Executive

"An excellent, down-to-earth, easy-to-use guide to the essentials of health and safety. The wealth of information should be invaluable to business managers."

Dr Rodger Evans MIOSH
Deputy Chief Executive
Constructing Excellence

"Bryan Toone helped us enormously by taking the jargon and the mystery out of health and safety language. He presented our programme simply and clearly so that our managers understood and accepted positively their role. It's an approach that really works."

Tony Coles
Managing Director
La Manga Club
Inmogolf SA

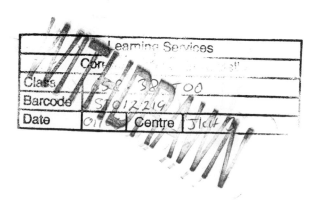

## Foreword from the Federation of Small Businesses

Today, health and safety policies are more than just a legislative requirement. Good practice within the workplace can bring genuine business benefits to the small firm. The majority of small businesses want to comply with health and safety legislation and consult with their employees on best practice in the workplace for a productive workforce and business. However, SMEs are not always well resourced to deal with the complexities of health and safety and do not necessarily see bodies such as the Health and Safety Executive as the first point of contact.

Small businesses need access to a health and safety infrastructure that is both effective and useful, with a minimum burden on their ability to operate. Within my own company, I know that the initial formalisation and production of a health and safety policy can be daunting for a small business. The work involved in maintaining and reviewing it to ensure that it continues to be relevant and effective is time-consuming for a small employer. *Protect your people – and your business* offers practical advice, which is very welcome.

The plain English style of writing and easy-to-follow navigation guide will be of benefit to small employers who need to be able to find information quickly and easily. We also believe the practical advice for dealing with employee health issues and the simple checklists within each chapter will be of use to businesses with fewer than 50 employees.

The Federation of Small Businesses supports the work of IOSH in making health and safety more accessible to small businesses.

Mary Boughton
Chairman
Health, Safety and Risk Management Committee
Federation of Small Businesses

The FSB is the UK's leading non-party political lobbying group for small businesses, existing to promote and protect the interests of all who own and/or manage their own businesses. With over 185,000 members, the FSB is also the largest organisation representing small and medium-sized businesses in the UK.

## About the author

Bryan Toone was born and brought up in Hertfordshire. He graduated from Queen Mary College, University of London in 1969 with a degree in civil engineering, and became a chartered civil engineer at the age of 25. He managed civil engineering and building projects in the UK and Middle East until, at the age of 37, he was appointed health and safety director of Bovis, an international construction company.

Bovis was part of the P&O group, with interests in shipping, ferries, cruises, ports, transport, leisure, hotels, exhibitions, catering, construction and property. Bryan was co-opted to the group safety committee and became a leading auditor and adviser to a diverse range of P&O companies worldwide.

At Bovis he gained a reputation for innovation in construction safety, introducing many then-new concepts such as safety management systems and weekly toolbox talks. He established a health and safety consultancy, held the post of planning supervisor for Terminal 5 at Heathrow Airport, and carried out work environment surveys and risk assessments for the Department of Transport. His current appointment is as health, safety and environment director for the Ardmore Group, a medium-sized, privately owned enterprise specialising in building, civil engineering, rail and plant hire.

Professionally, Bryan is a Chartered Safety and Health Practitioner and Member of Council of IOSH. He has presented papers at conferences in the UK, USA and Europe, and writes a health and safety newsletter for the Institution. He lives with his wife and children in Hertfordshire.

## Publisher's note

IOSH and IOSH Services Limited assume no responsibility for the contents of this book, in whole or in part, nor for interpretations or concepts advanced by the author. The views expressed in this book are the author's own, and do not necessarily reflect those of any employing or other organisation.

This edition is checked for technical updates regularly.
Visit **www.iosh.co.uk/publications** for any revisions.

# Acknowledgements

I am deeply indebted to the following people and organisations for their help, support, knowledge, patience and enthusiasm.

First and foremost, to my editor Trevor Anderson and publisher Caroline Brookes, for working so hard on this project and for truly understanding what this book is all about. And to Bill Edwards for creating so many excellent illustrations and layouts.

I must express my gratitude to the exceptional team at IOSH for their generosity, faith and guidance. Thank you especially to Rob Strange, Chief Executive, the IOSH Services Board for backing the project over more than two years, and Richard Jones, Director of Technical Affairs, for his review and constructive suggestions.

I must acknowledge, as my principal source, the superb publications of the Health and Safety Executive. We are lucky in the UK to have such a wealth of guidance available. The publications that I used for each chapter are listed in Appendix C, although of necessity I have been selective in choosing the material to include.

My other major source was the website of the Food Standards Agency, used in Chapter 9 in relation to food hygiene. In the same chapter the material on manual handling in laundries was sourced from the website of the Canadian Centre for Occupational Health and Safety. Other sources are referred to in Appendix C.

Above all, I must acknowledge the contribution of my wife Patricia in providing the environment, support and encouragement to get this book written.

Bryan Toone

Some figures in this book are based on material from the following HSE publications:

Health and safety in construction (HSG150)
Aching arms (or RSI) in small businesses (INDG171)
Health and safety in engineering workshops (HSG129)
Circular saw benches (WIS16)
Safety in the use of hand-fed planing machines (WIS17)
Health and safety in kitchens and food preparation areas (HSG55)
Health and safety in retail and wholesale warehouses (HSG76)

# Introduction

Six years ago I sat in the office of the managing director of a famous golf and leisure resort in southern Spain. He was explaining to me a problem that was causing him great concern. Some months before he had received the report of health and safety auditors from his group headquarters in London. Written in the technical language of risk management, the uncompromising message required him to set in place a plan for improvement immediately. He had struggled with the report, and remarked to me that "this mountain just seems to get bigger the more I look at it".

I examined the problem. The enterprise was huge: 2,000 villas, three championship golf courses, a tennis club with 21 courts, a professional football training centre with seven pitches, a fitness centre, a 5-star hotel, a water treatment plant, ongoing construction projects, roads, shops, 17 restaurants, three swimming pools, and the workshops and maintenance facilities to keep the whole thing running. It was a green oasis in a near desert, patronised by the rich and famous – and it all ran like clockwork.

So what was the problem? Of course there are health and safety issues in any organisation, especially one with such a range of activities. The management team had built the resort out of the arid landscape and had made it a success. Surely they could manage health and safety.

Well, we proved they could. Over the next few years I visited the resort twice a year, guiding them through the issues by showing them how to deal with them in a practical manner. Eventually the corporate auditors visited again, and this time they were delighted with the progress, judging the resort's health and safety to be "very satisfactory".

Which brings me to this book. Everything that was needed in Spain is written down here, and I know it works. It is based on over 20 years' experience helping managers address health and safety, experience that covers construction, exhibitions, transport, ports, offices, factories and, of course, leisure. It is not written as an examination text, but as a practical handbook for practical people, especially busy managers and supervisors in enterprises of any size and type. It is not intended to supplant the work of the health and safety professional, but its use will enable managers to help themselves, decide when they need assistance, and be able to judge the quality of the advice they are getting. I also hope the book will prove useful to the health and safety specialist, as I have gathered together as much useful data as possible to provide a ready source of daily reference.

This book explains how to identify and control hazards in the workplace. Much is common sense, but history is littered with examples where common sense was insufficient. Risk thinking is needed, and this book provides a foundation and guide through the subject in a concise and readable, yet thorough and authoritative manner. My reference throughout has been the publications of the Health and Safety Executive, and I both acknowledge this source and commend it to any reader who wishes to know more.

"When anyone asks me how I can best describe my experience of nearly forty years at sea, I merely say uneventful.

Of course there have been winter gales and storms and fog and the like, but in all my experience, I have never been in an accident of any sort worth speaking about.

I have seen but one vessel in distress in all my years at sea … I never saw a wreck and have never been wrecked, nor was I ever in any predicament that threatened to end in disaster of any sort."

From a paper presented by E J Smith in 1907.

On 14 April 1912, *RMS* Titanic sank with the loss of 1,500 lives. The captain went down with the ship.

His name – E J Smith.

## Using the book

The easiest and most systematic way of addressing health and safety in any business is to break the subject down into four components or stages:

- management

- premises

- fire

- operations.

This approach forms the structure of *Protect your people.*

The book is intended as an overview of health and safety for managers, and a broad source of reference for safety professionals. It cannot hope to cover every subject in sufficient detail to provide a solution to all the risks that each industry may face. Managers must therefore seek professional health and safety advice where appropriate.

We look first at the management issues that every organisation faces. This includes chapters on writing a health and safety policy and how to deal with risk, which form the foundation of the whole health and safety process. Next, we examine premises – the physical working environment – then look at fire protection and prevention. Finally, we focus on the physical activities that are carried out in the workplace – the operational issues.

The chapters covering operational issues focus on different sectors but, of course, many enterprises include elements from more than one. For example, you may be the manager of a workshop that has a canteen, in which case the 'Workshops and factories' and 'Hotels, restaurants and catering' chapters will be of particular relevance to you.

Three operational issues are covered in stand-alone chapters in their own right, as they apply to all of the sectors included in the book. These are health, maintenance and facilities management, and contractors.

Also contained in *Protect your people* are clear and succinct checklists to help you review systematically the health and safety of your organisation, assess the risks, and formulate a plan for improvement. These checklists are available to download at www.protect.org.uk. Finally, the book ends with supplementary appendices that provide a raft of useful information on health and safety tools, toolbox talks and legislation and guidance.

The following diagram illustrates the various stages and chapters in *Protect your people,* and at the same time represents an overview of the whole health and safety process for a typical enterprise.

## The four stages

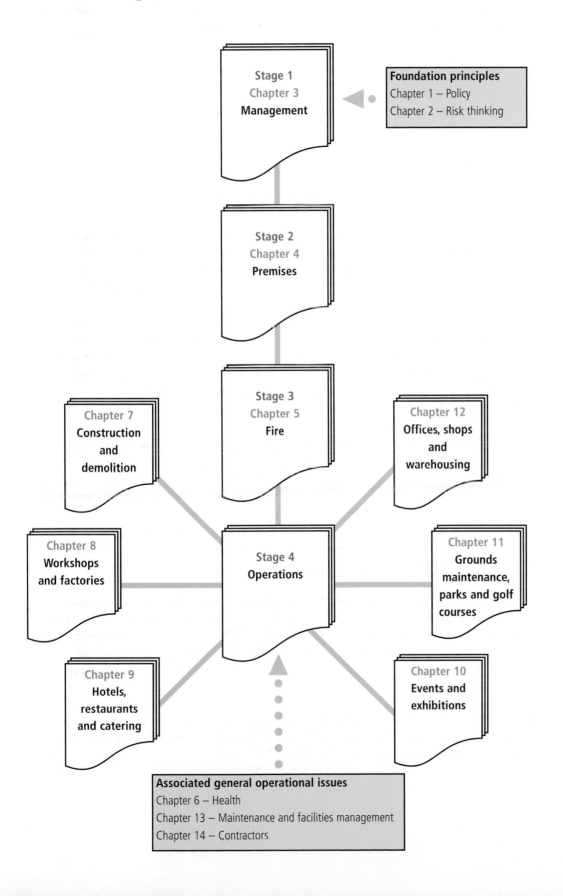

**Stage 1**
Chapter 3
**Management**

**Foundation principles**
Chapter 1 – Policy
Chapter 2 – Risk thinking

**Stage 2**
Chapter 4
**Premises**

**Stage 3**
Chapter 5
**Fire**

Chapter 7
**Construction and demolition**

Chapter 12
**Offices, shops and warehousing**

Chapter 8
**Workshops and factories**

**Stage 4**
**Operations**

Chapter 11
**Grounds maintenance, parks and golf courses**

Chapter 9
**Hotels, restaurants and catering**

Chapter 10
**Events and exhibitions**

**Associated general operational issues**
Chapter 6 – Health
Chapter 13 – Maintenance and facilities management
Chapter 14 – Contractors

# Navigation guide

*Protect your people* includes an icon system to help you find what you're looking for quickly and at a glance.

The human costs associated with health and safety failures can be an alarming wake-up call. These statistics and data boxes give you an idea of the real world downsides of bad health and safety management.

These give you the references for the printed checklists or other documents so that you can locate and download them from our dedicated website, www.protect.org.uk.

These boxes offer a concise summary of some of the key points in the preceding section. They typically focus on hard-and-fast legal requirements.

Health risks sometimes need more of an in-depth explanation. These boxes contain detail on specific health problems.

These jargon-buster boxes explain, in simple terms, words and phrases that are commonly used In health and safety.

Relevant sections are cross-referenced to ensure that you get the full picture on a particular issue.

# Contents

## Introduction

By law, if you employ five or more people you must have a written health and safety policy. This is not optional; you must have one. Even if fewer than five people work for you, it's good practice to have a policy.

There should be three components to the policy:

- a brief policy statement that expresses the organisation's commitment and approach to health and safety

- an organisational structure to discharge the statement; in other words, an outline of who does what

- arrangements to identify and manage risk that protect the health and safety of the workforce and others.

The policy statement is the major element that every organisation must produce. The organisational structure is also important and usually takes the form of a health and safety organisation chart and a description of the health and safety role of each category of employee in the organisation. All employees have at least some part to play and this should be stated.

The organisation chart and job descriptions should be produced in a form that can be detached and given to each employee, so that everyone is absolutely clear about their duties and responsibilities.

The arrangements to identify and manage risk are more difficult, as many organisations need manuals or management systems in order to describe their arrangements fully. There is often uncertainty, therefore, about what to include in a concise policy document. The solution is to summarise the main points and refer to other manuals and files of risk assessments.

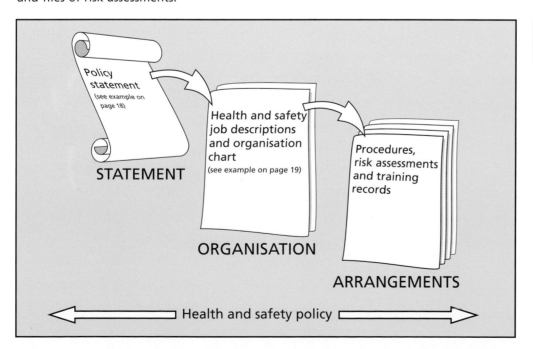

**Components of a health and safety policy**

## How to write a health and safety policy statement

A good health and safety policy statement will be inspirational. It is designed to be posted on notice boards to inform workers and clients alike that the organisation and its management are committed to health and safety, and often to the environment as well.

While the policy statement should be realistic, specific to the organisation, and reflect the environment in which the business operates, it should mention:

- the management's commitment to health and safety
- that health and safety contributes to the success of the organisation and is equal in importance to time, cost and quality
- that the organisation will comply with at least the minimum requirements of health and safety legislation, and is committed to progressive improvement
- the responsibilities of each level of management, eg that senior management will make financial and physical resources available; line management will assess risk and implement safe systems of work; and supervisors will ensure that safe systems are explained to the workforce and are implemented
- that the organisation will provide health and safety instruction and training, and will consult with and communicate to the workforce
- that a director or senior manager has been appointed to monitor health and safety performance, and state who is responsible to the board for health and safety policy
- who will provide expert health and safety advice
- the duty of employees and other workers to co-operate with supervisors and managers, not to interfere with health and safety provisions, to take care of their own health and safety and that of others, and report any health and safety concerns
- that the policy will be reviewed annually.

The statement should be signed and dated by the managing director.

## How to establish your organisational structure

Compile an organisation chart and outline the health and safety duties of the following:

- managing director
- health and safety director
- production directors
- commercial directors
- factory, facility or project managers
- line managers
- supervisors
- fire wardens
- commercial managers
- engineers
- health and safety adviser
- employees
- any other staff.

Ideally, the health and safety duties of staff should be set out in bullet point lists and each individual should be given a copy of the list that applies to their role in the organisation. A list of a typical manager's duties is included at the end of this chapter.

## How to set out your arrangements

Briefly outline the following:

- the purpose of risk assessments and the method by which they are to be carried out; make clear whose duty it is to carry out risk assessments and how they are to be recorded
- the results of generic risk assessments and how they are to be recorded
- the safe systems of work developed from the risk assessments and the organisation's health and safety procedures
- how consultation with employees will be carried out
- the means for ensuring that plant and equipment are safe and comply with statutory inspection requirements; make clear who has responsibility for maintenance, testing, monitoring and keeping records
- the means for ensuring safe handling and use of substances, including procedures, responsibilities and record-keeping
- what information, instruction, supervision, toolbox talks, task briefings and training should be provided to employees, who is responsible for this provision, and who is responsible for record-keeping
- accident reporting and health surveillance procedures
- monitoring arrangements, including workplace inspections and accident investigations
- fire and emergency procedures, and delegation of duties.

**Example of a health and safety policy statement**

---

EXAMPLE COMPANY LTD

# Health and safety policy statement

The Example Company Ltd is committed to working in a way that protects the health, safety and welfare of employees and others affected by our activities.

We will give equal regard to the environment, health and safety, production, quality and cost. We will act as good neighbours and provide employment that develops the potential of each employee. We will comply with legislation, as a minimum, and strive to improve performance on a continual basis.

We will promote equally the duties of management and employees. All employees, and others working on our premises, have a duty to co-operate with supervisors and managers, to maintain health and safety provisions, to take care of their own health and safety and that of others, and to report any concerns they may have or unsafe conditions they find. The company is committed to:

- providing a healthy and safe working environment
- identifying hazards and assessing risks
- providing safe systems of work
- providing information, training and instruction
- consulting with the workforce
- providing competent supervision
- providing personal protective equipment
- providing advice and monitoring
- providing adequate welfare facilities
- working with competent suppliers.

The company has appointed a director who is responsible for monitoring and reviewing this policy. However, all directors, managers and supervisors must accept responsibility for the health and safety at work of employees and others under their control. Directors are responsible for making available adequate physical and organisational resources. Managers must devise and implement safe systems of work, and supervisors must ensure that workers are briefed and consulted on the risks and comply with safe working practices. Ultimately, managers are responsible for ensuring that this policy is brought to the notice of all employees and others who may be affected by it.

The company has appointed safety advisers to provide monitoring, advice, training and instruction. They will carry out audits and inspections and bring to the attention of management any deficiency observed, and stop any operation that puts the company's employees or other persons at risk.

This policy will be reviewed annually.

**Managing Director**
**October 2004**

EXAMPLE COMPANY LTD

# Organisation chart

**Managing director (or board of directors in a large company)**
Has overall responsibility for the policy and establishing the health and safety culture of the organisation

**Health and safety director**
Monitors and reviews the implementation of the policy and leads the health and safety programme

**Production directors**
Provide adequate human and physical resources, and leadership in specific areas of operations

**Commercial directors**
Provide adequate financial resources to implement the programme

**Health and safety adviser**
Advises management on safe systems of work. Responsible for auditing and monitoring, and organising training

**Factory, facility or project managers, and engineers**
Devise and implement safe systems of work

**Commercial managers**
Procure competent suppliers and contractors, and safe, environmentally sound machinery

**Line managers, supervisors, fire wardens**
Consult with and brief employees, and ensure compliance with safe systems of work

**Employees**
Co-operate with supervisors, follow safe working practices, and report any health and safety concerns

This simplified organisation chart is an example of a workable structure for health and safety. The health and safety director is independent of operational management. Implementation of the policy is the responsibility of operational management. The role of the health and safety director will be full time in a large business, but can be carried out on a part-time basis by an appointed board director in a smaller organisation, who may not necessarily be a safety professional. In such cases, the director must have sufficient access to expert advice.

**Example of a typical manager's duties**

---

EXAMPLE COMPANY LTD

## Health and safety duties of a manager

- Implement the company's health and safety policy in the area being managed, eg facility, department or project.
- Administer the policy personally, or appoint a senior member of staff to carry out this function.
- Be aware of and implement the requirements of current legislation.
- Take professional health and safety advice where appropriate.
- Ensure that inspections and audits are carried out to monitor compliance with legislation and company standards and procedures.
- Insist that safe working practices are observed.
- Ensure that there are adequate resources, both in numbers of personnel and physical facilities, to carry out the policy.
- Delegate team duties and provide adequate health and safety instruction and training to enable the duties to be carried out properly.
- Investigate and, if appropriate, reprimand any member of staff who fails to discharge satisfactorily the responsibilities allocated to him or her.
- Ensure that the health and safety training needs of all staff are identified.
- Ensure that appropriate health and safety training is provided to all staff.
- Attend appropriate health and safety training courses.
- Appoint competent contractors and suppliers where required.
- Supervise a system of management to control and co-ordinate effectively the activities of contractors.
- Oversee accident and incident reporting and investigation, and promote action to prevent recurrence.
- Take advice and introduce measures to ensure a safe workplace.
- Ensure that welfare facilities are of a good standard and are well maintained.
- Liaise with external health and safety organisations.
- Encourage the distribution of relevant health and safety information.
- Establish or maintain a health and safety reference 'library' that is appropriate to the organisation.
- Chair a monthly health and safety committee meeting and produce minutes.
- Set a good example with regard to matters of health and safety.

### The bottom line

- By law, every organisation that employs five or more staff must write up a health and safety policy.
- There are three parts to a policy: a statement; an organisational structure; and arrangements to identify and manage risk.
- The policy is the tool that allows directors of an organisation to set out their commitment and approach, and to apportion duties to staff members.
- Policies should be communicated to everyone in the organisation and be reviewed regularly.

## Introduction

All employers and self-employed people have a legal duty to carry out health and safety risk assessments. Once the process is understood it is not difficult. If you can manage people you can certainly assess risks.

The object of the following diagram is to help you to evaluate what, in your organisation, could cause harm to people, the business or the environment. Then you can weigh up whether your existing precautions are adequate or more needs to be done.

## Risk thinking – the five stages

**Stage 1: Hazard identification**
Identify conditions or working practices that create a hazard. A hazard is anything with the potential to cause harm. Harm means injury, ill health or damage to equipment, premises, reputation or the environment.

**Stage 2: Risk assessment**
Decide who or what might be harmed by the hazard and assess the risk – high, medium or low – that harm will occur, and its severity.

**Stage 3: Plan risk control**
Decide on suitable measures to eliminate or control risk according to a 'hierarchy of risk control' that takes account of 'human factors'.

**Stage 4: Implement a safe system of work**
Write down a safe system of work in procedure or method statements, incorporating control measures. Provide training and implement the safe system.

**Stage 5: Monitor and review**
The safe system should be monitored and reviewed in operation and whenever something changes. It must be reviewed formally at least once a year.

**What are...**

**Human factors?**

Human factors is the term used to describe the organisational, environmental and job aspects, as well as individual and human characteristics, that can influence behaviour at work and, in turn, affect health and safety.

### Stage 1: Hazard identification

Examples of hazards include work at height, vehicles such as forklift trucks and delivery lorries, slips and trips on stairs or floors, chemicals, flammable materials, poor electrical wiring, work-related stress, repetitive activities, fumes from welding or vehicles, manual handling, use of vibrating tools, noise, poor lighting and food poisoning.

While hazard identification can be carried out simply by walking around the work premises and taking note of the hazards that are present, other ways of identifying hazards should not be overlooked, including:

- discussing tasks with your employees

- reading manufacturers' instructions and data sheets

- accident investigation and ill health records.

### Stage 2: Risk assessment

Risk assessment can be an onerous and complex process in high risk industries, but can be kept simple in most of the workplaces considered in this book. Risk is defined by the Health and Safety Executive (HSE) as follows:

Risk = Consequence severity × Likelihood of occurrence

The three categories of consequence severity are:

- Major – eg death or major injury, incapacitating ill health or dangerous occurrence, as defined by the HSE reporting regulations. Also included are lesser incidents that would excessively affect the business, such as food poisoning in a hotel.

- Serious – eg injuries or health problems that keep people off work for more than three days.

- Slight – lesser injuries or ill health than those noted above.

The three categories of likelihood of occurrence are:

- High – where it is almost certain that harm will occur, or where large numbers of people are exposed to the hazard.

- Medium – where harm will occur frequently.

- Low – where harm will occur infrequently.

The first step is to decide who or what might be harmed by the hazard.

The risk calculator opposite is a useful tool in assessing risk to those identified, taking the specific circumstances into account. It is unnecessary to follow the process exactly, as in many cases it will be sufficient to judge the risk level – high, medium or low – directly. But the process should include consideration of the aspects outlined above.

When assessing risk, do not overlook its potential impact on the public, contractors, young employees, trainees, pregnant women and nursing mothers, visitors, cleaners, maintenance workers and security guards. They all may be affected.

| Severity of harm | major | medium | high | intolerable |
|---|---|---|---|---|
| | serious | low | medium | high |
| | slight | low | low | medium |
| | | low | medium | high |
| | | Likelihood of occurrence | | |

**What is...**

**A risk calculator?**
The risk calculator can be used to convert the severity and likelihood values into individual high, medium or low assessments of risk, which can then be linked to required action. In certain circumstances, safety specialists use more sophisticated versions of this model.

### Environmental and reputation risks

For many employers, particularly large organisations and multi-nationals, reputation is everything. They need to be seen as good corporate citizens who do not harm the environment or the community, including the people who work for the organisation and those who use its products or services. However, a good reputation is important for all businesses, irrespective of size, so do not confine your risk thinking to injuries, but follow the leaders of industry and include this wider context.

### Stage 3: Plan risk control

Risk assessment is pointless unless the process leads to action to reduce risk. When deciding on control measures, you must observe the following principles:

- The object of the exercise is to make all risks 'low' or to reduce them 'so far as is reasonably practicable'.

- The first step is to comply with the requirements of the law, as many of these are absolute and must be complied with.

- Following this, the hierarchy of risk control applies:

  1. Avoid the process or change to one that is safer.

  2. Introduce collective measures to prevent people coming into contact with the hazard, eg guarding or edge protection to prevent falls, or engineering out the risk.

  3. Minimise risk by using safe procedures, including both training and supervision.

  4. Provide personal protective equipment (PPE).

**What is...**

**'So far as is reasonably practicable'?**
These words crop up constantly in health and safety law and guidance. They mean that you must do what is reasonable, in the eyes of a judge, to eliminate a hazard or reduce a risk. What is done should be proportional to the risk, so that a high risk will demand substantial expense, trouble and time to reduce it. By contrast, a low or medium risk would not demand an expenditure out of all relation to the benefit.

In the hierarchy it is necessary to work from one through to four in that order. It is much safer, for example, to have machines made with fixed guards than issue instructions on using PPE.

When looking at the risk calculator, an 'intolerable' risk means that the process is wrong and must be changed. Likewise, high risk must be reduced by going through the hierarchy, deciding on control measures, and then doing the risk assessment again to ensure that it has been reduced so far as is reasonably practicable. After a further review, it should be possible to reduce medium risks to low by seeking out best practice.

**Stage 4: Implement a safe system of work**
A safe system of work includes the following elements:

- a written risk assessment and method statement detailing the safe procedure, including a task briefing for employees and the control measures required, eg any PPE that may be required

- skills and health and safety training

- regular inspection

- systematic maintenance

- record-keeping, so that you can prove you assessed risks and briefed your employees accordingly.

**Stage 5: Monitor and review**
The safe system of work must be reviewed regularly, particularly after initial implementation or when a process changes. It is useful to put a review date on the procedure document or method statement, indicating at least an annual review.

## A practical risk assessment tool

The 'Risk assessment and method statement' in Appendix A contains all of the essential elements in a format that will guide you through the process. You could devise your own form, however this one shows you the processes involved. But remember – you know your organisation best, and only you can decide if the hazards listed apply to your situation. There may be other hazards that reveal themselves either through chance or by talking to your employees. So keep an open mind and do not get into the 'tick the box' mode too readily.

**The bottom line**

- The law requires that risk assessment is carried out, but does not prescribe how it should be done.
- There are five stages to risk thinking – identify hazards, assess risks, plan risk control measures, implement a safe system of work, and monitor and review.
- A hazard is anything with the potential to cause harm.
- A risk is the chance – high, medium or low – that someone or something will be harmed by the hazard.
- Risk = Consequence severity × Likelihood of occurrence.
- The hierarchy of risk control must be used to decide on the safe system of work.
- It is essential that employees receive a task briefing on the safe system of work.

# How to establish a positive health and safety culture

In order to manage health and safety in any organisation, it is essential to establish a positive health and safety culture. Central to this is the understanding, on the part of everyone in the organisation, that excellent health and safety is a priority of the directors, and that the managing director really means what he or she says in the policy statement.

Unfortunately, there is a deep-seated belief on the part of many employees, in enterprises both large and small, that profit is the main driver and that health and safety is low down the list of priorities. However, there are constant reminders that reputation is all important to business confidence and even survival. Combine that with ever-increasing fines imposed on organisations that have neglected their health and safety responsibilities and the threat of liability for corporate manslaughter, and the case for devoting extra effort and resources to health and safety becomes persuasive.

The problem is that it is not easy both to devise a practical health and safety programme and to stick to it. It requires investment, effort and discipline. It is no easier to persuade employees to follow a safe system of work than it is, say, to follow the Highway Code at all times and in all circumstances. It takes both encouragement and enforcement.

The single person most able to establish a positive health and safety culture is the managing director. He or she is the guiding force behind the organisation. If the managing director makes every effort to highlight the importance of health and safety issues, this will have a 'trickle down' effect on managers and employees alike.

The most direct action for a managing director to take is to appoint a good health and safety adviser, and then show 100 per cent support for that person.

### The health and safety programme and leadership
The health and safety programme needs to address the following if it is to be successful:

**1. Establish a health and safety policy and culture**
- Write a proactive health and safety policy statement.

- Allocate health and safety responsibilities to line managers and supervisors in writing, and explain the responsibilities to them.

- Nominate a board director to be responsible for the health and safety programme.

**2. Set up an organisational structure capable of controlling the risks**
- Appoint an expert health and safety adviser, either an employee or consultant, depending on the size of the organisation.

- Ensure that those with health and safety responsibilities are competent (see 'What is...' box on right), by providing adequate training and experience.

- Hold individuals accountable for poor health and safety performance, and reward good performance.

**Also read...**

Chapter 1 – How to write a health and safety policy statement

Chapter 1 – Health and safety duties of a manager

**What is...**

**A competent person?**
A competent person is someone who has the appropriate skills, training, knowledge, experience and personal qualities to carry out the tasks assigned to them. This could be an outside organisation, a consultant or an employee. Ultimately, the decision on who to appoint lies with the employer.

- Provide adequate supervision, instruction and guidance to employees. A workforce that is constantly changing will need extra supervision.

- Ensure that employees are trained and competent. Keep records of training.

- As implementing the various aspects of the programme can be time-consuming, allow people sufficient time to do so.

- Talk to your employees and follow up on any suggestions that they may have.

- Set up a safety committee.

3. Identify the hazards, decide on the best way to minimise the risks, and implement a safe system of work

- Complete the 'Health and safety programme' checklist in this chapter and ensure that each item is addressed – they are all legal requirements.

- Carry out a survey and risk assessment of your premises (see Chapter 4) and establish an action plan to correct any shortfalls.

- Carry out a fire precautions survey and risk assessment of your premises (see Chapter 5) and establish an action plan to correct any shortfalls.

- Carry out a risk assessment to identify the hazards associated with work tasks and put measures in place to reduce the risk to acceptable levels (see Chapter 2). This process must be recorded. Use Chapters 6 to 14 to guide you on specifics.

- Set targets for accident reduction, accident investigation, workplace health and safety inspections, training, and the involvement of managers and supervisors.

- Set up maintenance contracts or, depending on in-house expertise and time available, introduce an internal maintenance programme.

### 4. Check that the programme is working

- Health and safety advisers and managers (or supervisors) must carry out regular inspections of the workplace. The health and safety adviser's inspections should be carried out at least once a month. Weekly inspections are more appropriate if you work in a high risk environment. Reports must be produced and issued very soon after the inspection, and copies should be provided to senior management. Supervisors should inspect their areas daily, and take immediate action to correct any observed unsafe working practices or conditions. These inspections are known as 'proactive monitoring'. A 'Safety, health and welfare inspection report' form is included in Appendix A.

- Self-audit the programme (which can be done using the checklists provided in this book).

- Collect and report health and safety statistics.

- Report and investigate accidents to decide what remedial action can be taken to prevent a recurrence. This is known as 'reactive monitoring'.

### 5. Review performance

- Produce a monthly report for each part of the organisation that details:
  - assessment of physical conditions and the actions required
  - concerns
  - positive comments
  - accidents and near-miss incidents
  - accident frequency rate or incident rate
  - operations stopped on safety grounds
  - training achievement and needs.

  The health and safety adviser usually compiles this report, which should be considered and acted on by the directors.

- Produce an annual report and set new targets, striving for a year-on-year improvement.

- You may wish to follow the lead of some organisations and commission an external, independent audit of your health and safety programme, in order to set in place a plan for the following two or three years.

**Hard facts**

Getting health and safety wrong can land business owners in jail. A building boss was sentenced to 18 months in custody after being found guilty of double manslaughter. Following the collapse of a tunnel kiln, two men died after being buried under tonnes of rubble. The accused was charged under the Health and Safety at Work etc Act for failing to provide a safe system of work and information, instruction, training and supervision, as well as under the Construction (Design and Management) Regulations. The company was fined £125,000.

## Health and safety programme

The management issues noted above are all legal requirements that you must address. Use the following checklist to review them, and follow the guidance that illustrates good business practice.

www.protect.org.uk

PDF 01

| Item | Management action | Yes | No |
|------|-------------------|-----|-----|
| 1 | Write a health and safety policy statement | | |
| 2 | Carry out workplace risk assessments | | |
| 3 | Display the statutory 'Health and safety law' poster | | |
| 4 | Appoint health and safety representatives | | |
| 5 | Appoint a health and safety adviser | | |
| 6 | Publish fire and emergency arrangements | | |

| Guidance and good business practice |
|---|
| A health and safety policy statement must be produced and posted on a notice board (see Chapter 1). |
| There are various risk assessments that need to be carried out. These are:<br>• specific activities or tasks (see Chapter 2)<br>• premises (see Chapter 4)<br>• fire (see Chapter 5).<br>These chapters will lead you through the process in a straightforward manner and by completing the checklists you will record your assessments. |
| Obtain a 'Health and safety law' poster from The Stationery Office and put it on a notice board. Fill in the names of the appointed health and safety representatives and the name of the safety adviser. In addition, the address of the local Health and Safety Executive (HSE) office must be provided. |
| There is extensive legislation requiring employers to consult with their employees, to allow health and safety representatives to be appointed, and a health and safety committee to be formed. Health and safety committees that include both supervisors and employees, and are chaired by a senior manager, can prove to be an effective means of two-way communication and mutual understanding between management and employees. |
| Every business must have access to competent health and safety advice. Depending on the size of the organisation and the risks involved, this can be provided by a full- or part-time trained employee, or a consultant. |
| This requirement covers other emergencies apart from fire, such as the closure of plant in the event of an accident. You need to know how to contact the emergency services and any specialist rescue services needed, appoint fire wardens, carry out emergency drills and publish fire action instructions (see Chapter 5). |

## Health and safety programme (continued)

| Item | Management action | Yes | No |
|---|---|---|---|
| 7 | Make first aid provision | | |
| 8 | Record all injuries and put in place the means to learn from them | | |
| 9 | Provide health and safety information to employees, including office and field staff | | |
| 10 | Provide training | | |
| 11 | Consider agency workers, expectant mothers and young persons | | |
| 12 | Working time | | |

In addition to the items in the checklist, you may also wish to consider introducing an occupation health management programme or a drugs and alcohol policy. Typically, an occupational health management programme entails using the services of nurses or doctors, and associated services. A a minimum, a drugs and alcohol policy prohibits all intoxicants from the workplace; it may also incorporate random testing of employees.

## Guidance and good business practice

It is a requirement for every workplace to have at least a trained 'appointed person'. The exact provision depends on the hazards and risks in the workplace (see guidance and definitions of 'appointed person' and 'first aider' later in this chapter).

The safety representative must hold the statutory BI 510 accident book, available from HSE Books and stationers. Every injury must be recorded in this book and be reviewed by management. All reportable accidents must be fully investigated.

Display the following on a notice board:
- health and safety policy statement
- 'Health and safety law' poster
- employers' liability insurance certificate
- names and locations of first aiders
- fire and emergency instructions
- names and locations of fire wardens.

Any special information needed to ensure safety must be made available to employees in writing or on posters. Health and safety signs must also be provided in their prescribed colours (see guidance in Appendix A).

Health and safety training is a legal requirement for many tasks. Induction training must be provided, covering fire and emergency arrangements, and information on office, workshop or site rules. Other training may be necessary, eg to operate machinery safely (see Chapters 6 to 14 for training requirements for specific industry sectors, and the notes below).

For health and safety purposes, agency workers and self-employed people must be treated in the same manner as permanent staff. This means that their competency should be verified and any training needs addressed. Expectant mothers and young persons must be protected from hazardous work and given additional rest and facilities (see guidance later in this chapter, in the 'Health and welfare' section of Chapter 4, and in Chapter 6).

There are limitations on the hours that may be worked (see guidance later in this chapter).

# Accident reporting and investigation

### Accident reporting

By law, when an accident occurs you are required to take action.

Telephone your local HSE office immediately in the case of a fatal or major injury, or a dangerous occurrence. (For examples of major injuries and dangerous occurrences, see 'Reporting of injuries, diseases and dangerous occurrences' in Appendix A.)

Any accident that results in the injured party staying in hospital overnight counts as a major injury. An accident to a member of the public which results in that person going immediately to hospital must also be reported as major.

Follow up with a written report to the HSE. In some cases, eg shops and offices, the local authority is the enforcing authority, in which case the report should be submitted to them.

To report an accident or dangerous occurrence, use form F2508, available from HSE Books (t +44 (0)1787 881165). Occupational diseases are reported on form F2508A. Alternatively, visit the HSE website at www.hse.gov.uk or www.riddor.gov.uk, where F2508 and F2508A can be completed online and transmitted instantly. The report must be sent within 10 days – late reporting is an offence.

Over-three-day injuries require a written report on form F2508, but it is not necessary to telephone the authorities.

An over-three-day injury is one where the injured party is not available for work for more than the following three days, even where these days cover a holiday or weekend. The day of the accident is not counted. For example, if an accident occurred on a Thursday and the injured party returned on the following Monday, it would not be reportable as no more than three days are involved, ie including the weekend but excluding the day of the accident. However, if the injured party returned on the following Tuesday then it would be reportable, even though only two working days were involved.

All injuries that require first aid must be recorded in the accident book held in the workplace. The injured party is entitled to a copy of the entry. The accident book entry is not a report to the HSE but can be used in civil claims as evidence that the injury was sustained at work.

Also read...

Appendix A – Accident statistics

In addition to the above three reportable categories (fatal, major, over-three-day), many leading organisations also collate statistics of lost-time injuries. This is recommended as best practice. The definition of a 'lost-time' injury is one that results in absence from work on the shift following that of the accident.

### Accident investigation

All accidents should be investigated in an honest and open manner. The following should be present:

- the injured party (if available)

- witnesses

- the supervisor or manager

- the safety adviser.

In a blame-free atmosphere, discuss what went wrong, then consider ways in which work practices could be improved to avoid such an accident occurring in future. It is not enough to blame carelessness, as inevitably there will be organisational or physical improvements that can be made to prevent recurrence. For all reportable accidents, a safety adviser should be present, and the underlying and immediate causes identified. All relevant evidence must be collected in order to compile the report and provide the necessary documentation in case of enforcement action or a civil claim. In the event of a potential investigation by the enforcing authorities, the accident scene must not be disturbed until they arrive.

A suitable form for carrying out an accident investigation, and information on compiling accident statistics, are included in Appendix A.

## Information and training

There is a legal duty to provide information to employees on the risks and safe systems of work, and training in the skills and processes necessary to carry out a task. The means of doing this include:

- induction/orientation when joining

- recognised trade skills training schemes that provide registration cards

- health and safety awareness training

- toolbox talks

- task skills training

- health and safety signs.

### Induction/orientation training

Every organisation should carry out an induction programme. Ideally, the programme should begin when an employee starts work on his or her first day.

Adequate facilities must be provided in order to carry out a successful induction programme and a decision must be made on who will present the induction. Whoever presents the induction must be competent, enthusiastic and assertive, ensuring that the induction is relevant, well prepared and of a high quality. An agenda for safety induction/orientation training is included in Appendix A.

### Trade skills training schemes

There are many schemes operated by national registration bodies that provide proof of both skills and health and safety training. Schemes in this category include:

- Construction Industry Training Board (CITB) Construction Plant Competence Scheme (CPCS)

- Scaffolding Registration Scheme

- UK Accreditation Service for Gas Installers (CORGI)

- JIB Electricians Scheme.

**Health and safety awareness training**

This type of training is aimed at managers and supervisors, to provide them with the knowledge and skills necessary to demonstrate competence in health and safety matters. Two popular courses are:

- the five-day Managing Safely course run by IOSH

- the National Examination Board in Occupational Safety and Health (NEBOSH) 10-day National General Certificate in Occupational Safety and Health.

Both of these courses are recommended. The IOSH course should be taken by all managers; the NEBOSH course by those with organisational responsibility for health and safety. Other organisations offer comparable courses.

**Toolbox talks**

A toolbox talk is a 10-minute briefing given by a supervisor on a weekly basis to advise and instruct employees about a specific or general health and safety topic (a selection of toolbox talks is included in Appendix B). Such talks build up into a body of training, and are delivered in short sessions so that the content can be readily assimilated. Employees should record their attendance by signing a register.

Toolbox talks should be presented on the following:

1. General topics – those used for general, stand-alone, safety awareness training or integrated into task-oriented topics.

2. Task-oriented topics – those arising from the actual task being undertaken, including instruction in the risks involved and specific safe system of work or method statement. Where possible, they should be given in the workplace when a new task commences or when there is a change in risk or method. The supervisor giving these task briefings must use a simple, illustrated task sheet to brief the team. This should detail:

   - the hazards

   - how employees could be affected

   - how the risks are to be controlled

   - how to use work equipment safely

   - how to use personal protective equipment

- how to check equipment and look for faults

- the results of any exposure monitoring or health surveillance

- emergency procedures

- instructions to refer back to the supervisor if the method proves impractical or other dangers become apparent.

3. Topics arising from an incident – reference should be made to the circumstances of the incident and any appropriate listed talk. These talks should be given as soon as possible after an incident.

Task skills training

This form of training is given to employees so that they can carry out specific tasks safely, such as:

- changing abrasive wheels

- operating a mobile elevating work platform

- erecting mobile access towers

- using cartridge tools

- using chainsaws.

The precise type of training required varies from industry to industry, but if an employee has to undertake a hazardous task then the appropriate information and training must be given.

Health and safety signs

Regulations have standardised the colour and shape of health and safety signs with a view to communicating essential information in a uniform and standardised way that can be readily understood by all, regardless of reading ability or language.

Health and safety signs should be set up in cases where a risk cannot be eliminated. A table outlining the shape and colour of health and safety signs is included in Appendix A.

## First aid

By law, every workplace must have first aid provision, but the exact requirements are not specified. A list of the typical contents of a first aid kit is included in Appendix A.

The employer must weigh up the risks in the workplace and the injuries that may be caused, together with other factors such as the number of employees, their distribution about the premises, and any mutual aid that would be available. Mutual aid is where one party has first aid provision and agreement is made with one or other parties that this provision can be shared with them. This often takes place in buildings that are occupied by more than one organisation.

The table below gives an example of the first aid provision of a typical large organisation.

| Personnel at the location | Appointed person | First aider | Occupational nurse or medic | First aid kits | First aid room |
|---|---|---|---|---|---|
| 1–4 | 1 | – | – | 1 | – |
| 5–50 | 1 | 1 | – | 1 | – |
| 51–100 | 1 | 2 | – | 2 | – |
| 101–150 | 1 | 3 | – | 3 | – |
| 151–249 | 1 | 4 | – | 4 | 1 |
| 250+* | 1 | 5 | 1† | 5 | 1 |

*If you have more than 250 personnel, seek specialist advice.

†Suggested, depending on the risks.

### Appointed person

An appointed person is someone who has been trained to take charge of a situation (eg to call an ambulance) if a serious injury or illness occurs, and to be responsible for maintaining first aid equipment in the absence of trained first aiders. An appointed person's course covers basic first aid and normally takes one day.

### First aider

A first aider is someone who has received first aid training and holds a current 'First aid at work' certificate (valid for three years). The training course normally takes four days and a test of competence must be passed at the end.

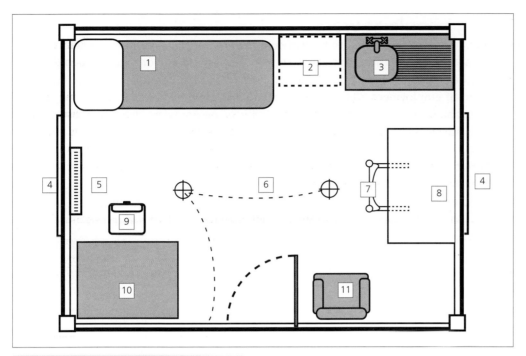

**Standard first aid room layout**

**2.7m × 3.6m**

1. Dorchester rest room couch
2. Smooth-topped base cupboard unit (lockable) and wall-mounted cupboard above
3. Sink unit with cupboard underneath
4. Obscure glazed windows
5. 3kw heater
6. Treatment area with two ceiling lights
7. Folding chair
8. Treatment table
9. Office chair
10. Office desk
11. Rest room chair

**Also read...**

Chapter 12 – Employment of young people in retail establishments

**Hard facts**

In 1998/99, 21 young people died and nearly 4,000 were seriously injured at work.

**Hard facts**

Over the past decade there have been 100 deaths and 644 major injuries to children playing on construction sites and in the railways and agricultural industries alone.

# Young people at work

Young people are considered to be particularly at risk because they are likely to have a lack of awareness, maturity and experience. Young people at work are those who have not reached the age of 18. Children under the age of 13 are generally prohibited from any form of employment. Children between 13 and the minimum school leaving age of 16 are prohibited from being employed in industry, except when on work experience schemes approved by the local education authority.

Businesses that employ young people are required by law to:

- assess the risks to young people under 18 years of age before they start work, taking into account their inexperience, lack of awareness of existing or potential risks, and immaturity

- address high risk activities of particular relevance to young people (see examples below)

- provide information to the young person's parent(s)/guardian(s) about the key findings of the risk assessment and the measures to be taken to keep their child safe

- consider and record whether the young person should be prohibited from certain work activities, except where: it is necessary for their training; the risks are reduced as far as possible; the young person is supervised by a competent person at all times

- tell young people about the risks to their health and safety identified by the risk assessment and the measures put in place to control the risks.

### High risk activities

Unless it can be fully justified as a training need, and all of the precautions mentioned above are documented and in place, including constant supervision, young people should not be employed in the following activities:

- heavy or awkward lifting or handling beyond the capacity of the young person

- production line work, where the young person has to keep up with stronger and more skilled adults

- stressful situations, such as dealing with aggressive behaviour

- work in high pressure atmospheres, such as diving or tunnelling

- work with asbestos, lead, biological agents (eg those used in cleaning cooling towers) or harmful chemicals, where a failure to follow safe practice could be disastrous

- work with ionising radiation or industrial gases

- demolition

- work with high voltages

- work in extreme cold or heat

- work that involves high levels of noise or vibration

- work with dangerous machinery, such as woodworking or metalworking machines, except as part of a training programme under supervision.

## Records

To keep a record of young people employed, the following register should be completed for all people under the age of 18.

| | |
|---|---|
| Surname | |
| Forename(s) | |
| Address | |
| Date of birth | |
| Trade/position | |
| Name and address of employer | |
| Risk assessment | |
| Name of supervisor responsible | |
| Date employment commenced | |
| Date employment finished | |

www.protect.org.uk

PDF 02

**Example of a record for a young person**

### Hard facts

Company car and van drivers who cover 25,000 miles a year for their employer are as likely to die at work as those in the coal mining industry.

### Also read...

Chapter 12 – Safe driving time

# Working time

Regulations have been introduced that seek to limit the duration of employees' working week. The regulations are complex but the main points are covered in the following sections.

### The working week

- The guiding principle is that employees should not work consistently more than 48 hours per week. A working period that regularly exceeds 48 hours per week is not acceptable under the regulations.

- A 17-week rolling reference period is used to calculate the average hours worked, so that employees can exceed 48 hours for short periods, provided that it is compensated for later in the 17-week period. If during the reference period the employee takes annual holiday or is sick, the reference period is extended by the equivalent number of days.

- Occasional work at home, travel time and company social events are excluded, provided they are undertaken of the individual's own free choice. A consistently heavy workload that forces employees to take work home should be taken into consideration under working time. Excessive daily travel should be treated in a similar manner.

### The opt out

Individuals may choose to opt out of the 48-hour limit. A written agreement must be in place, which can subsequently be withdrawn if the employee wishes. If an individual opts out, this must be of his or her own free choice.

### Breaks and holidays

- There are detailed provisions for rest periods. Essentially, employees are entitled to 11 hours' consecutive rest each day (24 hours), and two days off work each fortnight, which can be taken at any time during the fortnight. There are flexibilities provided in the regulations, including lieu time.

- Where the working day is longer than six hours, employees are entitled to an uninterrupted break of 20 minutes.

- Young people under the age of 18 are entitled to two rest days per week, consecutive if possible, and a 30-minute break each day, where the working day exceeds four hours. Additional restrictions apply to night work.

- Subject to a period of 13 weeks' qualifying service, an employee is entitled to four weeks' annual leave each year.

## Night work

The provisions for night work are detailed and complex.

- **Normal night work** – Night work is defined as the hours between 11pm and 6am. Employers are required to ensure that the 'normal' hours of their night workers do not exceed an average of eight hours for each 24 hours over a 17-week period.

- **Special hazards** – Where a night worker's work involves special hazards or heavy physical or mental strain, there is an absolute limit of eight hours on the worker's daily working time. The limit must be observed in any period of 24 hours during which the night worker performs such work. To comply with this requirement, it is necessary to undertake a risk assessment for night work activities so that special hazard activities may be identified. There is no opt out in this case.

- **Medicals** – Employers must offer a free health assessment to any of their employees who are required to work overnight on a regular basis. These health assessments should be made available annually to monitor the employee's health.

## Records

Legislation requires businesses to keep records for two years to demonstrate compliance with:

- weekly working times for those who have not opted out of the 48-hour limit

- night working hours and risk assessments

- night working health assessments

- young people's working time.

---

### The bottom line

**By law, every organisation must:**
- write a health and safety policy statement
- carry out workplace risk assessments
- appoint health and safety representatives from the workforce
- appoint a health and safety adviser (a staff member or a consultant)
- publish fire and emergency arrangements
- establish first aid arrangements
- record and investigate accidents
- provide essential health and safety information, including signage
- provide training relevant to the task
- have suitable arrangements for agency workers, expectant mothers and young people
- limit working time.

## Introduction

You are now ready to have a hard look at your buildings, offices, shops, workshops or other premises, including car parks, loading bays, yards and other external areas. This chapter provides you with the facts and figures you need to assess your premises. So take a walk around, looking and listening as you go, then work through the checklists and record your risk assessments. All of the items in the checklists are legal requirements.

There are four main building issues to consider, as shown in this diagram. In this chapter we will examine the first three. Fire requires more extensive coverage and will be looked at in Chapter 5.

What is...

**Sick building syndrome?**
The term 'sick building syndrome' was coined in the late 1980s to describe buildings that seem to cause a greater than normal incidence of ill health and a general lack of wellbeing. There is no single cause, but the following factors contribute:

- poor building and office design, particularly large open-plan offices without room dividers
- poor building services and maintenance, particularly air conditioning, high-glare or flickering lighting, windows that do not open, lack of heating control, poor maintenance and repair, and poor standards of cleanliness
- poor indoor environment and air quality, including high temperatures, high or low humidity, tobacco smoke and dusty atmospheres
- job factors, such as routine clerical work and work with display screen equipment.

## Building services

www.protect.org.uk

PDF 03

**What is...**

**Legionnaire's disease?**
Legionnaire's disease is a potentially fatal respiratory disease, named after the first identified case at a Legionnaires' convention in the USA. Legionella bacteria breed in air conditioning cooling towers and are dispersed over a large area by minute droplets of water that escape into the atmosphere from the spray-cooling process. These droplets can be breathed in, causing the bacteria to enter the respiratory system. Regular testing and specialist cleaning of cooling towers will prevent this hazard developing.

| Ventilation and air conditioning | Yes or no | Action to be taken |
|---|---|---|
| Is there an adequate supply of fresh air? | | |
| Is mechanical ventilation or air conditioning provided? | | |
| Is there any evidence of uncomfortable draughts? | | |
| Is the air conditioning/ventilation system regularly maintained and serviced? | | |
| Is testing for Legionella bacteria carried out? | | |

# Guidance
### Ventilation and air conditioning

| Guidance and good business practice |
|---|
| For many buildings, opening windows is adequate to provide fresh air. However, if there are complaints of high temperatures this may indicate a ventilation problem. Rooms without opening windows need mechanical ventilation. |
| The fresh air supply rate should be 5 to 8 litres per second for each person, depending on the activity. A simple test of adequacy is whether people complain of stale air, stuffiness or smells. If there is a problem, specialist help will probably be needed. |
| People cannot be made to work in uncomfortable draughts. The source of draughts must be identified (such as a badly fitting window) and put right. |
| This is an essential requirement of air conditioning and mechanical ventilation. |
| One of the main hazards with air conditioning is the potential for Legionella bacteria to develop, even in new systems. Annual testing of cooling towers is necessary, as is the testing of other spray-producing fitments such as taps and showers. |

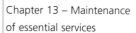

Also read...

Chapter 13 – Maintenance of essential services

Chapter 13 – Legionnaire's disease

## Building services (continued)

| Heating and lighting | Yes or no | Action to be taken |
|---|---|---|
| Is the temperature in each room reasonably comfortable without the use of special clothing? | | |
| Is there a conveniently situated thermometer? | | |
| Do very high or low temperatures occur? | | |
| Is there suitable and sufficient lighting in the workplace? | | |
| Has natural light been used wherever practical? | | |
| Is there emergency lighting? | | |

**Linear louvre light fitting**
This fitting produces widespread and downward light distribution for work on display screen equipment.

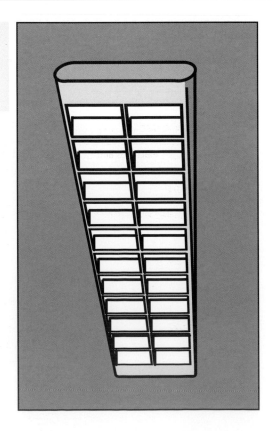

# Guidance
**Heating and lighting**

### Guidance and good business practice

The requirement for reasonably comfortable temperatures applies to workrooms in which people work for medium or long periods of time. The minimum temperature is 16°C for offices and non-physical work, and 13°C where severe physical effort is required. There is no stated maximum temperature.

This is a requirement, but not necessarily in every room.

People who work in foundries, cold stores, or work outdoors during the winter, for example, should be provided with personal protective equipment.

Lighting should:
- be sufficiently bright to allow work and any hazards to be seen
- be reasonably uniform
- not cast shadows and prevent work or hazards from being seen
- not cast excessive reflection
- not produce too much contrast between levels of illumination
- be of the correct directional quality for the task, eg work on display screen equipment requires widespread and downward light distribution.

Refer to the following table for the ideal lighting levels in different situations.

Windows must be kept clean and daylight should be made use of wherever possible. The lighting issues referred to in the bullet point list above also apply to daylight.

Emergency lighting must be provided on escape routes and in rooms where there are special safety needs.

### What is...

**Lux?**
Lux is the unit of measurement for illuminance on surfaces. Simple meters are available to measure lux.

### Recommended lighting levels in different locations

| Activity | Typical location and/or type of work | Average lux level in the area | Minimum lux level anywhere in the area |
|---|---|---|---|
| Fire escape | Emergency lighting on fire escape routes | 10 | 5 |
| Movement of people, machines and vehicles | Lorry parks, external yards, car parks | 20 | 5 |
| Movement of people, machines and vehicles in hazardous areas; work not requiring fine detail | Loading bays, bottling and canning plants, construction excavations | 50 | 20 |
| Work requiring limited visual detail; general access | Kitchens, canteens, corridors; factories where large components are assembled | 100 | 50 |
| Movement of large numbers of people | Staircases | 150 | 75 |
| Detailed work | Offices, metalworking, woodworking, bookbinding | 200 | 100 |
| Fine-detailed work | Drawing offices, textile production, electronic component assembly | 500 | 200 |

## Building layout, windows and traffic routes

| Floors, corridors and fire escapes | Yes or no | Action to be taken |
|---|---|---|
| Are all floors and corridors safe, with no unguarded holes and no uneven or slippery surfaces? | | |
| When floors get wet, is there a means of drainage? | | |
| Where access routes are on a slope or stairs, is a handrail provided? | | |
| Are all fire escapes clearly signposted and free from obstructions? | | |
| Do busy corridors and fire escape routes have fire doors that contain vision panels? | | |
| Are there two means of escape from each floor? | | |
| Are escalators and moving walkways equipped with readily identified emergency stop buttons and safety devices? | | |

# Guidance

**Floors, corridors and fire escapes**

### Fire escape signage

Fire escapes must be signposted with the green 'running person' and be visible from any position. Check the route yourself, all the way to the escape door. Are there any obstructions, or any extinguishers propping open fire doors? Does the escape door have a panic latch, and is the area behind the door safe and free from obstructions?

### Factory floor layout

Floors must be sound, with no unprotected holes or slopes, and no uneven or slippery surfaces. Where there are stairs and slopes, handrails must be provided. Floors near machinery must not be slippery – if necessary, an anti-slip coating or material should be used, and routes that get wet should be drained.

1. Escape door
2. Green 'running person' sign
3. Fire action sign
4. Panic latch
5. Fire extinguishers
6. Handrail on slope
7. Line on floor marking clear route
8. Edge guardrails
9. Machines
10. Drainage channel
11. Anti-slip matting

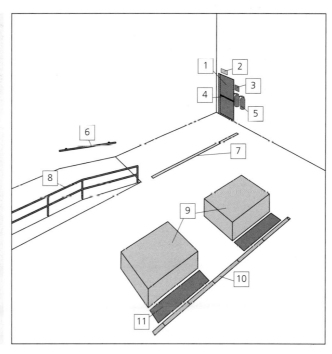

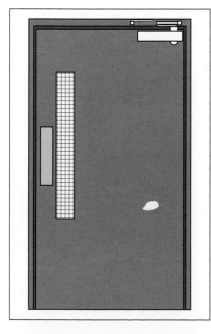

### Fire escape routes

Internal doors on fire escape and main access routes must be fitted with vision panels to allow people approaching on the other side of the door to be seen. Vision panels should also extend low enough to allow wheelchair users to be seen, as shown in the illustration on the left.

Access routes and exits must be clearly signposted and kept free from obstructions such as spare furniture, filing cabinets or rubbish. A blocked fire escape in a hotel, for example, is enough to get the owner prosecuted.

You need two means of escape from any floor. If you do not have two, seek advice.

www.protect.org.uk

PDF 04

## Building layout, windows and traffic routes (continued)

| Windows and window cleaning | Yes or no | Action to be taken |
|---|---|---|
| Are all windows and skylights capable of being opened safely without having to climb on desks, machinery and so on? | | |
| If you have roof lights, are they fragile? | | |
| Is the glass in windows, doors, partitions and/or walls made of safety material, where it is at waist level or below, or otherwise protected? | | |

### Hard facts

Since 1986, more than 300 people in the UK have died in falls through roofs and roof lights.

# Guidance

## Windows and window cleaning

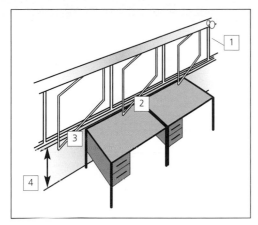

### Window opening

Where windows cannot be opened from floor level, anyone trying to open them is at risk of causing injury to themselves and/or others. For example, if a desk has been placed against a window and you have to climb onto the desk in order to open it, you are in danger of falling out. In such cases, safe ways of opening windows must be found, such as using poles. To be considered safe, the bottom edge of a window should be 800mm above floor level.

1. Window cleaning harness point set into building structure, not window frame
2. This window cannot be opened safely because to reach the handle someone has to climb onto the desk. This exposes a risk of falling out
3. This window can be opened safely as handles can be reached from floor level
4. 800mm is the minimum safe height

### View of an industrial roof (metal, pitched)

1. Fall arrest system. Running line permanently installed
2. Fragile Perspex roof light has the same profile as the roof sheets and so fits flush with the roof. This makes the roof light difficult to see. Almost all roof lights degrade with age
3. Roof edge

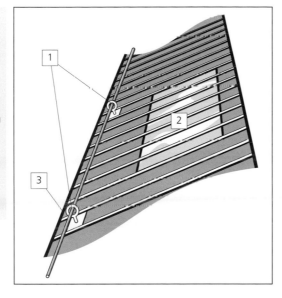

### Roof lights

Roof lights and ventilators must be capable of being opened safely. All roof lights must be considered to be fragile and unable to support the weight of someone standing on them. As a minimum, clearly mark them as fragile, and provide a means of anchorage so that anyone requiring roof access can use a safety harness. Running line anchorages can be readily installed by specialist companies. Any roof light that is in poor condition should be replaced.

### Window cleaning

To gain access to windows that need cleaning, it is unsafe to use a free-standing ladder that is longer than 6m. Similarly, leaning out of a window in order to clean it is also unsafe. Safe systems include:

- suspended cradles
- mobile elevating work platforms
- window cleaner harnesses, anchored from an internal point
- ladders up to 9m that are tied to fixing points.

All ladders and platforms must be placed on a firm base. Suspended cradles, mobile elevating work platforms and window cleaner harness anchorage points must be thoroughly examined and tested.

Windows, transparent sections in doors and so on must be made of safety material if they are at waist level or below (glasshouses are exempt from this requirement). Safety material includes glass or plastic manufactured in accordance with BS 6206:1981 – 'Specification for impact performance requirements for flat safety glass and safety plastics for use in buildings'. Alternatively, ordinary glass can be used in accordance with the following table.

| Thickness | Maximum size |
|-----------|--------------|
| 8mm | 1.1m x 1.1m |
| 10mm | 2.25m x 2.25m |
| 12mm | 3m x 4.5m |
| 15mm | Any size |

## Building layout, windows and traffic routes (continued)

www.protect.org.uk

PDF 04

| Prevention of falls | Yes or no | Action to be taken |
|---|---|---|
| Do your premises contain any pits or tanks that hold dangerous substances? | | |
| Are there any places on your premises where a person could be killed or injured if they fell from those places? | | |
| Do you have fixed ladders? | | |
| Do you have any fragile roofs or roof lights? | | |
| Do you have stacking or racking? If so, are there any hazards such as damaged racking or unsafe stacking that could cause falls of materials? | | |

Around 25 per cent of all fatal accidents involve falls from a height. Bearing this in mind, look at your premises – not just those areas that are regularly used but also awkward places that must be maintained.

# Guidance

## Prevention of falls

Obviously, tanks, pits and other similar structures that hold dangerous substances are confined spaces, and must be securely fenced or covered to prevent unauthorised entry. Roadways and traffic routes near such structures must be securely fenced off.

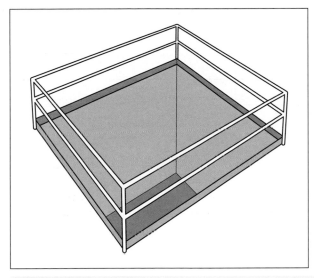

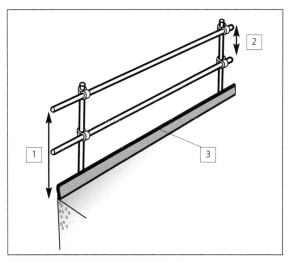

### Edge protection

Where there is the potential for falls that may cause injury or death, eg edges, openings and pits, protection or coverings must be provided – edge protection for large openings, covers for small. These measures are especially important where there are special risks, such as falling into chemicals, sewage or machinery. This applies only to places where people go regularly and does not normally apply to roofs.

### Edge protection dimensions

1. Top rail (minimum height: 1.1m for permanent fixtures; 950mm for construction works)
2. Mid rail (maximum gap: 470mm)
3. Toe board (minimum height: 150mm)

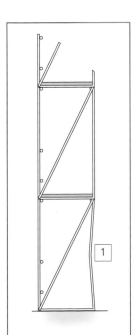

### Storage racking

There is a legal duty to ensure that racks used to store materials, components, goods and foodstuffs are safe and regularly inspected. Racks can be major structures, and if so need to be inspected by a structural engineer.
1. Damaged components should be replaced

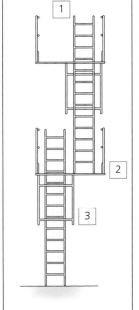

### Fire escape ladders

Stairs are much safer than ladders. Where practicable, stairs must be installed. Fixed ladders require:
- stiles extending 1.1m beyond the landing
- landings at 6m intervals
- safety hoops at a height of 2.5m then at 900mm intervals.
1. Stile
2. Staggered landing
3. Hoop

**Danger
Fragile roof**

### Fragile roofs

Many buildings have roofs that are made of fragile asbestos cement or some similar material, or contain roof lights, all of which are unable to support a person's weight. Roofs of this sort must be signposted as fragile, and specific arrangements should be made when access is required.

## Building layout, windows and traffic routes (continued)

www.protect.org.uk

PDF 04

| Outside your buildings – keeping people and vehicles apart | Yes or no | Action to be taken |
|---|---|---|
| Are the traffic signs adequate in your yard, car park, loading dock or other traffic route? | | |
| Do loading bays have escape routes for personnel? | | |
| Are pedestrian crossings provided so that people can cross busy roads? | | |
| Are there any 'blind' crossing points for pedestrians? | | |
| Are there physical barriers, such as gateways, doorways, tunnels and bridges, to prevent pedestrians coming into contact with vehicles? | | |
| Are safe routes for forklift trucks marked on the ground? | | |
| Has vehicle reversing been minimised? | | |
| Have appropriate speed limits been set? | | |
| Are roads wide enough to allow vehicles to pass safely? | | |
| Are there any blind bends? | | |
| Are there any dangerous pits that dumpers or other vehicles have to approach or drive close to? | | |
| Are all doors to the building safe and free from traps? | | |
| Are power-operated doors and/or gates fitted with safety controls? | | |
| Are all external gates robust, free from traps, and fitted with vision panels (so that when someone opens a gate they can see any hazards on the other side)? | | |

## Guidance
### Outside your buildings – keeping people and vehicles apart

This section is concerned with the delivery of goods and materials, loading bays, yards, car parks, and routes for forklift trucks and the like. It also includes a section on doors and gates, and yard gates and doors into areas such as loading bays. The guiding principle is that people and vehicles have to be kept apart, and you have to plan and arrange access to your factory, shop, office, construction site, or other facility to ensure that this happens. Doing so is not always easy, particularly on older premises, but you are legally obliged to do so.

**Signs**

Potential hazards such as sharp bends, junctions, crossings, steep gradients and roadworks should be signposted, as should building and department locations. Speed limits must also be clearly signposted.

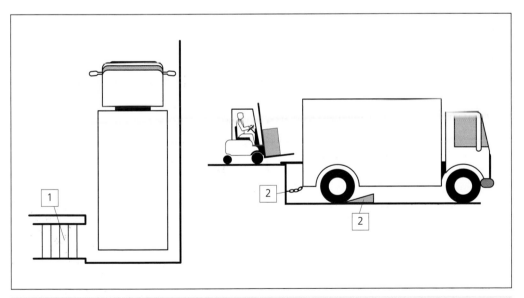

**Loading bays**

1. Loading bays must have at least one escape route or refuge to ensure pedestrians are not trapped by reversing vehicles
2. Lorries must be anchored to loading bays or their tyres wedged so that they cannot move

## Guidance
### Outside your buildings – keeping people and vehicles apart

**Crossings and the separation of people and vehicles**

Pedestrian crossings should be provided to allow people to cross busy traffic routes.

Where an enclosed walkway meets a road, an open space of at least 1m should be allowed before the road edge or kerb to allow pedestrians to see any oncoming vehicles.

Vehicle routes and pathways should be wide enough to allow vehicles and pedestrians to pass each other in safety.

Inside buildings, routes for forklift trucks and other vehicles should be marked on the floor.

In doorways, gateways, tunnels, bridges and other such openings, there should be a physical kerb or barrier. This is especially important at site entrances.

1. Buildings
2. Walkway – people cannot see vehicles
3. 1m minimum pathway – people can see vehicles

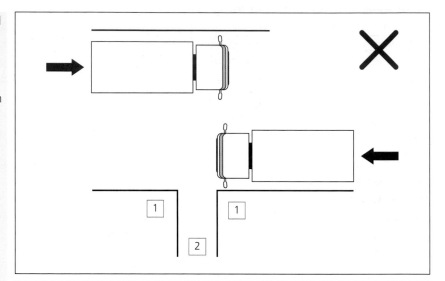

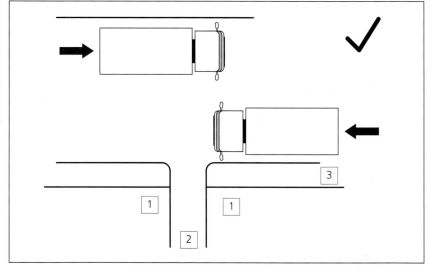

# Guidance
## Outside your buildings – keeping people and vehicles apart

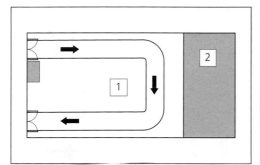

**One-way systems that minimise reversing in service yards**
1. Vehicle hardstanding
2. Workshops

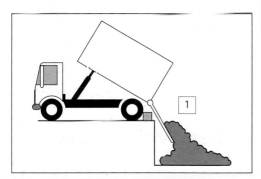

**Tipping into a pit**
1. Stop block fixed to structure

### Vehicle routes
When organising your roadways, yards and car parks, look at the areas of reversing, speed limits, and road widths and layout.

### Reversing
- Minimise reversing, particularly if vehicles have restricted rear vision; if necessary, create a one-way system.
- Provide high-visibility jackets to people working in reversing areas.
- Fit reversing alarms or flashing lights to vehicles.
- Employ a trained banksman if reversing is frequent.
- Ensure that all vehicles are fitted with good mirrors.

### Speed limits
- Set a safe and practical speed limit that you are prepared to enforce.
- If necessary, install speed humps, but not in areas used by standard forklift trucks; speed humps must be signposted and be visible from both directions.

### Road widths and layout
- Make roads wide enough so that vehicles can pass each other and park safely.
- Avoid creating blind bends and dangerous obstructions; if vehicles have to tip into an open pit, a physical stop must be provided.

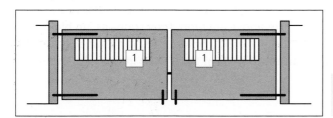

**Gates that swing in both directions**
1. Vision panels

### Doors and gates (both inside and outside)
Doors and gates are often the cause of serious accidents. Typically, the main gate into a service yard is large and heavy. If the gate were to fall over, passers-by or vehicle drivers may be severely injured or even killed. To prevent such accidents, the following legal requirements must be adhered to:

- doors and gates must be well constructed and robust
- sliding doors must have end stops
- an upward sliding door must be fitted with a counterbalance or something similar to prevent it from falling back when released

- power-operated doors/gates must be fitted with detectors or controls that must be held down while the door/gate closes slowly, so that it is not possible to trap someone or cause injury (if the person operating the control removes their finger from the button, the door/gate should stop moving); these doors/gates must also be capable of being opened manually if the power fails
- doors/gates that swing in both directions must have vision panels to allow the person opening the door to see any obstruction or person on the other side.

# Health and welfare

### Cleaning

Work through the following checklists to ensure that you comply with legal requirements.

There is a statutory duty to keep premises clean. For example, floors and corridors must be cleaned at least weekly, kitchens and canteens daily; rubbish must be removed from the workplace on a daily basis, and walls and ceilings must be cleaned periodically.

www.protect.org.uk

PDF 05

| Cleaning | Yes or no | Action to be taken |
|---|---|---|
| Is the workplace clean and free from rubbish? | | |
| Are there containers for waste materials? | | |
| Are floors and stairs clean, well drained and non-slippery? | | |
| Are cleaning materials available to mop up spillages promptly? | | |
| Is there a need for a documented schedule that covers the cleaning of all surfaces, furniture, machines and equipment, eg in kitchens and washrooms serving the public? Is the schedule provided and maintained? | | |
| Can the windows and any roof lights be cleaned safely, eg using reversible windows, short ladders, cradles or harnesses? | | |
| Are there contracts for the cleaning of windows and office/premises, and arrangements for the removal of rubbish? If not, how are the premises kept clean and how is rubbish removed? | | |

### Room dimensions and space

There are regulations to prevent overcrowding in workplaces. Rooms should allow free access and easy escape in the event of an emergency. Each person should have a volume of at least 11m³. Where ceilings are above 3m high, they count as 3m high for the purpose of the calculation. In workplaces existing before 1992, and which have not been altered, regulations allow a height of up to 4.2m to be used in the calculation.

**What is...**

**Sufficient space?**

The following examples illustrate the amount of space required by each employee.

- In a typical room 2.4m high, a minimum floor area of 4.6m² (2.0m × 2.3m) is required.
- In a room 3.0m high or more, a minimum floor area of 3.7m² (2.0m × 1.85m) is required.
- In a room 2.0m high, a minimum floor area of 5.5m² (2.2m × 2.5m) is required.

These rules do not apply to meeting rooms, temporary construction site offices, retail sales kiosks or machine control cabs.

## Workstations and seating

All workstations, not just those in offices, must be designed with both the task and the person in mind. Chronic injury or ill health can be caused by lack of movement, awkward posture, the use of excessive force, an uncomfortable hand grip and the absence of a footrest, particularly if coupled with repetitive work over long periods.

| Workstations and seating | Yes or no | Action to be taken |
|---|---|---|
| **Indoor and outdoor workstations** | | |
| Have workstations been risk assessed? | | |
| Is there any evidence of ill health that could be attributable to the use of workstations? | | |
| Have you talked to the operators to discuss their workstations? | | |
| Are footrests provided where necessary, and do seats have adjustable back support? | | |
| Do operators have freedom of movement and the ability to stand up and stretch? | | |
| Do operators have adequate working space, and are controls within easy reach? | | |
| Is the work surface at a sensible height? | | |
| Are repetitive hand or arm movements avoided? | | |
| **Outdoor workstations – additional considerations** | | |
| Are they weather protected? | | |
| Can they be left quickly in an emergency? | | |
| Are there any obvious tripping hazards? | | |

www.protect.org.uk

PDF 06

**What is...**

**A workstation?**
A workstation is a facility where the user or operator remains in one location in order to perform tasks that are often repetitive. Workstations include office computer terminals, supermarket checkouts and machine-operating workstations in factories.

## Welfare requirements

Poor welfare is a cause of employee dissatisfaction and an indication of a poor health and safety programme. Every manager should address welfare as a priority.

www.protect.org.uk

PDF 07

| Welfare requirements | Yes or no | Action to be taken |
|---|---|---|
| Are there sufficient and adequate sanitary conveniences and washing facilities? | | |
| Is there a good supply of drinking water? | | |
| Is accommodation for clothing adequate? | | |
| Are rest and eating facilities adequate? | | |
| Are there facilities for pregnant women and nursing mothers? | | |
| Is there a smoke-free rest room? | | |
| Does each employee have sufficient space in their work area? | | |

## Guidance
Welfare requirements

**Sanitary conveniences and washing facilities**

**Men**

**Women**
(or men if no urinals)

| Number of men | Number of toilets | Number of urinals | Number of washbasins |
|---|---|---|---|
| 1–5 | 1 | 1 | 1 |
| 6–15 | 1 | 1 | 2 |
| 16–25 | 2 | 1 | 2 |
| 26–30 | 2 | 1 | 3 |
| 31–45 | 2 | 2 | 3 |
| 46–50 | 3 | 2 | 3 |
| 51–60 | 3 | 2 | 4 |
| 61–75 | 3 | 3 | 4 |
| 76–90 | 4 | 3 | 5 |
| 91–100 | 4 | 4 | 5 |

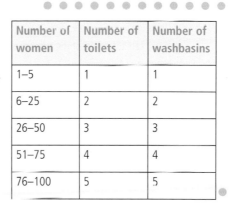

| Number of women | Number of toilets | Number of washbasins |
|---|---|---|
| 1–5 | 1 | 1 |
| 6–25 | 2 | 2 |
| 26–50 | 3 | 3 |
| 51–75 | 4 | 4 |
| 76–100 | 5 | 5 |

Above 100, an additional toilet, urinal and two washbasins should be provided for each additional 50 men or part.

Above 100, add an additional toilet and washbasin for each additional 25 women or part.

- Facilities must be adequately ventilated, well lit, and kept clean and tidy.
- Washbasins must have hot and cold (or warm) running water.
- Showers should be made available for dirty work or emergencies.
- Soap and towels or hand driers should be provided.
- Skin cleansers and barrier creams should be supplied, if required.
- Washing facilities must be near the toilets.

**Drinking water**

- Must be supplied to every workplace.
- Must be clearly marked as such.
- Must not be installed where contamination is possible, and ideally not in washrooms.
- Disposable cups or a water fountain should be supplied.

**Accommodation for clothing**

- Secure accommodation for home clothing must be provided for every worker.
- Secure accommodation must be provided for work clothing such as overalls.
- The room should have sufficient space for clothes to hang in a clean, warm, dry, well-ventilated place, where they can dry out during the day or overnight.

**Rest and eating facilities**

- Rest facilities must be provided, including separate facilities to eat food that would otherwise become contaminated; at the very least, a microwave and water boiler must be provided.
- Separate canteens or rest rooms are not required in clean facilities such as offices, so long as undisturbed breaks can be taken.
- There must be non-smoking areas or rooms in rest facilities, or a complete ban on smoking.

**Pregnant women and nursing mothers**
- Rest areas must be provided near to washrooms and should include facilities to lie down.

**Also read...**

Chapter 13 – Asbestos

## Asbestos

Many thousands of tons of materials containing asbestos remain in buildings all over the world. If in good condition and encapsulated, asbestos poses no threat to workers; if its condition deteriorates, then a risk develops. There is a particular risk to maintenance workers, who may disturb the material. The building occupier is required to inform employees and others of the risks. This is done by means of an asbestos register, training and signage.

**www.protect.org.uk**

**PDF 08**

**Hard facts**

Asbestos is the biggest-ever single cause of insurance claims. Worldwide, there have been an estimated 600,000 claims relating to asbestos, with over 60 manufacturers of products incorporating asbestos and dozens of insurance companies bankrupted. $200 billion has been paid out so far.

| Asbestos | Yes or no | Action to be taken |
|---|---|---|
| Is there an asbestos register for the building? | | |
| Does the register indicate the presence of asbestos in the workplace? | | |
| If so, is asbestos properly managed or are there plans for its removal? (Indicate timescale.) | | |
| If there is no asbestos register, are you sure that no asbestos is present? Should an asbestos survey be carried out by a specialist? (If in doubt, seek advice.) | | |
| Are workers informed of the presence of asbestos by signage and task briefings? | | |

## The bottom line

**To comply with current legislation:**

- it is necessary to provide a well-ventilated, clean, warm and properly lit working environment
- corridors must be free from obstructions, with clearly signposted fire escape routes and vision panels in doors
- windows must be capable of being cleaned without undue risk
- edges, openings and other places that have the potential for falls that may cause injury must be protected
- dangerous pits must be fenced off or provided with a load-bearing cover
- traffic routes in yards, car parks and factories must be designed to provide pedestrians with a clear view of, and keep them apart from, vehicles
- external gates that open both ways must have vision panels so that oncoming traffic can be seen
- rooms must meet minimum dimensions and standards
- workstations must be assessed for health hazards
- welfare facilities must include:
  - sanitary conveniences and washing facilities
  - a good supply of drinking water
  - sufficient space for clothing
  - rest and eating facilities
  - special rest areas for pregnant women and nursing mothers
  - a smoke-free rest room
- the presence of asbestos must be identified and action taken to prevent exposure to employees and maintenance contractors. Where relevant, an asbestos register must be maintained.

## Introduction

If there is a fire, people need to be able to evacuate the building to reach a place of safety. It cannot be emphasised strongly enough that, if there is a fire, the primary aim is to ensure that everyone reaches safety. Putting the fire out is secondary. An essential requirement is that people's ability to escape should not depend on makeshift arrangements, such as the use of portable ladders or rescue by the fire brigade, but on properly planned provision.

If you have a fire certificate for your premises, have a look at the attached plan. It will tell you exactly what is required by way of fire escape, fire doors and signage. Make sure you get permission from the fire officer before any alterations are made to the premises.

## Fire – the essential factors

Three factors are necessary for a fire to start – fuel, oxygen and a source of ignition (the 'fire elements'). When assessing fire risk, you need to consider which items on your premises fall into these three categories:

- fuel, eg wood, paper, rags, petrol, propane cylinder

- oxygen, eg air, oxygen cylinder, oxidising chemicals

- source of ignition, eg flames, hot surfaces, sparks from grinding wheel, blow lamp, static electricity, smoking.

**The fire triangle**

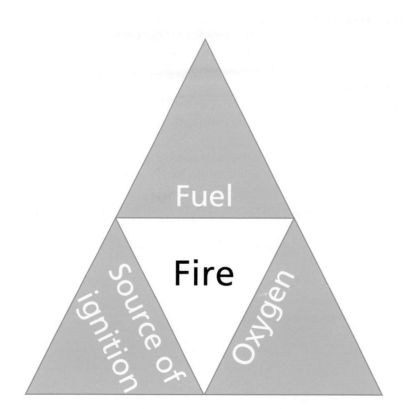

## Fire risk assessments and fire certificates

A fire risk assessment is required for every workplace, and must be formally recorded where five or more people are employed. By following through the checklists in this chapter, you will have carried out and recorded a fire risk assessment.

At the time of printing, the need for fire certificates still exists (see box for requirements), but will be replaced by the duty to conduct a fire risk assessment. Those premises with existing fire certificates may use them to base their fire risk assessments on, provided they are not too old or there have not been any significant changes to the building or processes.

Before altering premises or spending money on items identified following your fire risk assessment, it is advisable to discuss your proposals with the fire authority or other competent adviser.

A fire certificate is required if any of the following apply:

- more than 20 people are employed at any time

- more than 10 people are employed at any time elsewhere than on the ground floor

- flammable or explosive substances are stored or used on the premises

- premises are used as a hotel or boarding house that sleeps more than six people (including employees), or if sleeping accommodation is other than on the ground or first floors

- premises are 'special premises', designated and controlled by the HSE because of their high risk (in such high hazard installations, the HSE issues and enforces the fire certificate, not the fire authority).

In a multi-occupancy building, it is the total number of people working on the premises that is used to decide if a fire certificate is needed.

In all cases except 'special premises', the local fire authority issues and enforces fire certificates.

# Fire precautions survey and risk assessment

**The five steps of the fire risk assessment process**

**Step 1** Identify the hazards from the quantity and nature of combustible materials in the workplace, work processes, and the potential sources of ignition.

**Step 2** Identify the location of those people at significant risk in the event of a fire.

**Step 3** Make a survey of general fire precautions that are present in the premises in order to ensure that they comply with building regulations and statutory standards. To do this, use the checklists in this chapter. Assess the risk to people and property, taking into account the hazards identified in Steps 1 and 2, and carry out any necessary improvements.

**Step 4** Put in place emergency procedures and provide training to make sure that the physical measures will work effectively if they are ever needed. Complete the fire plan model (later in this chapter).

**Step 5** Keep the assessment under review and revise if the situation changes.

### Compartmentation?

To stop a fire spreading, a building can be subdivided using fire-resistant walls, floors and/or ceilings. This is called 'compartmentation'. One example is a protected escape stairway in which internal fire doors help form compartments that restrict fire to a specific part of the building.

In large or complex buildings, compartmentation is often a major part of the strategy to limit the spread of fire. Unfortunately, it is quite common to find these measures breached. This can happen where building services such as drainage and power supplies run vertically through the floors, leaving gaps in the structure around them. If these gaps or other holes are left at floor level or in walls in service risers and the like, a route is created for fire to spread. In such cases, the openings must be filled with non-combustible material ('fire stopping') to maintain fire resistance.

A half-hour fire resistance can be provided with 12.5mm plasterboard on timber studwork, with joints filled with plaster. Alternatively, proprietary mineral fibre-reinforced cement boards or similar can be used.

**Step 1. Identify the hazards from combustible materials and sources of ignition**
Assess the risk, noting any existing precautions that are in place. Tick the relevant boxes. Any risks that are high or medium will need to be reconsidered and additional precautions or management systems put in place to reduce them. Detail these separately as part of your organisation and arrangements (see Chapter 1).

www.protect.org.uk

PDF 09

| Combustible material | Location and activity | Number of people at location | Quantity of combustible material – high, medium or low | Name sources of ignition | Risk – high, medium or low |
|---|---|---|---|---|---|
| Timber | | | | | |
| Paper | | | | | |
| Furniture | | | | | |
| Flammable chemicals | | | | | |

**Flammable and explosive substances – what are the hazards?**
Some gases, liquids and solids can cause explosions or fire. For a fire to start, fuel, air and a source of ignition are needed. Some materials will burn violently in an oxygen-rich atmosphere, such as when an oxygen cylinder is leaking. Therefore, store cylinders separately. Some dusts form an explosive cloud that can destroy a building. Serious explosions can occur in boilers, ovens and the like. Explosives, including fireworks, need special precautions and require licensing.

**Sources of ignition**
Isolate all potential sources of ignition from storage areas that contain flammable and/or explosive substances. Potential sources of ignition include smoking, naked flames, propane use and heaters, electrical equipment that has no spark protection, overloaded or defective power circuits, static electricity and bonfires. Also, protect storage areas from arson.

Carry out a survey of general fire precautions (Step 3), taking into account the hazards identified here. Note here any specific action required.

| Action required to reduce risk | Guidance |
|---|---|
| | 1. Stored combustible materials constitute a fire load and increase both the chance of a fire occurring and its size. Therefore, it makes sense to minimise the quantity of stored materials such as paper, timber, furniture, paint, old tyres, fertilisers, oils, fuel, chemicals, flammable liquids and gases and rubber mats. In joinery premises, wood dust is a potent fuel. |
| | 2. Ideally, combustible materials should be stored outside main buildings. Internal stores should be positioned away from main escape routes and have at least a half-hour fire resistance. |

Storage

- Some chemicals react together and therefore must be stored separately – refer to suppliers' data sheets for information.

- Separate storage from the workroom or process, where fire or leakage is more common.

- Store all flammable and explosive substances in a safe, well-ventilated place, at least 3m from buildings.

- Prevent incompatible chemicals being mixed by spillage, damage to packaging and so on, by providing bunded storage areas.

- Store cylinders in an upright position (if stored horizontally they are a potential missile).

- Stores must be fire resistant.

- Carefully store empty drums as well as full ones; both can be hazardous.

What is...

**Bunded storage?**
A bund is a type of wall or bank around a tank or other container. Bunding acts to prevent the substance in the container from escaping. The bund should have sufficient capacity to accommodate the entire contents plus a further 10 per cent.

**Step 1. Identify the hazards from combustible materials and sources of ignition (continued)**

www.protect.org.uk

PDF 09

| Combustible material | Location and activity | Number of people at location | Quantity of combustible material – high, medium or low | Name sources of ignition | Risk – high, medium or low |
|---|---|---|---|---|---|
| LPG | | | | | |
| Oxygen | | | | | |
| Acetylene/ propane | | | | | |
| Other flammable gases | | | | | |

**Oxyacetylene set**

1. Outlet pressure gauge
2. Cylinder contents gauge
3. Flashback arresters
4. Non-return valves

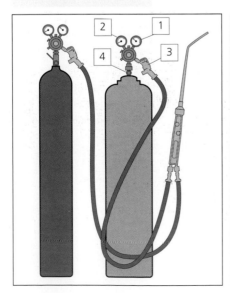

**Use of oxyacetylene (and propane) equipment**

- Workers must be trained and competent in the use of equipment.
- Equipment must be marked with a recognised standard and be formally maintained.
- Hoses should be colour coded as follows:
  - blue – oxygen
  - red – acetylene
  - orange – propane.
- Use proprietary hose assemblies – jubilee clips can damage hoses, causing them to leak.
- Fit non-return valves and flashback arresters.
- Use cylinders secured in special trolleys.
- Check equipment for damage before each use, and make sure that oil and grease do not contaminate the oxygen supply.
- Turn off valves at the end of each day.
- Change cylinders in a well-ventilated place, away from sources of ignition.
- Use soap to test for leaks; never use a flame.

| Action required to reduce risk | Guidance |
|---|---|
| | **Use of LPG equipment**<br>• Turn off cylinder valves before connecting or disconnecting any equipment.<br>• Check before use and never kink hoses.<br>• Secure equipment vertically during use.<br>• Follow lighting-up procedures, normally closing the appliance valve before opening the equipment valve.<br>• Handle cylinders carefully to avoid damage.<br>• Appliances such as room heaters should be fitted by a CORGI-registered fitter; ideally, cylinders should be fitted outside the building.<br>• Fit a flame-failure device to heaters.<br>• LPG heaters must be well ventilated at both floor and ceiling level.<br>**Transport of LPG**<br>• Use open vehicles to transport upright cylinders.<br>• Any other flammables that are transported must be kept in a closed steel box.<br>• Carry two dry powder extinguishers, nominally 2kg and 6kg.<br>• Drivers carrying more than two cylinders must have received instruction and carry a Transport emergency card (Tremcard) detailing the load carried and action required in the event of an emergency. |

**Gas cylinder compound**

1. 1.5m separation
2. 9kg dry powder extinguisher by gate. Gate opens outwards
3. Signs:
   ○ Highly flammable LPG
   ○ No smoking. No naked lights

**Storage of gas cylinders**

• Store both full and empty cylinders upright, in a secure outdoor compound with a 1.8m high (minimum) wire-mesh fence. Only one exit is required up to 300kg of gas stored; greater than this, two exits are required. Keep compound weed-free using non-chlorate weed killer.

• Never store liquefied petroleum gas (LPG) in unventilated metal boxes or huts. If there is a leak, gas will build up to a dangerous level.

• Avoid placing cylinders in basements or nearby pits, drains or excavations, as most gases are heavier than air and may accumulate.

• For flammable gas and oxygen cylinders stored internally, ventilation openings to the open air are necessary, representing 2.5 per cent of the total wall and floor area.

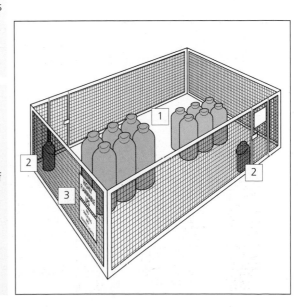

Step 1. Identify the hazards from combustible materials and sources of ignition (continued)

| Combustible material | Location and activity | Number of people at location | Quantity of combustible material – high, medium or low | Name sources of ignition | Risk – high, medium or low |
|---|---|---|---|---|---|
| Bitumen | | | | | |
| Oils | | | | | |
| Fuels | | | | | |
| Flammable paint | | | | | |
| Other flammable liquids | | | | | |

| Action required to reduce risk | Guidance |
| --- | --- |
| | **Bitumen boilers**<br>• Bitumen boilers should be kept at least 3m from LPG cylinders.<br>• Never leave a boiler unattended or move it when it is alight.<br>• Where possible, avoid taking bitumen boilers onto roofs. If necessary, place the boiler on an insulating base and keep under constant supervision.<br>**Flammable liquids, including paints**<br>• The safest place to store flammable liquids is in a separate building or in the open air.<br>• In a workroom, a maximum of 50 litres of highly flammable liquids may be stored on their own in a specially constructed steel cupboard or box.<br>• Dispense and use flammable liquids in a safe, well-ventilated place.<br>• Openings totalling 1 per cent of the total wall and floor area are necessary to provide the required ventilation for storing flammable liquids.<br>• Keep containers closed and contain spillage by dispensing over a tray and having clean-up materials ready, such as sand.<br>• Prohibit smoking and naked flames; spark-proof electrics are required in areas of use.<br>• Place rubbish in a closed steel box.<br>• Have a fire extinguisher available, either dry powder or foam.<br>• Use non-sparking tools when scraping deposits from spray booths and the like. |

Step 1. Identify the hazards from combustible materials and sources of ignition (continued)

www.protect.org.uk

PDF 09

| Combustible material | Location and activity | Number of people at location | Quantity of combustible material – high, medium or low | Name sources of ignition | Risk – high, medium or low |
|---|---|---|---|---|---|
| Explosive dusts | | | | | |
| Fine wood dust | | | | | |
| Flammable solids | | | | | |
| Plastic foam | | | | | |
| Rubber | | | | | |
| Polystyrene | | | | | |
| Polythene | | | | | |
| Other flammable solids | | | | | |
| Explosives | | | | | |
| Protection materials | | | | | |
| Packaging materials | | | | | |
| Household materials | | | | | |
| Rubbish | | | | | |
| Other | | | | | |

| Action required to reduce risk | Guidance |
|---|---|
| | **Dust explosions**<br>• Dusty materials that can cause explosions include aluminium powder, flour, bone meal, cotton fly, paper dust, polystyrene and fine sawdust.<br>• Keep plant enclosed so that dust cannot escape.<br>• Use exhaust ventilation with dust collectors.<br>• Keep areas clean.<br>• Prohibit smoking, welding and the use of space heaters.<br>• Reduce sparking by using enclosed and dust-tight electrical equipment, and earthing sources of static electricity.<br>• If a major risk is present, incorporate explosion vents into plant design.<br>**Flammable solids**<br>• Plastic foams, rubber mats, polystyrene and similar products are all high risk.<br>**Oxygen**<br>• Air is necessary for fires to start, but pure oxygen makes fires worse.<br>• Store oxygen cylinders on their own, away from other flammables and gases.<br>**Kitchens**<br>• Remove grease from cooker hoods and extract duct.<br>• Ensure thermostats on deep-fat fryers are regularly maintained and free from the build up of grease.<br>**Special cases**<br>• You must notify the HSE if you use or store certain 'major hazard' dangerous substances, such as large quantities of highly flammable or toxic chemicals.<br>• If you think that this may apply to your operations, seek specialist advice.<br>• In such cases, the HSE (not the local fire authority) issues the fire certificate and enforces health and safety standards.*<br>**Rubbish**<br>• Rubbish is usually combustible and constitutes a serious fire hazard.<br>• General rubbish should be cleared daily into skips that are sited at least 3m from the building.<br>• Flammable rubbish such as contaminated rags must be kept in a close-topped metal dustbin or similar container.<br>• All skips and bins must be emptied regularly. |

*See 'Fire risk assessments and fire certificates' on page 70

**Step 2. Identify the location of people who are at significant risk in the event of a fire**
It is important to locate systematically every person at work and ensure that they can be warned in the event of a fire and can escape. Many premises contain a labyrinth of passages and remote rooms where people may be working. All such locations must be evaluated.

Night workers may be at greater risk because they are working alone, perhaps on an intermittent basis. Similarly, security guards working at night should understand the safety procedures in the event of a fire. Visitors and contractors must also be considered.

Induction training should include fire precautions, alarms, escape routes and assembly areas (see later in this chapter).

| Location | Names of people at significant risk in case of fire, and reasons for significant risk | How will they be warned of fire? | How will they escape? |
|---|---|---|---|
|  |  |  |  |
|  |  |  |  |
|  |  |  |  |
|  |  |  |  |
|  |  |  |  |
|  |  |  |  |
|  |  |  |  |

www.protect.org.uk

PDF 10

**Step 3. Premises survey of fire precautions**

When undertaking a survey of fire precautions, take into account the hazards identified in Steps 1 and 2. The standard required will be relative to the risk identified in those steps.

Make sure that any required action is recorded here (or separately), and is followed up in a timely manner.

www.protect.org.uk

PDF 11

| Fire certificate | Yes or no | Action to be taken and comments |
|---|---|---|
| Does the workplace require a fire certificate? State why. | | |
| If so, is it available? | | |
| After careful inspection, state if the premises have been altered in any way that would materially affect the relevance of the fire certificate. This includes both the layout and use of the workplace. | | |
| Has the local fire authority added any special requirements or limitations, and if so are they being complied with? | | |
| Do the general fire precautions set out in the fire certificate correctly address the current level of fire risk? State the risk level with these in place – high, medium or low. | | |

### Guidance and good business practice

Refer to 'Fire risk assessments and fire certificates' at the beginning of this chapter.

It is not unusual to find premises that require a fire certificate but do not have one. Application must be made to the local fire authority on Form FP1(REV) 1989. In any event, all of the general fire precautions must still be in place; you cannot wait for a certificate. So carry on with this survey and risk assessment.

Almost all workplaces are in a continual state of change. Therefore, you must decide if there are significant changes in layout or use, and if so apply for an amended fire certificate. Be particularly vigilant about change of use, such as introducing a spray booth using flammable paint. In any event, relevant precautions must be implemented immediately.

There may be limitations on the number of personnel in the workplace. Special maintenance may be required to ensure that the means of escape is always kept clear. You may also require training or other additional fire precautions relevant to a specific hazard.

Current law does not allow you to rely entirely on a fire certificate; you must also assess the risk. However, if you have a reasonably up-to-date fire certificate in place that is closely followed, it would be reasonable to conclude that the resultant risk is low. If you have concluded that the risk is other than low, then you need to examine ways of reducing it by following the guidance in this chapter.

www.protect.org.uk

PDF 11

**Step 3. Premises survey of fire precautions (continued)**

| Escape routes and fire exits | Yes or no | Action to be taken and comments |
|---|---|---|
| Are all escape routes clear, uncomplicated passageways, of adequate width, properly maintained and free from obstructions? | | |
| Are there at least two escape routes, in different directions, from each floor, section or workshop? | | |
| Are the travel distances adequate to reach safety? | | |
| Are there sufficient protected stairways from each upper storey or basement? Note the number. | | |
| Is the construction and condition of all protected stairways satisfactory? | | |
| Is the construction and condition of all fire doors and final exit doors satisfactory? | | |
| Can all external fire escapes be reached easily, and are they unobstructed throughout (including at ground level), with fire-resistant windows and doors adjacent to them? | | |
| Are all assembly points adequately sized and signposted, and safe in the event of fire or other emergencies? | | |
| Are all escape routes adequately signposted? | | |
| Are all escape routes provided with adequate emergency lighting? | | |

## Guidance and good business practice

- See table on 'Widths of escape routes, exits and stairs' later in this chapter.
- Ramps are acceptable up to a 1:10 slope, provided they have a non-slip floor and a handrail. Stairs greater than 1.4m wide need a central handrail.

A basic principle of escape routes is that any person confronted by a fire can turn away from it or pass it safely to reach a place of safety. People working in dead ends should not have to pass a place of high fire risk to reach safety.

The distances given are as a person walks. Where there is a protected stairway, the travel distance is measured to the stairway. See 'Travel distances to reach a place of safety from fire' at the end of this section.

See 'What is?' box on the right for a detailed explanation.

When inspecting, always follow the stairway right down to the bottom and open the final exit door to see if it is blocked.

- Do the doors fit properly, with no gaps through which fire could pass?
- Do the door closers work efficiently?
- Are doors propped open?

External fire escapes are not desirable but are sometimes necessary. The same applies to fire escapes via a roof, but if this is unavoidable the route should be protected from smoke, fire and falls.

Check that the assembly points are clear of windows (which may fall out in the event of a fire) and are situated away from the arriving fire appliances. Can assembly points be reached safely from the fire exits?

Required signposting will be indicated on the fire certificate (see 'Fire risk assessments and fire certificates' earlier in this chapter). Fire exit signs (comprising a white pictogram on a green background) must be visible from every point in the building (see 'Fire exit and equipment signs' later in this chapter).

If the power supply fails there must be adequate light on escape corridors and stairs to allow evacuation. This is usually by means of a battery- or generator-powered supply, which must be maintained and tested on a regular basis in accordance with the manufacturer's instructions. Check that you have emergency lighting, a back-up power supply and a test regime.

---

## What is...

### A protected stairway?

A protected stairway is made of non-combustible construction, such as concrete and plaster, with non-combustible or flame-retardant floor and wall coverings. The stairway should be continuous, have standard risers and treads, be ventilated, have at least half-hour fire-resistant doors and glazing, and be fitted with handrails on both sides.

- Small two-storey buildings that have travel distances well within those given for dead ends do not necessarily need protected stairways.
- Low-rise buildings up to four storeys must have at least one protected stairway, although two is normal good practice.
- Buildings of more than four storeys must have at least two protected stairways.
- Basements must have at least one protected stairway exiting to the open air at ground level.

When evaluating a building for the purpose of risk assessment, consider this information together with that for travel distances – you must comply with both sets of legal requirements.

### Step 3. Premises survey of fire precautions (continued)

 What are...

Two or more directions of escape?

1. This angle must be 45° or greater.

In other words, if you are at point 'X' you should have two different escape options, with a minimum of 45° between the two.

| Travel distances to reach a place of safety from fire | | |
|---|---|---|
| Use of the premises or part of the premises | Maximum travel distance, in metres, where travel is possible in: | |
| | one direction only or dead end | two or more directions at least 45° apart |
| **Institutional** | 9 | 18 |
| **Other residential and hotels** | | |
| • Bedrooms | 9 | 18 |
| • Bedroom corridors | 9 | 35 |
| • Elsewhere | 18 | 35 |
| **Offices, shops and commercial** | 18 | 45 |
| **Assembly and recreation** | | |
| • Buildings primarily for people with disabilities, except schools | 9 | 18 |
| • Schools | 18 | 45 |
| • Areas with seating in rows | 15 | 32 |
| • Elsewhere | 18 | 45 |
| **Industrial storage and other non-residential** | | |
| • Normal risk – some flammables and combustibles, but any fire is likely to be localised | 25 | 45 |
| • High risk – significant quantities of flammable materials, so that any fire would be serious, with copious smoke or fumes | 12 | 25 |
| **Place of special fire hazard** Oil-filled transformer and switchgear rooms, boiler rooms, storage space for fuel or other highly flammable substances, and rooms housing a fixed internal-combustion engine. Also, school laboratories, kitchens, stores for chemicals and mats used in physical education. | 9 | 18 |
| **Plant room or rooftop plant** | | |
| • Distance from the most remote point in the plant room to the door | 9 | 35 |
| • Escape route not in open air (overall) | 18 | 45 |
| • Escape route in open air (overall) | 60 | 100 |

| Widths of escape routes, exits and stairs | | |
|---|---|---|
| Maximum number of persons | Minimum width in mm | |
| | Escape routes/exits | Escape stairs |
| 50 | 750 | 800 |
| 110 | 850 | 1,000 |
| 220 | 1,050 | 1,050 |
| More than 220 | Seek specialist advice | Refer to building regulations |

Fire doors, including final exit doors

Fire doors must have a fire resistance equal to that of the building – 30 minutes minimum. They must:

- have fire-resistant vision panels so that wheelchair users can be seen (with the exception of the final exit door)

- open in the direction of escape

- not be revolving or sliding doors, which can jam

- be capable of being opened without keys

- be protected from fires in adjacent premises or a basement

- be of adequate width – a standard width (750mm) door is adequate for 50 people.

Preferably, final exit doors should not open onto steps but give direct access to an unenclosed space in the open air at ground level, from which the assembly point can be reached safely.

www.protect.org.uk

PDF 11

### Step 3. Premises survey of fire precautions (continued)

| Raising the alarm | Yes or no | Action to be taken and comments |
|---|---|---|
| Decide on and note the risk level for the occupants, and choose an appropriate detection and alarm system. | | |
| If a modern fire alarm system is installed, does it have sufficient call points and sounders? | | |
| Is the fire alarm system tested on a regular basis? | | |
| Do the premises, or that part of the premises requiring automatic fire detection and alarm, have an appropriate system? | | |
| Does the fire alarm/detection system have a regular maintenance contract? | | |

**Fire exit and equipment signs**

| Guidance and good business practice |
|---|
| See 'Fire alarm systems' below. |
| There should be a call point beside each exit and enough sounders so that the alarm can be heard in every part of the building, including toilet areas, conference rooms and so on. |
| Sound the alarms weekly, at a defined time, to ensure that they are all working, and record these tests, detailing any action required. Check that the sounders can be heard in every room. |
| In a hotel or large building, this includes a display board indicating the location of the fire. Consider any unoccupied areas. Systems can be based on smoke, heat or radiation detection, as appropriate. |
| There should be written evidence of annual inspection and maintenance, or in accordance with the supplier's recommendations that are provided on installation. |

### Fire alarm systems

As part of the fire risk assessment of your premises, consideration must be given to the most suitable fire alarm/detection system.

All buildings should have arrangements for detecting fire. People in some buildings may detect fire either through observation or smell, and often nothing more will be needed. In small buildings or premises, the means of raising the alarm may simply be someone shouting "Fire!". In such cases, it must be determined that the warning can be heard and understood throughout the premises. In certain circumstances, a hand bell, air horn or simple manual call point, combined with a bell, battery and charger, may be suitable.

In all other cases, buildings should be provided with a fire warning system that is electrically operated, with manual break-glass call points situated next to exit doors, and sufficient sounders so that the alarm is clearly audible throughout the building. Where people might not respond quickly, a voice alarm should be installed. In premises such as shopping centres and entertainment venues, an initial general alarm may be undesirable because it may cause the public to panic. A two-stage system may then be used, initially to alert trained staff discreetly, followed by full evacuation by sounders or voice alarm.

Automatic fire detection and alarm systems are mandatory in institutional and other residential occupancies such as hotels. They are not mandatory in offices and shops, or commercial, assembly, recreation, industrial, storage and other non-residential premises. However, current good practice is to install such systems in larger premises of these types. They may also be required as part of an overall fire safety strategy that is an integral part of the design of the building, or to protect unoccupied parts of premises such as basements, storage areas or lofts.

### Step 3. Premises survey of fire precautions (continued)

www.protect.org.uk

PDF 11

| Fire-fighting equipment | Yes or no | Action to be taken and comments |
|---|---|---|
| Are there adequate fire extinguishers provided:<br>• by each exit?<br>• within the building or premises?<br>• adjacent to hot works, such as welding or flame-cutting?<br>• in places of special fire hazard, such as boiler rooms and LPG storage areas? | | |
| Are hose reels provided? | | |
| Is there a maintenance contract to examine extinguishers and hose reels at least annually, in accordance with a recognised procedure? Is every extinguisher satisfactory? | | |
| Do sprinklers cover all areas where sprinkler protection is appropriate? | | |
| Are sprinkler systems maintained on an annual basis? | | |

**Typical fire instruction notice**

Has space for entering clear and concise instructions on what to do if there is a fire.

## Guidance and good business practice

Extinguishers should be appropriate to the nature of the potential fire (see 'Which fire extinguisher to use' below). The following level of cover is considered reasonable for average conditions per 200m² of floor area:
- one 9-litre water or foam extinguisher
- one $CO_2$ extinguisher.

There should be no fewer than two of each type of extinguisher per floor in case one proves to be defective or is in a location where a fire prevents it from being used.

A hose reel can supplement water-based extinguishers only, but make sure it can reach all parts of the area and will be accessible in a fire. Up to 800m² can be covered.

Check each extinguisher to verify the date of the most recent inspection and which organisation carried out the work. Also, check that any maintenance contract lists all of the extinguishers.

Institutional and other residential occupancies, such as large hotels, will normally require sprinkler protection, and it is good practice for most large buildings.

Check that the maintenance contract lists all of the sprinkler heads to be maintained.

## Which fire extinguisher to use

The purpose of fire extinguishers is to enable people to extinguish small fires before they get out of control, or enable them to escape before this happens. Putting out fires that have taken hold is the role of the fire service.

| Fire class | | | | |
|---|---|---|---|---|
| | **A**  Solids  Materials with glowing embers, eg wood, paper and cloth | **B**  Liquids  B1 – soluble in water, eg methanol  B2 – liquids not soluble in water, eg petrol and oil | **C**  Gases  Methane, butane, liquefied petroleum gas and so on | Electrical fires |
| **Extinguisher type** **Water** | ✓ | | Use water to cool leaking container and dry powder or foam to extinguish fire | |
| **Foam** | ✓ | ✓ B2 only | ✓ | |
| **CO₂** | | ✓ B1 and B2 | | ✓ |
| **Dry powder** | ✓ | ✓ B1 and B2 | ✓ | ✓ |

*Note: extinguishers are not suitable for use on fires involving deep-fat fryers or chip pans – use a fire blanket. Class D fires, which involve burning metals (eg aluminium, magnesium, sodium and potassium), represent a special risk, and specialist advice should be sought if such materials are on your premises.*

### Step 4. Making emergency plans

Emergency procedures and plans need not be complex or lengthy, but they must be appropriate, clearly understood by all, and practised. On multi-occupancy sites, it is necessary to have effective co-ordination and liaison. Emergencies other than fire, such as bombs or terrorist attacks, will need to be considered by some organisations and should be incorporated into the plan. For most organisations, however, fire remains the biggest risk they face.

www.protect.org.uk

PDF 12

| A simple fire plan model for normal risk premises | | |
|---|---|---|
| **Management action** | **Notes** | **Plan** |
| Appoint fire officer | Name: | Duties<br>• Ensure that the general fire precautions are adequate and maintained, and that the fire certificate is up to date<br>• Appoint fire wardens, as appropriate<br>• Take charge of any emergency<br>• Ensure that the emergency services are contacted<br>• Ensure that a head count is carried out<br>• Meet and brief the emergency services on the situation and relevant information, such as the location of fire hydrants and hazardous materials<br>• Maintain liaison with emergency services and other affected parties to ensure that the site and its risks are fully understood by all concerned<br>• Maintain discipline and control re-entry after consultation with the emergency services<br>• Ensure records are kept of fire drills and lessons learned<br>• Appoint a deputy. |
| Appoint fire wardens | Names: | • Sufficient fire wardens (plus deputies) should be appointed to allow a sweep of the building while people evacuate. Fire wardens must have the authority to instruct people to leave the premises and are responsible for a head count of the people in their area.<br>• Fire wardens are responsible for checking that escape routes in their area are kept clear and free from obstructions, and that fire-fighting appliances are in place, in good condition and tested. These inspections should be carried out weekly (or more or less frequently, depending on risk) and recorded. |

| A simple fire plan model for normal risk premises (continued) | | |
|---|---|---|
| Management action | Notes | Plan |
| Weekly sounding of fire alarms | Name of person who will test alarm: | This check should be made at the same time each week, to ensure that the alarm works and can be heard. Keep basic records. |
| Fire drills | Frequency: | Normally carried out once or twice per year, with the entire workforce evacuating the premises. These drills provide invaluable training and testing of procedures, and every attempt should be made to carry them out, although in some situations this is not practicable. Record the test, evacuation time and other relevant information. If possible, involve the emergency services. |
| Fire instruction notices | Locations: | Fire instruction notices must be permanently and prominently displayed on major escape routes, places where people meet, circulation spaces and so on. They must detail:<br>• action to be taken, including raising the alarm and using fire extinguishers and hoses only when safe to do so<br>• action to be taken on hearing the alarm, including the location of the assembly point. |
| Information, instruction and training | Name of person(s) who will provide basic fire induction training:<br><br>Name of person(s) who will train fire wardens: | The fire instruction notices act only as a reminder. All people at work must be trained on what to do in the event of a fire. Fire wardens and others need training in the fire plan procedures and the use of fire extinguishers. |

**Step 5. Keep premises under review**
Review the assessment before you make any large change to your premises, and at least annually.

## Fire precautions induction

Employees need to be told about the following when they join an organisation:

- the location and safe use of the escape routes from their working area

- what the fire alarm sounds like

- that evacuation is compulsory on hearing the alarm

- not to collect personal belongings when the alarm sounds

- the location of the assembly point

- when to tackle a fire and when to leave it

- the use of different types of fire extinguisher

- the name of their fire warden

- to report any defects or escape route obstructions to the fire warden

- when they hear the alarm and before evacuating, to turn off any high risk equipment such as oxyacetylene tools or LPG, but only where this can be achieved without risk.

**The bottom line**

By law, your organisation must:
- carry out a fire risk assessment
- comply with any fire certificate that exists for the premises
- store and use gas cylinders in the prescribed manner
- maintain escape routes and fire exits
- install an appropriate fire alarm system
- provide fire extinguishers
- make emergency plans.

## Introduction

In this chapter we examine some of the main health issues that face workers on a daily basis.

Health issues can be summarised under the following headings:

- manual handling

- upper limb disorders

- noise

- hand–arm vibration

- hazardous substances

- solvents

- radiation

- lead

- asbestos.

> **Hard facts**
>
> Each year in the UK, an estimated 2 million people suffer from ill health caused by work, resulting in 18 million days lost, at a cost to the economy of up to £11 billion.

> **Hard facts**
>
> More days are lost through ill health than through accidents, and many more fatalities if we include exposure to asbestos

Some health issues are dealt with in other chapters as they have particular relevance to specific industries. Thus, in Chapter 8 we look at metalworking fluids and oils, welding fume and wood dust; repetitive strain injury in Chapter 12; and asbestos in Chapter 13.

## Manual handling

Generally, manual handling injuries are caused by incorrect or excessive use of bodily force, leading to sprains and strains. Poor posture and repetitive movement are common factors and injuries can be cumulative, at times leading to permanent disability.

The law requires that:

- hazardous manual handling operations should be avoided if reasonably practicable, and other means of handling found, eg mechanical handling

- hazardous manual handling operations that cannot be avoided must be assessed, and the risk of injury reduced as much as possible by practical means, eg reduced load or providing hand grips

- people carrying out manual handling should be given training and relevant information, eg the weight and distribution of the load.

**Hard facts**

Manual handling injuries account for more than a quarter of all reportable accidents and 10 per cent of major accidents.

To illustrate these points, take the example of a large television that is awkward, heavy and unevenly distributed within its box. In the factory, the TV will be moved on conveyor belts and made ready for transportation by pallet movers, thereby avoiding any unnecessary manual handling. However, when the set is installed in the home, manual handling cannot be avoided. Consequently, the box is labelled with its weight, and there are hand grips in the correct position to balance the load.

**Risk assessment**

If a general risk assessment indicates that manual handling is unavoidable, then a competent person should carry out a manual handling assessment. Where applicable, employees and their safety representatives should be involved in this process. The manual handling assessment must identify the problems likely to arise during handling and the measures necessary to deal with them. A review of accident and/or ill health records will be useful in this respect.

Assessments must be recorded and need to be reviewed in the light of experience, when there is a change in manual handling operations, or if an accident occurs. An assessment form is included in Appendix A.

**Reducing the risk**

Once the risks have been identified, they will have to be reduced if practicable, and the following measures introduced:

- avoid the need for manual handling by not doing the process, or by doing it differently, eg having the load delivered direct to the point of use

- make use of mechanical handling, eg forklift trucks or pallet movers

- reduce the load or make it lighter by changing specifications, eg in the construction industry, cement that has to be handled by hand is usually supplied in 25kg bags, much smaller than the 50kg bags that used to be the norm

- improve the working environment by ensuring that there is adequate space for handling operations; good housekeeping and clear access routes are essential.

**Training**

Training on safe handling techniques should be given, including taking employees' individual capabilities into account, how to recognise dangerous or unfamiliar situations, and the use of handling aids. A toolbox talk on basic lifting is included in Appendix B.

**Information**

Where practicable, precise information on the weight of each load, and on the heaviest side of any load where this is not centred, must be provided. Where items are likely to be handled manually, manufacturers and suppliers are required to provide such information on the box or packaging, or on the load itself.

## Guidelines for lifting and lowering

Basic guidelines for manual handling that involves lifting and lowering are set out in the diagram below. The guidelines assume that loads are readily grasped with both hands, the working conditions are reasonable, and that the handler is in a stable body position. The capability to lift or lower is reduced significantly if the load is held at arm's length or the hands pass over shoulder height. If the hands enter more than one of the weight guideline boxes during the lifting operation, the lowest weight figure should be used.

### Twisting

The figures for lifting and lowering should be reduced if the handler twists his or her back to the side during the operation: reduce by 10 per cent if twisting through 45° and by 20 per cent if twisting through 90°. Movement on a swivel chair may avoid twisting of the back.

### Frequent lifting and lowering

The figures for lifting and lowering are for relatively infrequent operations (30 operations per hour), where the pace of work is not forced, rest is possible and the load is not supported for any length of time. The figures should be reduced by 30 per cent if the operation is repeated once or twice a minute, by 50 per cent if the operation is repeated around five to eight times a minute, and by 80 per cent if the operation is repeated more than 12 times per minute.

### Carrying loads

The figures for carrying loads are similar to those given for lifting or lowering, if the load is held against the body and is carried no further than 10m without a rest. Where the load can be carried securely on the shoulder without first having been lifted (eg unloading from a lorry), the assessment may show that it is acceptable to exceed the guide figure, depending on the strength of the person involved.

Also read...

Appendix B – Basic lifting

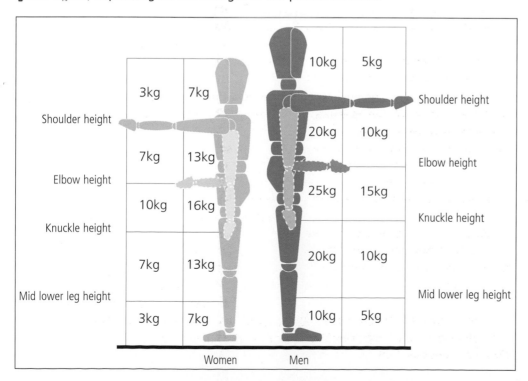

Women     Men

**Guidelines for lifting and lowering**

*Note: these weights do not represent 'safe' loads – they are merely guidelines to indicate where risk assessment may be needed*

**Pushing and pulling loads**

The guideline figures for pushing or pulling loads, whether the load is slid, rolled or on wheels, are a force of 25kg for starting or stopping the load and a force of 10kg to keep the load moving. If the force applied is not with the hands between knuckle and shoulder height, the figure needs to be reduced.

**Team handling**

Handling by two or more people may make possible an operation that is beyond the capability of one person. However, team handling may introduce additional problems that the assessment must consider, eg the proportion of the load that is borne by each member of the team will vary when handling on rough ground.

As a guide, the capability of a two-person team is two-thirds of the sum of their individual capabilities; for a three-person team the capability is half the sum of their individual capabilities. However, if steps or slopes are to be negotiated, most of the weight may be borne by the handler at the lower end, thereby reducing the capability of the team as a whole.

Additional difficulties can arise if team members impede each other's vision or movement, or if the load has insufficient handholds.

## Hard facts

Musculoskeletal disorders, including upper limb disorders and hand–arm vibration, account for more cases of work-related ill health than any other. It is estimated that 1.2 million people in the UK suffer from musculoskeletal disorders, resulting in the loss of some 10 million working days each year.

# Upper limb disorders (ULDs)

ULDs cause aches and pains, difficulty in movement, and swelling in the neck, shoulders, arms, elbows, wrists, hands and fingers. If left unchecked, permanent disability can develop, preventing the sufferer from performing the task that caused the injury in the first place, and often from performing similar tasks. Even simple household tasks, such as lifting a kettle, can become difficult. Some sports injuries fall into the ULD category, eg tennis elbow.

ULDs can occur if tasks require repetitive finger, hand or arm movements; twisting, squeezing, hammering or pounding; or pushing, pulling, lifting or reaching movements. Repetition, force, awkward posture and insufficient recovery time all increase the risk.

The checklist opposite will help you decide if any of the tasks carried out by your employees need closer examination.

| Upper limb disorders – initial assessment | | |
|---|---|---|
| **Does the job involve frequent, forceful or awkward action of any of the following or combination of the following:** | **Yes** | **No** |
| gripping of a tool or work piece? | | |
| squeezing of tool handles or other parts? | | |
| twisting? | | |
| reaching? | | |
| pushing, pulling or lifting things? | | |
| finger or hand movement, such as keyboard work? | | |
| **Are there any warning signs, such as:** | | |
| cases of ULD associated with this or similar work? | | |
| complaints by employees of aches and pains in hands, wrists, arms, shoulders or the neck? (If necessary, ask your employees) | | |
| home-made, improvised changes to workstations or tools, eg handles that have been cushioned or made longer? | | |

www.protect.org.uk

PDF 13

If the answer to any of these questions is 'yes', then there may be a problem that needs investigating and correcting. Solutions include:

- providing training in good working techniques and posture

- varying or rotating tasks

- allowing rest periods and self-paced work

- providing adequate space for the workstation

- providing an adjustable chair

- redesigning the workstation to avoid twisting or reaching

- moving controls to a more convenient position

- avoiding overhead or awkward work, or providing good working platforms for overhead work, eg a mobile access tower rather than a stepladder

- using good quality industrial tools, not DIY tools

- replacing hand tools with power tools, eg electric screwdrivers

- maintaining tools properly.

**Examples of bad practice**

1. A joiner constantly having to apply overhead pressure to the drill and with a bent wrist.
2. A painter constantly reaching and stretching overhead.
3. A machinist constantly twisting the wrist when placing heavy fabric into a sewing machine.
4. A production line worker constantly twisting and stretching to load a box.

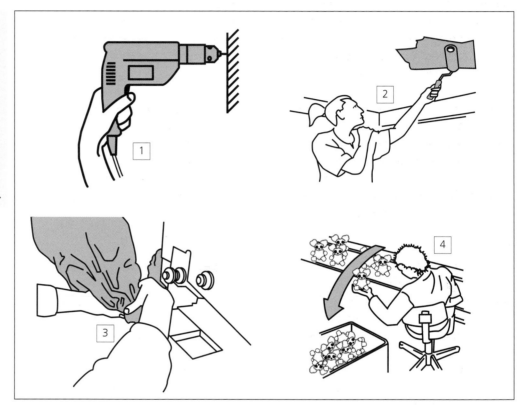

 **Also read...**

Appendix B – Noisy environments

## Noise

Workers are often exposed to noise from a wide variety of sources, including power presses and guillotines, power saws, pneumatic breakers, compressors and piling hammers. Although individuals are affected to varying degrees, exposure to high noise levels can cause incurable hearing loss and permanent tinnitus (ringing in the ears). Noise can interfere with working efficiency by inducing stress, by disturbing concentration and by increasing the risk of accidents.

### Noise measurement

Noise levels are measured in decibels (dB). The human ear is more sensitive to some noise frequencies than others and so noise-measuring instruments normally incorporate a filter that mimics the response of the human ear. Instrument readings using this filter give a better guide to the potential of noises to cause hearing damage and are given in terms of 'A-weighted decibels' – dB(A). The dB(A) scale is logarithmic, which means that every increase of 3 dB(A) amounts to a doubling of the noise level. Thus, 93 dB(A) is twice as loud as 90 dB(A).

### Action values

Regulations in force from April 2006 require specific action to be taken when the following action values are reached (daily values are measured over an 8-hour working day, weekly over 5 days):

#### Lower exposure action values

A daily/weekly personal exposure of 80 dB(A), and a peak sound pressure of 135 dB(C).

At this level, a noise assessment should be made, any significant findings recorded, and the situation monitored over the long term. Employees should be told about the risk of damage to their hearing from exposure to loud noise, and suitable ear protection should be made freely available on request. Employers do not have to force employees to wear hearing protection at this level, but must advise them about the risks. There is also a general duty to reduce noise levels if reasonably practicable.

If conditions are so noisy that people have difficulty speaking to each other over a 2m distance, then this exposure value has probably been reached. Noise measurements need to be taken in order to make an assessment. For most organisations it is worth acquiring a basic noise meter in order to do this, recognising the limitations of such meters if short-duration, high-peak noise levels are involved. Where an assessment indicates that there is a risk to the health of employees, hearing checks and health surveillance should be carried out.

#### Upper exposure action values

A daily/weekly personal exposure of 85 dB(A), and a peak sound pressure of 137 dB(C).

At this level, take measures that will reduce the noise exposure without the use of hearing protection, eg enclosing noisy machines or reducing the working time exposed to noise. There is a duty to eliminate the problem at source rather than rely on ear protection, which most people find oppressive to wear for extended periods. If, following this action, the level of noise remains at 85 dB(A) or above, hearing protection must be provided free of charge and be worn by employees. Ear protection zones should be marked with signs showing that ear protectors must be worn. In addition, provide employees with training and information on the use and care of ear protectors, and ensure that they are properly maintained.

High-peak noise levels must be measured using specialist equipment. In such cases it is advisable to employ a consultant to take the necessary readings and specify the appropriate hearing protection. Where specific machines produce a noise level at or above 85 dB(A), or a peak sound pressure of 137 dB(C), then a 'High noise machine' sign should be fixed to the machine.

#### Exposure limit values

A daily/weekly personal exposure of 87 dB(A), and a peak sound pressure of 140 dB(C).

At this level, reduce exposure to as low a level as is reasonably practicable using a programme of measures (not including hearing protection). Taking account of hearing protection, employees must not be exposed above this level. If the exposure limit value is exceeded, identify the cause and introduce measures to prevent a recurrence.

'Ear protection zone' sign

'High noise machine' sign

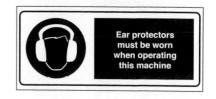

### Health surveillance

Where a risk to health from noise is anticipated, besides providing specific ear protectors, health surveillance is also advised. This involves:

- regular hearing checks by a medically competent person

- informing those people at risk about the results of the tests

- keeping records for 40 years

- providing medical advice to employees.

### Reducing noise exposure

The following are some typical noise exposures in the construction industry. Many factories produce noise levels that equal or exceed these levels, eg caused by woodworking machines or dust extraction equipment.

- compressors              91 to 120 dB(A)

- pile drivers              94 to 147 dB(A)

**Earmuffs**

- concrete breakers              101 to 112 dB(A)

The methods used for reducing exposure fall into four main categories:

### Silencing noise at source

Use modern equipment, fit silencers or baffles, or fit noise-reducing enclosures. This is the first step that must be taken, particularly where people are exposed to high noise levels on a daily basis.

**Earplugs**

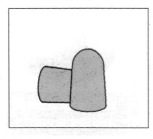

### Controlling the spread of noise

Increase the distance between the noise source and the receiver. Sound levels fall off between 3 dB(A) and 6 dB(A) for each doubling of distance from the source. Alternatively, naturally occurring or specially erected barriers can be used. To cut down on the transmission of noise, insulate walls, floors and ceilings with sound-absorbent material.

### Reducing exposure duration

It may be possible to avoid excessive noise exposure by job rotation, so that a short duration exposure to high levels is followed by a longer period of work in a quiet area. In such cases, ear protection should still be worn in the noisy environment.

**Semi-inserts**

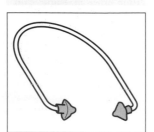

### Ear protection

The main types of ear protection are:

- earmuffs, which completely cover the ear

- earplugs, which are inserted into the ear canal

- semi-inserts (or 'canal caps'), which cover the entrance to the ear canal.

The ear protection selected must:

- reduce the employee's daily/weekly personal noise exposure to below 87 dB(A). Most general purpose ear protection will reduce noise exposure by 5 dB(A) only, so if the noise level is likely to be above 92 dB(A), you will need to match the ear protection to the noise characteristics. To do this, specialist measurements and advice are necessary

- be suitable for the employee's working environment – consider comfort and hygiene

- be compatible with other protective equipment such as hard hats, dust masks and eye protection.

Wherever possible, offer a choice. People have different preferences and some may not be able to fit earplugs properly, eg because of ear infections.

Regardless of the ear protection that is chosen, employees must be provided with instruction, training and supervision to ensure that they are wearing ear protection, and wearing it correctly. A toolbox talk on noisy environments is included in Appendix B.

Correct use

Trapping long hair, safety glasses, spectacles or earrings between the earmuff seal and the head reduces its efficiency. Check that earmuffs are clean, their overall condition is good, seals are undamaged, headbands are correctly tensioned, and that no-one has made any unwarranted modifications to them.

Check that compressible earplugs are soft, pliable and clean, and provide a ready supply of new earplugs.

**Long hair reduces seal**

**Safety glasses reduce seal**

**Earrings reduce seal**

**Correct**

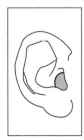

**Incorrect**

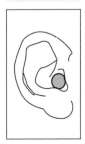

**Hard facts**

In the UK, around 36,000 people currently have an advanced disability from vibration white finger, the most common form of HAVS. Vibration white finger costs the state more each year than any other industrial disease.

**Also read...**

Appendix B – Vibrating equipment

**Hard facts**

Since the UK government assumed responsibility for British Coal's health liabilities in 1998, it has paid out more than £360 million in compensation. There are an estimated 124,000 claims lodged, with an estimated future cost of £1,900 million.

# Hand–arm vibration

People whose hands are regularly exposed to vibration can suffer from several kinds of injury to the hands and arms, including impaired blood circulation and damage to the nerves and muscles. This type of painful injury is known as hand–arm vibration syndrome (HAVS) and is widespread in those industries where vibrating tools and machines are used.

**Effects of HAVS**

HAVS can cause:

- vascular disorders, caused by impaired blood circulation and blanching of affected fingers and parts of the hand

- numbness and tingling in the hands and fingers, reduced grip strength and dexterity, and reduced sensitivity to touch and temperature

- pain and stiffness in the hands, wrists, elbows and shoulders.

**Recognising the onset of vibration white finger**

The first stage of vibration injury is a tingling sensation in the fingers accompanied by numbness. With continued exposure, the injured party may suffer periodic attacks in which the fingers change colour when exposed to the cold. In mild cases, only the tips of the fingers are affected. As the condition deteriorates, fingers down to the knuckles become white and attacks occur even in warm surroundings. In very severe cases, blood circulation may be permanently impaired and the fingers take on a black and blue appearance.

The first noticeable symptoms may occur some time after regular exposure to vibration has begun. In the early stages, improvement may occur if activities associated with vibration cease. If activities continue, however, the condition is likely to become permanent.

**Work activities associated with hand–arm vibration**

The primary cause of vibration white finger is work that involves holding vibrating tools or work pieces, eg:

- percussive metalworking tools

- grinders and other rotary tools

- percussive tools used in stonework/construction

- timber and wood machining tools.

**Several other factors also affect the severity of the risk, including:**

- the grip, push and forces used to guide and apply vibrating tools or work pieces (a tight grip increases vibration energy to the hand)

- the exposure pattern, ie length and frequency of work and rest periods

- how much of the hand is exposed to vibration

- factors that impair blood circulation, such as low body temperature and smoking

- individual susceptibility.

**Hand–arm vibration technology**

As with noise, the art of assessing the impact of vibration is to know when to use common sense and when to call in a specialist.

First, it is worth getting to know the following formula:

$$\text{Allowable working time in hours} = 8 \text{ hours} \times \left( \frac{2.5}{\text{tool vibration level}} \right)^2$$

For a tool used throughout an 8-hour working day, 2.5m/s² is the current acceptable tool vibration level. The tool vibration level is obtainable from the manufacturer or hirer.

For example, if a tool has a quoted vibration level of 5.0m/s², it can be used for 2 hours per day (8 hours × (2.5/5.0)²). In other words, if the vibration level is doubled, then the user time is quartered. The ready reckoner below provides some examples of safe usage times.

| Tool vibration level (m/s²) | Hours of 'safe' use | Tool vibration level (m/s²) | Hours of 'safe' use | Tool vibration level (m/s²) | Hours/minutes of 'safe' use | Tool vibration level (m/s²) | Minutes of 'safe' use |
|---|---|---|---|---|---|---|---|
| 2.5 | 8.0 | 4.0 | 3.1 | 7.0 | 1.0 | 11.0 | 25 mins |
| 2.8 | 6.4 | 4.5 | 2.5 | 8.0 | 47 mins | 15.0 | 13 mins |
| 3.0 | 5.5 | 5.0 | 2.0 | 9.0 | 37 mins | 20.0 | 7 mins |
| 3.5 | 4.0 | 6.0 | 1.4 | 10.0 | 30 mins | 25.0 | 5 mins |

Typical vibration levels of certain tools are included in the table below, but because these vary you must find out the exact vibration levels of your own equipment.

| Tool | Vibration level (m/s²) | Tool | Vibration level (m/s²) | Tool | Vibration level (m/s²) |
|---|---|---|---|---|---|
| Circular saw | Less than 2.5 | Jigsaw | 3.0 | Clay digger | 8.7 |
| Grinder | 2.5–4.0 | Cartridge gun | 7.0–10.0 | Concrete breaker | 10.0–25.0 |
| Cordless drill | Less than 2.5 | Large drill | 8.0–11.0 | Pole scabbler | 23.9 |
| Diamond drill | Less than 2.5 | Disc cutter | 9.0 | Rock drill | 25.0 |

In reality, the situation is more complicated in that manufacturers quote vibration levels for new equipment that is tested in a laboratory and in perfect working order. In actual use, tools are rarely well maintained, and are often fitted with consumables such as chisels or points that may be blunt and increase vibration enormously. However, due to advances in technology, improvements are being made all the time, eg concrete breakers are now available with vibration levels of less than 4.0m/s².

**Action plan**

If your employees have a significant exposure to hand–arm vibration, then you need to take action. Here is what you should do:

- First, try to change the way of working to avoid the use of hand-held vibrating tools. This is often possible, but is sometimes not done because of cost implications or lack of planning. In construction, for example, high-strength concrete up to 1m in length can be trimmed down using 'pile crackers', which use hydraulics and perform the task effortlessly. However, much of the time pile crackers are not used because there are insufficient piles to justify the hire charge of the equipment. Instead, the job is done by hand using concrete breakers, taking several hours. A glance at the ready reckoner illustrates how unsatisfactory this is.

- Buy or hire new equipment and consumables and make sure that they are maintained properly. Modern equipment is far more efficient and produces much lower vibration levels than old equipment. You need to insist on buying or hiring the lowest vibration equipment available, equipment that is CE marked to indicate that it complies with the relevant harmonised European Product Safety Directives. Make sure that consumables such as discs or concrete-cutting points are in good condition and, where necessary, sharp.

- Survey and list your vibrating equipment. On a spreadsheet, list the plant number, description, vibration level, and maximum safe use time per working day of all equipment. Use this in training and in choosing the most suitable equipment for specific jobs.

- Provide employees with warm clothing, particularly gloves, and well-heated welfare facilities where they can keep their work clothes in warm, dry conditions, and where they can get warm at break times. This greatly helps blood circulation and therefore helps to avoid the onset of vibration white finger. Avoid pneumatic exhausts that discharge towards the operator's hand, making it cold. Instead, fit a flexible hose to lead the exhaust away. Anti-vibration gloves are often considered ineffective, although some operators report favourable results when using them.

- Minimise the time working with vibrating tools by job rotation, working within the limits given in the ready reckoner.

- Train and provide information for employees and supervisors on:

  1. The nature of the risk and the signs of injury.

  2. Why any injury or concern should be reported.

  3. The action employees should take to minimise risk, including:

○ good working practice to minimise vibration being directed at the hands

○ maintaining good blood circulation

○ making sure that tools are properly maintained

○ reporting defects and problems with equipment and obtaining replacements where necessary.

A toolbox talk on the safe use of vibrating equipment is included in Appendix B.

### Specialist advice

If your employees regularly work with tools or equipment with a vibration level above 5m/s$^2$, then you probably need to consult a specialist to take vibration readings in the workplace. This is not a simple procedure, as vibration can occur in three directions and all three have to be measured and combined. The specialist will also take into account the different types of vibrating equipment used throughout the working day. Ultimately, a health surveillance programme may have to be put in place, involving regular medicals, the recording of exposure times on vibrating equipment and the keeping of long term records.

## Hazardous substances

When dealing with substances that are hazardous to health, you are required by law to carry out a risk assessment. The substances are governed by the Control of Substances Hazardous to Health (COSHH) Regulations, and the risk assessments that are required are known as COSHH assessments.

Examples of hazardous substances include some paints, industrial cleaners and degreasers, wood dust, metalworking fluids, chemicals, and substances that cause cancer, asthma and dermatitis. COSHH applies to all chemicals with a warning label on the container. Manufacturers of all such chemicals must also provide a material safety data sheet, which is needed in order to complete the assessment.

'Hazardous substances' warning label

COSHH also applies to substances with workplace exposure limits, biological agents such as those encountered in farming, sewage treatment and healthcare, any kind of dust, and other toxic substances. It does not apply to asbestos and lead, which have their own regulations. Lead is addressed later in this chapter and asbestos is covered in Chapter 13.

### Four steps to managing hazardous substances

### Step 1: Carry out a COSHH assessment

See overleaf for details on how to conduct a COSHH assessment. Complete the 'Hazardous substance assessment' form that is included in Appendix A to make sure that you have not missed anything.

### Step 2: Decide what action to take

Prevent or adequately control the exposure of people to the hazardous substance.

Physical control measures that may be used include:

• substituting for a less hazardous substance

- isolating or enclosing the substance

- local exhaust ventilation

- good general ventilation

- good housekeeping

- welfare and personal hygiene

- personal protective equipment (PPE).

Examples of these physical control measures are given in Chapters 7 to 14.

### Step 3: Take action

- Ensure that control measures are used and maintained.

- Keep your employees informed.

- Provide employees with adequate training so that they understand the health effects, recognise the symptoms of exposure, know how to use the equipment, and are aware of the measures in place to protect their health.

- Provide good supervision.

### Step 4: Check that what you have done is effective

- Monitor the level of exposure to employees. Where applicable, take air or other samples to ensure that workplace exposure limits are not exceeded.

- Monitor the general health of employees.

- Provide employees with training and refresher training courses.

- Carry out appropriate health surveillance where your assessment has shown this to be necessary or where COSHH sets specific requirements. If you are involved with hazardous substances at this level you will need expert advice to ensure that your control measures are suitable. Records of exposure and health checks have to be maintained for 40 years.

- Regularly review your assessment and control measures.

Also read...

Chapter 13 – Confined spaces

### COSHH assessment

The key to any assessment is to weigh up not just the potential harmful effects, but the situation in which a substance is used. For example, a paint may be relatively low risk when used in the open air, but an entirely different proposition when used inside a closed tank. The steps you must take are as follows:

- Obtain the manufacturer's safety data sheet for the substance. This essential preliminary action is often overlooked. Also, read the label on the container.

- Form a clear view of the hazards involved and weigh these up along with the circumstances of use.

- Now think about the hierarchy of risk control. Are there any less risky substances available? Keep an open mind, as technical advances are being made all the time. If you are choosing between two substances, one of which requires personal protective equipment, you must choose the substance that is inherently safer and does not require PPE.

- Having selected a substance, make sure that you understand the concentration or conditions likely to cause ill health, including the route into the body (breathed in, swallowed, or taken in through the skin, particularly through cuts and abrasions). Also, identify the worst health outcome if things go wrong, the first symptoms of over-exposure, and the first aid arrangements.

- Consider everyone who could be exposed, including staff, maintenance staff, young people, pregnant women, contractors and the public, and the numbers involved.

- Consider the length and continuity of exposure, and any cumulative effects.

- Ensure that you know how to clean up any spills safely.

- Write all of this down and make it readily available, together with data sheets, to employees.

- Carry out training.

The 'Hazardous substance assessment' form included in Appendix A also covers flammability, which is not included in COSHH but which can be considered conveniently at the same time. The form should be regarded as a starting point (or cover sheet), backed up by the material safety data sheets and a full description of the control measures, in a format that can be readily provided to employees in a toolbox talk.

### Occupational asthma

Work-related asthma is an extremely distressing and potentially life-threatening disease caused by breathing in hazardous substances called respiratory sensitisers. The symptoms of asthma are attacks of coughing, wheezing, tightness of the chest and breathing difficulties.

Sensitisation normally takes months or years to develop, but can be caused by a single exposure. Once the symptoms occur, they may not immediately be associated with work, so the exposure continues. However, once sensitised, continued exposure can result in permanent lung damage.

**Key health risk**

Using any hazardous substance inside a confined space creates a major risk that requires specialist assistance to resolve. Ensure that you take expert advice.

**Also read...**

Chapter 2 – Stage 3: Plan risk control

**Hard facts**

In the UK, it is estimated that up to 150,000 people suffer from work-related asthma. There are up to 3,000 new cases each year.

The following table lists the main substances that cause occupational asthma and the industries/activities most commonly associated with them.

| Hazardous substance | Industry/activity |
| --- | --- |
| Isocyanates | Vehicle spraying, foam manufacturing, construction |
| Flour/grain/hay | Bakeries, grain handling, milling, malting |
| Soldering flux | Soldering, electronic assembly; similar diseases are caused by welding fume and metalworking fluid mists in workshops |
| Laboratory animal-related sensitisers | Research, education |
| Wood dusts | Sawmilling, woodworking |
| Some glues and resins | Curing of epoxy resins used in manufacturing and construction |

Ways of controlling exposure to these substances are central to the COSHH assessment process described above. Specific matters relating to workshops are discussed in Chapter 8.

## Work-related dermatitis

Work-related dermatitis can be a very serious and debilitating skin disease. Symptoms include redness, itching, scaling and blistering of the skin. If the condition gets worse, the skin can crack and bleed, and dermatitis can spread all over the body. How quickly it develops depends on the substance that causes the condition, its strength or potency, and how long and how often it touches the skin. The effects may be immediate, or may take months or years to develop.

With care, most cases of dermatitis can be avoided. Ways of doing this are discussed in Chapter 8 in relation to metalworking fluids and wood dust, the key points being to:

- maintain good personal hygiene

- keep overalls and protective equipment clean

- keep the workplace clean

- use gloves, if practicable, and other appropriate protection in specific circumstances, eg face shields

- avoid cuts and abrasions to the skin

- use a moisturising cream before and after work, to replace natural skin oils

- dilute chemicals such as cleaners to the recommended strength – if they are over-strength they are more likely to cause dermatitis.

**Hard facts**

There are estimated to be some 66,000 occupational dermatitis sufferers in the UK alone. Each year, the condition accounts for the loss of around 500,000 working days to the UK economy.

Occupational dermatitis occurs in industries as diverse as hairdressing and construction. The main hazardous substances are:

- cement

- certain shampoos and detergents

- metalworking fluids

- lubricants and oils

- chemicals

- certain printing inks

- the sap from some agricultural crops.

### Work-related cancer

If chemicals are carcinogenic, the law requires that the containers they come in should be labelled as such. It is essential that any process using such chemicals is strictly controlled in accordance with COSHH. Expert advice will be needed to establish a robust regime of preventing exposure, monitoring, and possibly health surveillance.

## Solvents

### Effects on health

Serious health effects can result from even short periods of exposure to high concentrations of solvents, or from prolonged exposure to lower concentrations. The main effects are irritation of the skin, eyes and lungs; headaches; nausea; dizziness; and light-headedness. Co-ordination is impaired and this is made worse by drinking alcohol. Very high exposures, such as may be received when working inside a degreasing tank, may even cause unconsciousness or death. Matters are compounded where more than one solvent is used, as in some paints.

Solvents affect health by:

- Inhalation of vapour (fumes) or mist. This is always possible where solvents are handled.

- Ingestion (through eating). Deliberate ingestion is rare; accidental ingestion as a result of contaminated food or fingers is more common.

- Skin contact. Some solvents are absorbed through the skin, with effects similar to those following inhalation. With many solvents, skin contact can also lead to dermatitis.

**Hard facts**

In the UK, there are about 6,000 deaths each year from work-related cancer. About half of these are caused by exposure to asbestos; the remainder are caused by chemicals, the sun and ionising radiation.

**What is...**

A solvent?

A solvent is a liquid that has the ability to dissolve, suspend or extract other materials, without chemical change to the material or solvent. Solvents are used in:

- paints
- degreasing operations
- printing
- chemicals
- adhesives
- pesticides
- toiletries
- dry cleaning.

Typical industrial solvents include acetone, ethyl acetate, methanol, perchloroethylene, butanol, methylene chloride, trichloroethylene, toluene and white spirit. They are all hazardous substances and require a COSHH assessment.

**Effective management of solvents**

Step 1: Undertake a COSHH assessment

Consult the supplier's safety data sheet to determine immediate or long term health effects. Understand how easily the solvent can vaporise. As a general rule, high-volatility solvents have a boiling point of less than 50°C, while low-volatility solvents have a boiling point greater than 150°C. The lower the boiling point the easier the solvent will evaporate and be inhaled by someone who has no respiratory protection. Caution is still needed even if the solvent does not readily form a vapour, as it may be harmful at low air-borne levels.

Find out if there is a workplace exposure limit and if so how this will be monitored. Also, determine whether the solvent can be absorbed through the skin, in which case urine tests will indicate the amount absorbed.

Watch the process and talk to those who work with solvents. Ask about maintenance, working in confined spaces and how to clean equipment. It is often the non-routine or end-of-shift tasks that lead to the highest exposures. Think about how the solvent vapour or mist is created and how people come into contact with it, and for how long. There may be obvious improvements that can be made at this stage, such as using a chemical direct from its container using a pump, rather than having to pour it into a machine tank.

Finally, complete the 'Hazardous substance assessment' form that is included in Appendix A to make sure that you have not missed anything.

Step 2: Decide on what action to take

Modify or enclose the process to reduce the exposure, or if this is not possible use local exhaust ventilation. The best example of this is the spray booth, which is dealt with in Chapter 8. The design of local exhaust ventilation depends on the substance; some substances are heavier than air and require low-level extraction. Specialist suppliers of ventilation equipment should be employed to design the facility.

Practice good housekeeping, keeping lids on cans and solvent-soaked rags in closed bins to limit evaporation.

Finally, supply effective personal protective equipment, including respirators, gloves, aprons, boots, safety glasses and so on, to take care of any remaining risk. Respirators should normally be used in spray booths even though they have local exhaust ventilation. Respirators normally have a cartridge that filters the solvent. Filters have a short life and soon become saturated when exposure is high. Always leave respirators in sealed containers when not in use, so that they do not continue to absorb solvent.

In high concentrations of solvent, such as inside a tank or in continuous paint-spraying work, air-fed respiratory protection is the solution, as it provides a constant supply of clean air. When working with solvents in a confined space, get specialist advice before proceeding.

Solvent-resistant gloves, boots and aprons may be needed, especially gloves. Guidance on the various types is available from manufacturers. Different gloves are required for different solvents.

Step 3: Take action

Keep your employees informed and give them adequate training so that they understand the health effects, recognise the symptoms of exposure, know how to use the equipment, and are aware of the measures in place to protect their health.

Step 4: Check that what you have done is effective

- Monitor the health of employees.

- Employ a specialist contractor to test and clean the ventilation systems routinely.

- Replace filters regularly and maintain the plant properly. A poorly maintained plant will inevitably pose a risk to health.

- Provide employees with training and refresher training courses.

- Monitor employees' personal exposure to solvent/vapour mist, where necessary. A consultant chemist may be employed to take the necessary readings.

- Regularly review your control measures.

- Monitor your solvent usage, as a reduction may indicate that your improvements are working.

# Radiation

### Hazards

Radiation in industry is most commonly encountered as follows:

- sunburn and skin cancer (typically due to outdoor workers removing their shirts in hot sunny weather)

- burns to the skin and eyes caused by industrial lasers

- burns, dermatitis and skin cancer caused by repeated exposure to X-rays or radiography, eg in medicine and dentistry

- work activities in the nuclear industry

- mining in areas of naturally occurring radon.

### Sunburn

Excessive exposure of the skin to ultraviolet radiation from the sun can increase the risk of developing skin cancer. Those most susceptible to risk have fair, sensitive skin, and the work sectors most affected include construction, agriculture and other outdoor industries. Outdoor workers should not be allowed to remove shirts on hot summer days; they should wear a short-sleeved tee-shirt as a minimum. Hats and sun screen may be needed as well.

### Lasers

Lasers vary greatly in their strength and dose of use, therefore once expert advice has been obtained, an assessment must be made of the specific equipment and circumstances of use.

When working with lasers, the following precautions are required:

- workers must be made aware of the hazards, be trained in the use of the equipment and authorised in writing to use it

- suitable eye protection (depending on the outcome of the risk assessment)

- work areas should be marked with signs prohibiting entry to all unauthorised personnel

- laser targets should be non-reflective, as should other objects in the work area that may also reflect the laser beam

- toxic gases may be emitted by the target, so ventilation requirements must be assessed

- the beam-emitting equipment must be securely fixed down so that it cannot be inadvertently moved out of position

- when in use, the equipment must be attended at all times.

### Microwaves

- Door seals on microwave equipment must be inspected and maintained regularly to ensure that there are no leakages.

- All sources of radiation must be clearly identified and signage erected.

- Personal protective equipment that is suitable for the task must be provided.

### Radiation management

- A radiation protection adviser should be appointed to monitor and advise on the use, precautions and controls of radiation, and levels of exposure. For smaller organisations, this will usually be a specialist consultant.

- Provisions for radiation release must be included in emergency plans.

- Workers should be classified according to their level of training and exposure. Those potentially exposed to ionising radiation (found in X-rays and certain radioactive materials) should be classed as 'persons especially at risk'. In such cases, specialist advice should be sought.

# Lead

Lead has long been known to have the potential to damage health. Excessive exposure can cause lead poisoning. Lead alloys and compounds can be found in paint coatings and plumbing materials. When carrying out renovations or demolitions, working with materials that contain lead – eg burning, welding or abrasion with hand or power tools, or grit blasting and hot cutting of lead-painted structures – may give rise to high levels of lead in the air. This can take different forms, eg dust, fumes or vapours, and can be inhaled or ingested. However, there is little risk when handling cold metallic lead, such as that used in roof work.

Other industrial processes that create lead dust, fume or vapour include lead smelting, battery manufacture, lead soldering, manufacturing lead compounds, and manufacturing certain pigments, glazes and enamels.

Lead enters the body through inhalation of dust, fume or vapour, or by ingestion when eating contaminated food or eating with contaminated fingers. Once in the body, lead circulates in the blood. Some is removed but some stays for years, mainly in the bones, and builds up with continued exposure.

Lead causes headaches, tiredness, irritability, constipation, nausea, stomach pains, anaemia and loss of weight. Ultimately kidney, nerve and brain damage result. Lead is particularly dangerous to unborn children. Consequently, women need to be especially careful and protected.

### Safe working with lead

By law, the following measures must be taken:

- Assess the risk to health and decide if the exposure is 'significant'. To do so, measurements are needed of fume, dust and vapour. A 'significant' exposure exceeds one half of the workplace exposure limit (currently 0.15mg/m³) of air, a rating of 0.075mg/m³. A specialist consultant will normally take these readings and provide advice.

- Put in place extraction ventilation equipment to prevent or control employees' exposure.

- Provide clean welfare facilities.

- Provide information and training.

If the exposure is significant:

- Provide protective equipment and clothing.

- Measure the level of lead in the air and advise employees of the results.

- Where the workplace exposure limit is exceeded, provide employees with respiratory protection and ensure that it is used.

- Provide ongoing health surveillance every three months using blood and urine tests (taken by a doctor at the place of work). Maintain long term records.

- If the amount of lead in an employee's blood reaches the 'action level' of 50 micrograms per decilitre, review all control measures and ensure that they are working properly. Check that employees are making use of good hygiene practices and consult with the doctor about any further measures that could be taken to improve levels of hygiene.

- If the amount of lead in the blood reaches the 'suspension level' of 60 micrograms per decilitre of blood, suspend that person from working with lead.

- Women capable of having children have an action level of 25 and a suspension level of 30 micrograms per decilitre. For young people under the age of 18, the limits are 40 and 50 micrograms respectively. Both groups are prohibited from working in lead smelting and refining, and in manufacturing lead-acid batteries.

## Asbestos

As asbestos is not used in manufacturing and is principally a risk to maintenance and facilities management workers, it is dealt with in Chapter 13.

**The bottom line**

**Your legal duties as a manager are to:**

- manage your activities in such a way that prevents work-related ill health
- reduce the risks associated with manual handling by considering how materials and/or goods will be moved, and either reduce the weight or provide manual handling aids
- reduce the likelihood of upper limb disorders caused by repetitive, awkward or forceful arm/wrist actions
- reduce noise and vibration to acceptable levels by using modern equipment and adapting work processes to reduce or eliminate the problem
- assess and reduce the exposure of hazardous substances and solvents to legally defined control levels
- control employees' exposure to radiation, lead and asbestos
- provide personal protective equipment where necessary, although other measures should supplement its use – it should not be relied on as the sole or initial measure.

## Introduction

Everyone involved in the construction process, including the client who commissions the work, is legally responsible for ensuring construction safety.

After reading this chapter, you should:

- understand your role in the construction process

- know how to cope with demolition

- know what to expect from contractors

- understand some key elements of construction and demolition safety.

## Commissioning construction works

If you are the client for construction works, such as the owner of business premises or a developer, you have the following duties in law:

- Appoint a planning supervisor to oversee health and safety in the design of the building and prepare a health and safety plan at the pre-tender stage. This initial plan will include information from the designers about any special risks that they have identified, as well as information from the client about risks within the premises and any client site rules and interface issues. The initial plan is included with the tender documents that the contractor prices.

- Provide the planning supervisor with existing information on health and safety issues in your premises that may affect the construction works, eg the presence of asbestos or a weak roof. If you suspect the presence of asbestos, but are not certain, you should ensure that a survey is carried out and give the results to the planning supervisor. Normally, the planning supervisor will organise this survey.

- Appoint a principal contractor to carry out and manage the construction work, including the management of subcontractors. The principal contractor retains overall responsibility for the health and safety of the construction works, including the interface with the client's premises and the public. For example, the renovation of a store while it is still trading may affect both the store staff and customers, and the principal contractor must manage the interface. For this reason, the principal contractor should always have a supervisor on site, even when all works are carried out by subcontractors.

- Ensure that the planning supervisor, designer and principal contractor are competent and have adequate resources to carry out their health and safety responsibilities. The planning supervisor usually carries out this check on the principal contractor on the client's behalf, but the client retains the responsibility in law.

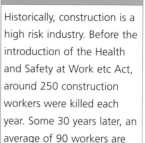

**Hard facts**

Historically, construction is a high risk industry. Before the introduction of the Health and Safety at Work etc Act, around 250 construction workers were killed each year. Some 30 years later, an average of 90 workers are killed each year.

**Hard facts**

A steelwork design company was fined £100,000 following the death of a 16-year-old. The ground worker was the victim of an incident in which two inadequately supported structural steel columns fell over in high winds. He had only been at work for two weeks.

- Ensure that the principal contractor has prepared a suitable health and safety plan before construction work commences. This plan should take account of the pre-tender plan and include detailed arrangements for identifying and managing risks and for organising the project. The planning supervisor normally reviews this document on behalf of the client. If the project starts before the plan is prepared, the client runs the risk of prosecution.

- Ensure that a health and safety file is handed to you at the end of the project and that it is kept up to date and available. The health and safety file contains operation and maintenance manuals and other information needed to maintain the facility safely. Drawings that record the detail of the finished building (including structure, services and architectural details) should be included, as they will be needed if the building is altered at a later stage or demolished. The planning supervisor has to ensure that a health and safety file is prepared. In practice, the principal contractor accumulates information from the contractors, collates the file and hands it to the planning supervisor for review.

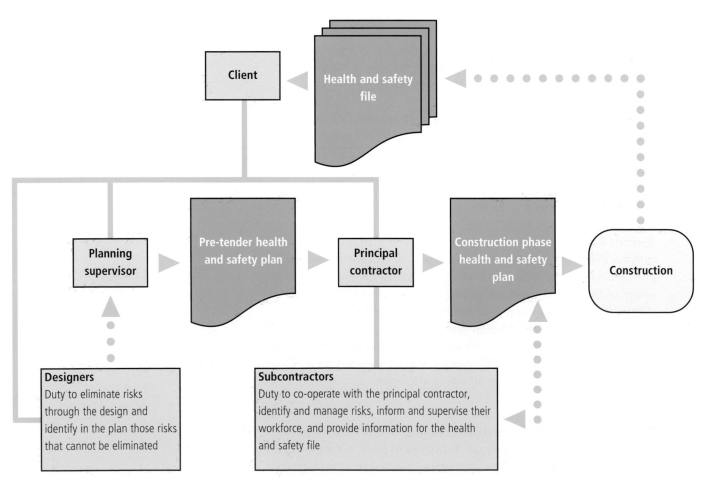

Client

Health and safety file

Planning supervisor

Pre-tender health and safety plan

Principal contractor

Construction phase health and safety plan

Construction

**Designers**
Duty to eliminate risks through the design and identify in the plan those risks that cannot be eliminated

**Subcontractors**
Duty to co-operate with the principal contractor, identify and manage risks, inform and supervise their workforce, and provide information for the health and safety file

Typical contractual links

Flow of information

## Construction health and safety process

The diagram shown on the preceding page reflects statutory requirements and not necessarily contractual arrangements. Each party shown has individual duties, and a duty to co-operate with other parties in the process and supply information on the risks. The arrows indicate the flow of information.

### Planning supervisor

The planning supervisor can be an independent consultant, one of the design team, the principal contractor, a project management organisation, or a member of the client's own staff. Whoever is appointed must have knowledge of both health and safety and the design process. As the client, you can make a choice to suit your needs. The Association of Project Safety provides details of planning supervisors and professional standards (t +44 (0)131 221 9959, www.aps.org.uk). IOSH maintains a register of health and safety consultants, many of whom act as planning supervisors (t +44 (0)116 257 3100, www.iosh.co.uk).

### CDM Regulations

The management framework for dealing with construction safety is prescribed in great detail in law. The Construction (Design and Management) Regulations 1994 (the 'CDM Regulations') require that health and safety is taken into account and managed at all stages of a construction project: from conception, design and planning through to site work and any subsequent maintenance and repair of the structure.

The CDM Regulations apply to all demolition and most construction projects, but do not cover:

- construction work that lasts 30 days or fewer and involves fewer than five people on site at any one time

- construction work for a domestic client

- construction work inside offices, shops, in setting up exhibitions, sports premises and other premises where the local authority is the enforcing authority, provided the construction work is done without interrupting the normal activities in the premises and without the need to separate the construction activity

- the maintenance or removal of insulation on pipes, boilers or other parts of heating or water systems

- site surveys (although site investigation and clearance is included).

All demolition and dismantling is included, even that which is short in duration.

It is important to note that even if the CDM Regulations do not apply, the work must be carried out in compliance with all other health and safety legislation.

**Notification of the project**

It is the duty of the planning supervisor to notify the local HSE office if the construction project is to last for more than 30 days, or involves more than 500 person days of work. To do so, a Form 10 (rev) must be completed (obtainable free from HSE Books; t +44 (0)1787 881165, www.hsebooks.com; or via the HSE website, www.hse.gov.uk). The planning supervisor and principal contractor must declare their appointments by signing the form. It also has to be returned promptly. For this reason it is usually returned twice: first, when the planning supervisor is appointed; and again, once the principal contractor is appointed (unless, of course, they are one and the same person or organisation). It is worth bearing in mind that, as a result of neglecting to appoint a planning supervisor, and hence failing to notify the HSE, some clients have been successfully prosecuted.

**Summary of planning supervisor's duties**

- Notify the HSE of the project.

- Ensure co-operation between designers.

- Ensure that designers comply with their duties to eliminate risk in construction and maintenance by designing out risks where practicable, and highlighting those that remain.

- Prepare an adequate pre-tender health and safety plan.

- Advise the client, if requested, on the competence of designers and the principal contractor, and the adequacy of the construction stage plan.

- Ensure that a health and safety file is completed and handed to the client.

**Summary of principal contractor's duties**

- Review the pre-tender health and safety plan and use all relevant information in the development of a construction phase health and safety plan.

- Ensure that the risks are assessed and method statements explain how to control them.

- Ensure co-operation and exchange of information between contractors.

- Take a positive leadership role by ensuring that interactions between contractors (such as site transport) and common risks (such as temporary electrics) are dealt with safely. This entails the principal contractor assessing the risks and producing a plan to deal with them.

- Ensure that contractors and employees comply with the site rules.

- Secure the site and protect the public.

- Ensure that employees receive adequate information and training (see 'Workforce information and training' later in this section).

• Make arrangements for collating the views of employees.

• Provide information for the health and safety file.

**Construction phase health and safety plan**
The construction phase health and safety plan must be prepared by the principal contractor, taking into account the information contained in the pre-tender health and safety plan that is prepared by the planning supervisor. The client must ensure that the plan is in place before allowing the construction work to start. This check is usually made by the planning supervisor on the client's behalf.

## Content of the construction phase health and safety plan

The HSE recommends that the following items are included in the health and safety plan:

1. Description of the project
   - Project description and programme details.
   - Details of client, planning supervisor, designers, principal contractor and other consultants.
   - Extent and location of existing records and plans.
   - Information about any restrictions that may affect the work.

2. Communication and management of the work
   - Management – an outline of the structure and responsibilities of the team, and arrangements for directing and co-ordinating contractors, including meeting schedules.
   - Health and safety goals and standards for the project, and arrangements for monitoring and reviewing health and safety performance.
   - The site rules and the means of communicating them.
   - Emergency procedures, particularly fire and first aid arrangements.
   - Selection procedures – an outline of the procedures for ensuring that contractors are competent and have adequate resources for health and safety.
   - Information for contractors – measures to ensure that any relevant information that the client, designers or the principal contractor have identified is passed on to the contractors affected by it.
   - Information from contractors, particularly information on specialist materials and methods that the contractor may use that will affect the overall construction programme, or that will need to be included in the health and safety file to inform the future maintenance of the building or structure.
   - Arrangements for handling design changes.
   - Arrangements for regular liaison between all parties to the project, including the production and approval of risk assessments and method statements.
   - Arrangements for consulting with the workforce.
   - Arrangements for security, site induction, on-site training, welfare, and accident and incident reporting.

3. Arrangements for controlling significant site risks
   - Safety risks

   This is one of the most important sections as it identifies, in overview, the principal risks of the project and how they are to be eliminated, minimised or controlled. Topics may include:
     - fall prevention
     - pedestrian/vehicle segregation and traffic routes
     - control of lifting operations
     - poor ground conditions
     - excavation sequence
     - confined space entry
     - storage of hazardous materials

- ○ waste removal
- ○ common access
- ○ common plant and logistics
- ○ temporary works and structural support
- ○ demolition
- ○ protection of adjacent structures
- ○ dealing with existing unstable structures
- ○ fragile roofs, roof lights and other fragile materials
- ○ working in occupied premises
- ○ temporary power
- ○ water, gas and electricity services
- ○ building services and commissioning
- ○ maintenance of plant and equipment
- ○ protection of the public
- ○ accommodating clients' and neighbours' activities
- ○ security.

The above list is not definitive and each project should be examined on its merits. Standard everyday construction risks need not be highlighted at this initial stage, as a short relevant document is better than a long volume that is not read.

- • Health risks
  - ○ Presence of asbestos.
  - ○ Removal of asbestos.
  - ○ Working on contaminated land, including its removal or remediation.
  - ○ Hazardous substances left in disused buildings or structures.
  - ○ Working with hazardous substances.
  - ○ Reducing the exposure to noise and vibration through the design and construction method used, and ways to deal with any residual risk.
  - ○ Reducing the need for manual handling through the design and construction method used, and ways to deal with any residual risk.
  - ○ Other significant health risks.

4. Health and safety file

- • Contents.
- • Layout and format of the information to be provided.
- • Arrangements for collecting and gathering information.
- • Storage of information.

## Workforce information and training

By law, everyone working in the construction industry must be given information about the risks of the site in general, and any risks specific to their tasks. Personnel must also be provided with the necessary training in order to discharge their duties safely. This takes several forms, as outlined in the table below.

| Training | Employees concerned | Responsible provider | Frequency of training/ certification | Monitoring | Records |
|---|---|---|---|---|---|
| Project induction | All principal contractors and contractors' workforces | Principal contractor | Before starting on first day | Check records/ sample monthly | Employee to sign register to confirm attendance |
| Method statement briefing – task-specific, detailing risks and safe work method | Contractor's workforce | Contractor's manager/ supervisor | Before starting on first day (follows project induction) and when starting a new task | Principal contractor to check records and spot-check talks | Employee to sign register to confirm understanding of the task |
| Toolbox talks – a short general talk about a topic relevant to the task | Contractor's workforce | Contractor's supervisor | One 10-minute talk each week | Principal contractor to check records and spot-check talks | Attendees' signatures to be obtained and kept by contractor |
| Mobile plant operators and slinger/ signaller (banksman) training and competence certification | Plant operators | Plant operator's employer | Construction Industry Training Board (CITB) Construction Plant Competence Scheme (CPCS) or equivalent | Principal contractor to check certification | To be kept with machine; copies contained in a site file held by principal contractor and contractor |
| Abrasive wheels/ cartridge tools/mobile access towers | People who mount wheels, use tools or towers | Contractor | Certificate of training | Principal contractor | To be kept by contractor and made available for inspection on site |
| First aid | All first aiders | Principal contractor and contractors | HSE-approved 'First aid at work' certificate (four-day course) | Principal contractor | Principal contractor |

## Demolition, dismantling and structural alteration

Demolition, dismantling and structural alteration are extremely high risk activities. The main risks are:

- falling from edges that are exposed during demolition

- falling through holes produced by the demolition, or existing holes such as service risers

- falling through fragile materials, especially roofs

- premature collapse of the structure or a part of it, endangering both workers and the public

- high levels of dust and noise affecting breathing and hearing

- asbestos contamination of both workers and the public

- harm caused by chemical or biological waste

- contamination caused by needles and the like left by drug misusers who have occupied derelict buildings.

If you are the client for demolition works, or if such works will affect your premises, there are a number of things you should do:

- Appoint a competent contractor. This is more important in demolition than in almost any other activity. A good contractor will provide a competent site manager who has both knowledge and experience. You should meet the site manager before awarding the contract.

- Make every effort to identify the risks. All demolition is within the scope of the CDM Regulations, so you need to appoint a planning supervisor. You must provide the planning supervisor with details of any hazards such as fragile roofs or suspected asbestos. It is an offence to withhold this information. Typically, the client will commission an asbestos survey and provide this to tendering contractors so that they can allow for the removal works. As with construction projects, the planning supervisor must notify the HSE of the works.

- Create an exclusion zone, thereby ensuring that your workforce and the public are kept well away from the demolition. The contractor must erect substantial barriers; at times these have to be altered as the work proceeds, in which case extreme care is needed with planning.

- Make sure that your life safety systems – such as fire alarms and escape routes – remain operational throughout the demolition process. This is most important because the risk of fire is increased with demolition activities, eg cutting and burning.

- At the tender stage, make sure that the contractor employs a demolition method that minimises the need for workers to stand on the structure that is to be demolished. For example, it is completely unacceptable for a demolition worker to stand on a wall and at the same time attempt to knock it down with a sledgehammer. Instead, remotely operated breakers should be used.

- Ensure that all services are isolated, or that the contractor is made aware of any that are live.

- Satisfy yourself that the planned sequence of demolition will retain stability of the structure. If it will not, ascertain any necessary propping. Any failure of this type can be disastrous, and many demolition methods require input from a structural engineer.

- Decide how demolition debris will be removed. Floors can easily become overloaded and collapse if stacked with rubble, so it must be removed safely. It is dangerous to throw waste and rubble directly out of a window into a skip, as it can bounce out and injure passers-by. So if a chute is to be used, devise a method for controlling it and place a warning at ground level indicating that debris is being dropped down.

**Demolition machine allowing remote demolition without endangering people**

A risk here is the collapse of the structure onto the machine, which is why the cab is protected by the cage. All demolition machines working underneath or at a lower level than a structure should have this protection.

1.  Concrete-breaking attachment
2.  Reinforced cage over cab and windscreen

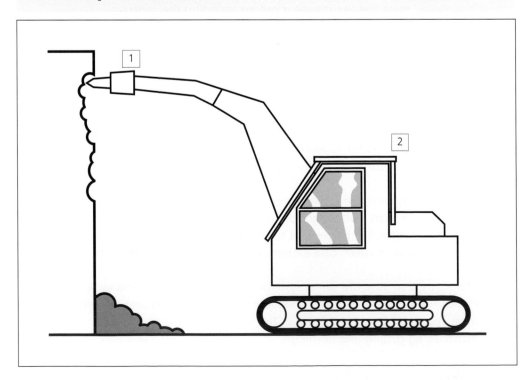

# Construction's number one risk – falls from a height

Year on year, statistics tell us that falls from a height cause up to half of all fatal accidents in the construction industry. All we have to do is eliminate them. The best way of doing so is to obey the law and pay the financial costs involved.

**Preventing falls from a height – the rules**

By law, the following hierarchy of risk must be followed at all times.

- Where possible, avoid work at height.

- Where work at height is unavoidable, properly constructed working platforms must be used. The platform must have all-round edge protection, comprising a guardrail, mid rail and toe board. Examples of working platforms include scaffolds, mobile towers, mobile elevating work platforms (known as 'MEWPs', 'scissors lifts' or 'cherry pickers') and suspended cradles.

- Where it is impracticable to erect a working platform, rope access techniques may be used, subject to strict controls, eg access to a high level wall of a building for a short task or inspection, where the time and risks involved in building a scaffold would be excessive.

- Where it is impracticable to use working platforms or rope access, nets or anchored safety harnesses may be employed. Personnel who use these methods include industrial roofers, metal deckers and scaffolders. Steel erectors, however, can usually use MEWPs.

- Ladders and stepladders may only be used if an assessment indicates that the risk of harm associated with their use is low.

**Hard facts**

From 1996/97 to 2002/03, falls from height accounted for 51 per cent of fatal accidents (294 deaths) in the UK construction industry. Other major causes of fatalities included being struck by a moving object (14 per cent), transport (11 per cent) and the collapse of a structure or machine (7 per cent). In 2002–2003, 10 per cent of fatal accidents (7 deaths) in construction were caused by electricity.

## Safe working platforms

The following pages give examples of safe and unsafe working platforms and set out legal requirements and best practice.

### Guardrails and toe boards – required dimensions

Note that the guardrail must be strong enough to maintain these dimensions if someone falls against it.

1. Guardrail at least 950mm high
2. Mid rail
3. Toe board at least 150mm high
4. Gap between toe board and mid rail, and between guardrail and mid rail, not more than 470mm
5. Standards fixed securely with edge clamp system or similar

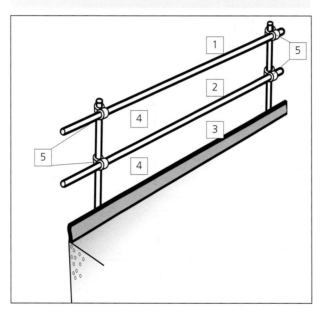

| Checklist of typical scaffolding faults to check | | | | | | | | | | |
|---|---|---|---|---|---|---|---|---|---|---|
| **Elements of scaffolding** | Footings | Standards (vertical load-bearing member) | Ledgers (horizontal members along elevation) | Bracing | Transoms and putlogs (cross members) | Couplers (join members) | Ties (secure scaffold to structure) | Boards | Guardrails, toe boards | Ladders |
| **Typical faults** | Soft and uneven | Not plumb, joined at same height | Not level, loose | Some missing | Wrongly spaced | Wrong fittings | Some missing, not enough | Damaged, incomplete | Incomplete, wrong height | Not tied |
| | No sole/base plates | Wrongly spaced | Joints in same bay | Loose | Loose | Loose, damaged | Ring ties have loose anchorage | Traps (ie unsupported boards) | Excessive gap to wall | Too short |
| | Undermined | Damaged | Damaged | Wrong fittings | Wrongly supported | No check couplers | Reveal ties loose | Insufficient supports | Not strong enough | Damaged |

## General access scaffolds

By law, scaffolds must be formally inspected (with records kept) before being used for the first time, after alteration, after any event likely to have affected stability, and at seven-day intervals.

1. Guardrail
2. Mid rail
3. Toe board
4. Working platform – minimum 4 boards, usually 5
5. Positive tie to structure – 8m apart on alternate lifts
6. Scaffold boards supported every 1.2m by scaffold tubes (transoms), which are fitted below the boards
7. Cross-bracing to alternate pairs of standards
8. Ledgers with staggered joints
9. Standards with staggered joints
10. Facade bracing to full height
11. Lift height 2m maximum, unless specifically designed
12. Bay length
    - 1.8m for demolition/masonry loading
    - 2.0m for bricklaying loading
    - 2.4m for painting/light duty loading
13. Base plates (every standard)
14. Sole plates (boards on soft ground)

Also read...

Appendix B – Fixed scaffolds

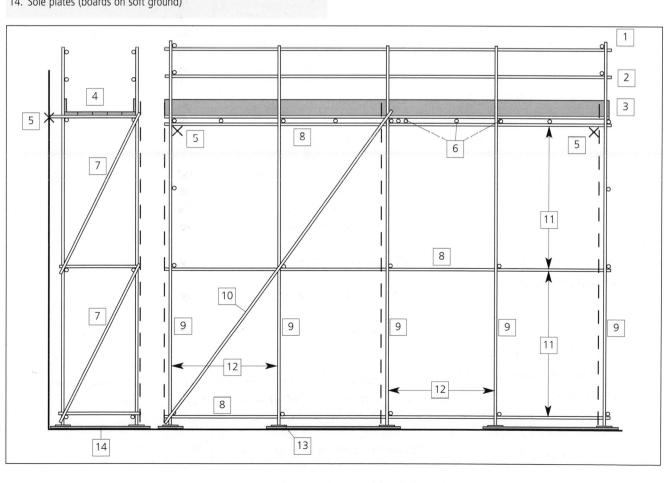

### Mobile tower scaffolds

Mobile access towers can give quick and safe access, but they are involved in many accidents each year because of poor erection or incorrect use. The following points must be borne in mind:

1. Internal hatchway
2. Ladder (used internally)
3. Outrigger. The outriggers increase the base width/area and so allow a higher tower to be used

*Rules for mobile tower scaffolds*

- As a general rule, towers must not be higher than three times the minimum base width when used externally, and three-and-a-half times when used internally.
- Workers should be trained in how to erect towers. Manufacturers' instructions should be available and followed.
- Towers must be fitted with double guardrails, a toe board and an internal ladder.
- Climbing on the outside of a tower can pull it over.
- The tower must be based on firm, level ground.
- People must not remain on the platform when it is being moved (watch for power lines).
- Casters must always be locked before the tower is used.
- Towers should be tied if sheeted, used for grit blasting, exposed to strong winds, or if heavy materials are pulled up externally.

**Also read...**

Appendix B – Mobile tower scaffolds

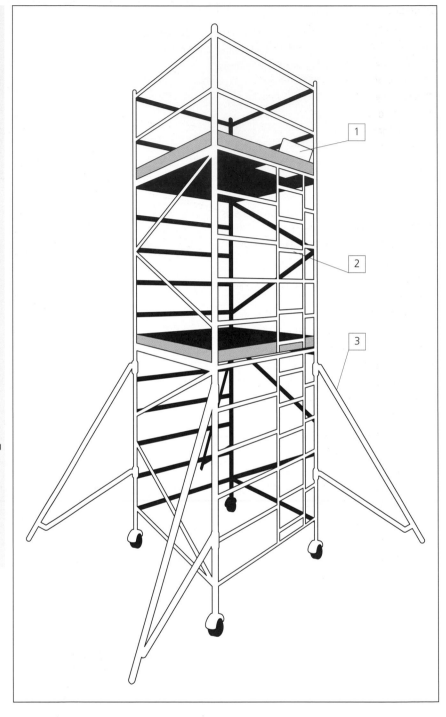

### Ladders

The main use of ladders in construction is for access. At all times three points of contact should be maintained (normally two feet and one hand), which means ladders cannot be used for carrying tools or materials from floor to floor, or for any work that requires more than one hand to operate the tool or equipment. In these instances, the correct approach is to use a mobile access tower or MEWP.

*Rules for ladders*

- Both stiles must be tied securely.
- Check stiles and rungs for damage. If there is any damage, the ladder must be discarded.
- The ladder must extend three full rungs or 1m above the place of landing so as to provide a handhold when getting on and off the working platform.
- To use a ladder for painting, for example, the painter should be able to reach the work area from a position 1m below the top of the ladder.
- The correct angle for a ladder is 75° (a ratio of 1:4) – see illustration.
- A second person should 'foot' the ladder while it is being tied. If it cannot be tied then it should be footed at all times. In such cases, the length of the ladder should be limited to that which can be easily handled.
- By law, ladders above the height of 9m must have intermediate landings.

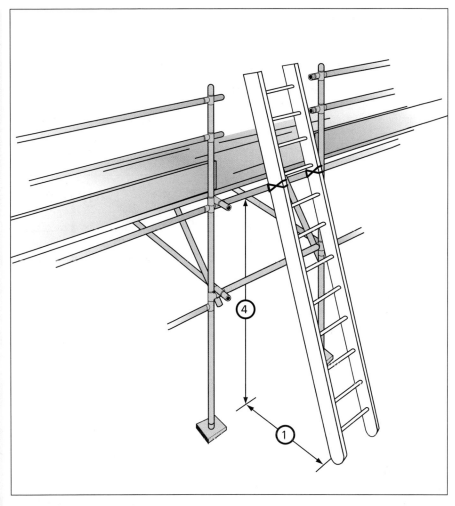

### Stepladders

Stepladders are a free-standing means of access, frequently used by electricians and services engineers when working on ceilings. They are only safe for short duration work and where the person does not have to climb higher than thigh height below the top of the platform, as shown in the diagram (left).

Mobile tower scaffolds are a safer alternative to stepladders and should be used wherever practicable.

### Mobile elevating work platforms (MEWPs)

There are two basic types of MEWP:

- cherry picker
- scissors lift.

There is a wide range of machines available, and the choice of which machine to use must be based on the needs of the job in hand.

Large cherry pickers are used to gain access to awkward-to-reach places both above and in front of the base unit, and can therefore be sited well away from hazards such as excavation edges. A smaller machine of the same type would have to be sited closer to the hazard and would be less safe.

By contrast, scissors lifts move vertically only but have the benefit of a much larger working platform. This is useful in wall cladding and internal finishing operations.

### Safe operation of MEWPs

MEWPs can provide safe access to high level work, but there are hazards, particularly of the machine turning over. The following rules should be observed:

- operators must be trained, competent and hold a certificate of training
- the machine must have a current test certificate
- the machine must be based on firm, level ground, prepared if necessary
- tyres must be in good condition and properly inflated, and any outriggers should be extended and chocked onto firm ground
- the machine must not be operated close to overhead cables or dangerous machinery
- the machine must not be moved with the platform raised, unless designed for this purpose
- the machine must not protrude into traffic routes, as it could be hit by a passing vehicle.

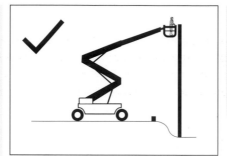

**Safe operation of a cherry picker**
A safety harness is required for use with this type of machine as the operator can be thrown out by jerky operations or ground movement, or by collisions with other vehicles or cranes.

**Unsafe operation of a cherry picker**
Risk of falling into excavation

**Unsafe use of a cherry picker or scissors lift on a slope greater than 5°**

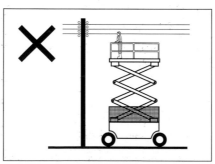

**Unsafe operation of a scissors lift under power cables**
The minimum safe distance is 15m to power lines mounted on steel towers and 9m to those mounted on poles.

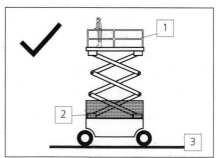

**Safe use of a scissors lift**
Scissors lifts should not be used to gain access onto structures or roofs. The operator must work from the platform at all times. A safety harness is not normally required, unless the operator has to lean over the guardrail.

1.  Fully guarded platform
2.  Guarding for mechanism
3.  Firm, level ground

## Fall protection

Pitched roofs and fragile roofs feature in many thousands of premises. When repairing or replacing these roofs, the risks must be assessed and appropriate precautions taken to prevent falls. A client for such works should make it clear that compliance with legislation is required, which means provision as illustrated below.

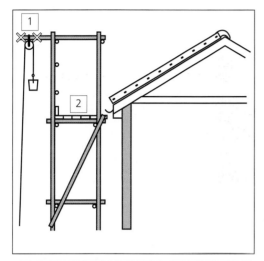

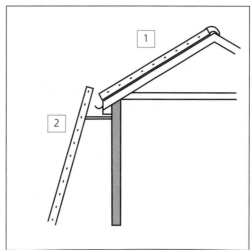

**Traditional pitched roof – long duration work**
1. Gin wheel with double check fittings (to haul up materials)
2. Working platform

**Traditional pitched roof – short duration work**
1. Roof ladder
2. Tied access ladder

A scaffold platform with edge protection is required, as shown above. Chimneys require their own access platform. For work of short duration on a pitched roof, such as replacing a few tiles, the minimum standards are:

- a safe means of access to roof level

- a properly constructed and supported roof ladder

- that roof workers must not work directly on tiles or slates unless they are wearing a safety harness that is securely anchored.

## Fragile roofs and roof lights

Many roofs are either fragile in themselves or contain roof lights, which must be assumed to be fragile. Asbestos cement roofs must also be assumed to be fragile and great care must be taken with metal roofs, which may be corroded. When replacing or overcladding roofs of these particular types, they must be treated with the utmost caution and specific methods must be developed to eliminate or reduce the risk when undertaking work on or to these roofs.

Also read...

Chapter 13 – Roof work

Appendix B – Roofs

## Groundworks

Groundworks are a major cause of fatal accidents. The risks to workers include:

- **Collapse of trenches** – use a trench box, trench sheets and props, or sheet piles, depending on depth and ground. Engineering design is necessary when working in poor ground and for all trenches more than 2m deep. Batter the sides of shallow trenches to a 45° angle.

- **Collapse of bulk excavations** – batter the sides to a 45° angle or shallower, depending on the ground.

- **Contact with buried underground services** – check utility drawings and use a cable-locating device before excavation.

- **Materials falling onto people working in the excavation** – provide edge protection and toe boards. Keep the edges clean. Do not stack spoil close to the edge of an excavation.

- **People and vehicles falling into the excavation** – provide guardrails to protect personnel. Do not approach excavations with dumpers; instead, use tracked excavators to lower in materials.

- **Vehicles running close to excavations** – vehicles impose extra loads on support systems and they must be taken into account in the design.

- **Vehicles reversing up to or approaching excavations** – if unavoidable, use a heavy and anchored stop block.

- **Undermining nearby structures** – when excavating closer to a structure than 1.5 times the excavation depth, an engineered support scheme is essential. For example, if an excavation is 2m deep, an engineering support scheme is required if it is dug closer than 3m (2m × 1.5) to a building. In poor ground, a support scheme may be necessary at greater distances.

- **Water inflow** – check soil reports and have pumps ready.

- **Premature removal of supports** – have a written method statement and task briefing if the shoring scheme has been engineered.

**Also read...**

Appendix B – Excavations

By law, excavations must be inspected:

- at the start of each shift

- after any accidental fall of rock, earth or any other material

- after any event likely to have affected their strength or stability.

In addition, records of the inspection must be kept. Registers for this purpose are available from safety equipment suppliers.

The best way to ensure safety in groundworks is to use an experienced specialist contractor who, in turn, has competent supervisors.

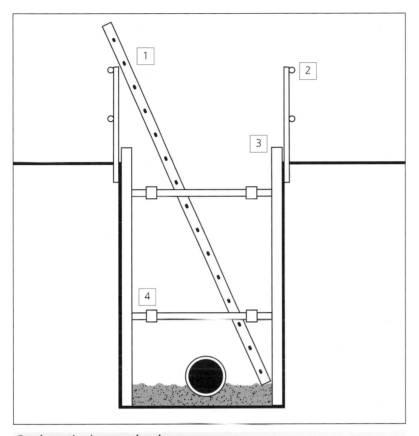

**Good practice in groundworks**

1. Access ladder
2. Guardrail
3. Trench box – projects above ground level to prevent materials falling into the trench
4. Hydraulic props prevent sides from collapsing

## The bottom line

**By law, the client for a construction or demolition project must:**

- appoint a competent principal contractor, planning supervisor and designers
- provide information to the planning supervisor about any risks
- ensure that a health and safety plan is in place before work starts
- ensure that a health and safety file is received at the end of the project.

The main cause of fatal accidents in construction is falls from a height. To prevent these, the law requires that proper working platforms are provided to workers wherever this is reasonably practicable and that safety harnesses are used only as a last resort.

Demolition and groundworks are also high risk activities that need to be carefully planned. Workforce training in the construction industry is a key issue for clients and contractors alike, and is a legal requirement for safety-critical activities such as driving plant and machinery.

## Introduction

Workshops are found in a wide range of enterprises. Some use workshops to produce their own goods; others are used to maintain or repair equipment, eg grass-cutting equipment and tractors.

Irrespective of a workshop's size, some or all of the following hazards may be present:

- metalworking machines and metalworking fluids and oils

- cleaning and degreasing solvents

- paint spraying

- welding

- woodworking machines and wood dust

- movement of vehicles in adjacent yards

- loading, unloading and handling of heavy objects

- overhead cranes, forklift trucks and other similar vehicles

- noise and vibration

- fumes, dust, mists and sprays

- fire and storage of hazardous and/or flammable materials

- vehicles and/or plant maintenance.

## Metalworking

Metalworking machines include presses, drilling machines, milling machines, lathes, metal-cutting saws, guillotines and grinding machines. Most accidents occur when:

| Also read... |  |
| --- | --- |
| Appendix B – Metalworking | |

- loading or unloading components

- removing swarf (waste metal that has been cut away)

- taking measurements or making adjustments, particularly to the flow of cooling fluid.

Accidents typically result in hand injuries and amputations of fingers, eye injuries, fractures and dislocations. Often, fatalities occur as a result of an operator becoming entangled in machinery. This can happen more readily if loose clothing or jewellery is worn.

Skin contact with metalworking fluids can cause irritation and dermatitis. Breathing in aerosols, oil mists or fumes from metalworking fluids can result in severe irritation of the eyes, nose and throat, often leading to serious conditions such as bronchitis and asthma.

**Also read...**

Chapter 6 – Noise

Appendix B – Noisy environments

Chapter 6 – Hand–arm vibration

Appendix B – Vibrating equipment

Chapter 6 – Manual handling

Appendix B – Basic lifting

High noise levels can cause deafness. This is most likely to occur to those who work at or alongside machines that use impacts as part of their process, or high-speed machines or groups of machines running together. Vibration, particularly when grinding, may also lead to hand–arm vibration syndrome (HAVS). The most common symptom associated with HAVS is reduced blood flow to the fingers, causing them to take on a grey/white appearance, with reduced feeling and nerve damage. Attacks are painful and can result in the loss of the ability to grip properly, which can be permanent.

Finally, unsafe loading and unloading of heavy components can cause back injury, and where an operator has to perform awkward repetitive tasks, arm injuries can develop that, if severe, may lead to permanent disability.

### Drilling machines, lathes, and milling machines
The main cause of injury using drills and lathes is that of hair, clothing or jewellery becoming entangled in the rotating parts.

### Safe working practices
1. Wear eye protection to safeguard against flying waste metal and fluids.

2. Do not wear jewellery or loose clothing, and tie back long hair.

3. Gloves should not be worn unless all rotating parts are enclosed. Gloves can be trapped in rotating parts, causing serious hand injury.

4. Ensure that chuck keys are removed from chucks, as they may become detached when the machine is started and cause injury.

5. Do not handle swarf, which can cut hands and increase the likelihood of dermatitis.

6. Make sure that the machine has an emergency stop button and that it is routinely tested.

7. Ensure that the machine is fitted with fixed adjustable guards.

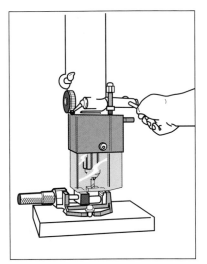

**Fixed adjustable guard and vice for a drill**

### Drill specifics
1. A securely fixed vice should be used to hold the work piece. A loose work piece can become detached at high speed and cause injury.

2. Fit the drill with a fixed adjustable guard that covers the spindle and drill tip as far as is practicable, and ensure that the guard is in place. Alternatively, fit a vertical tripping device not more than 75mm from the drill bit and positioned within the first 90° of rotation from the operator's position. These devices cut the power when tripped by anything that comes into contact with them, such as a hand or arm.

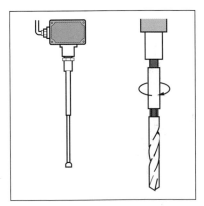

**Vertical tripping device (left), and drill bit (right)**

### Lathe specifics
1. Emery cloth is often used to smooth the work piece, but should never be used on computer-controlled or automatic lathes. If possible, avoid using hand-held emery cloth on a lathe; if

unavoidable, use a backing board that keeps fingers away from the rotating surface.

2. Ensure that there is a fixed guard at the rear of the machine, a chuck guard, and a guard for the feed and lead screws. A splashguard for suds and swarf should also be fitted.

### Grinding machines
The main cause of injury is the abrasive wheel bursting or shattering.

#### Safe working practices
1. Abrasive wheels usually burst or shatter because they have been damaged or incorrectly mounted. Because of this, the law requires that someone who has been specifically trained in this task, and therefore understands the risks and correct procedures, should mount abrasive wheels. The requirement also applies to hand-held tools such as disc cutters.

2. At a small grinding machine used for tool sharpening, a guard must be fixed that is strong enough to contain fragments of a bursting wheel. The guard must be close fitting with just enough room for the work piece.

3. The workrest must be well adjusted. The revolutions per minute of the spindle must be clearly marked (so that a matching wheel can be fitted – there is a danger of bursting the wheel if the spindle has a higher speed than the wheel rating). There must be an easily accessible on/off switch, and the floor must be kept clear to ensure that no-one trips and stumbles onto the wheel.

4. At a large grinding machine, dust extraction is necessary to minimise risks to health and prevent explosions.

**What is...**

**Guarding?**
Regulations require measures to be taken to prevent access to dangerous parts. There are four levels of protection:

- fixed enclosing guards
- other guards such as interlocking guards and pressure mats
- protection items such as jigs, holders and push sticks
- provision of information, instruction, training and supervision.

All four may be needed in specific cases.

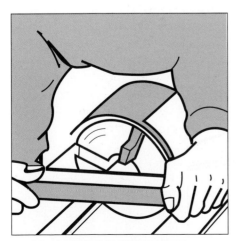

**Backing board used with a lathe**

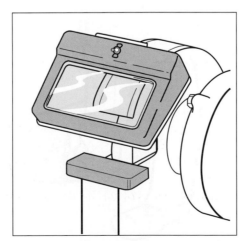

**Small grinding machine guard**

## Key health risk

### Metalworking fluids and oils

Machining creates heat and so requires cooling and lubrication. The fluids that perform this function are called metalworking fluids (MWFs). MWFs also prolong the life of the tool, carry away swarf, and protect the surfaces of the work pieces. They are held in the machine sump, pumped to the machining point and flow back to the sump. MWFs often contain oils and other hazardous substances that can damage health through skin contact or inhalation.

The machining process produces aerosols, mists and vapours that can irritate the eyes, and if inhaled can cause irritation and breathing difficulties, at times leading to conditions such as bronchitis and asthma.

In some instances, prolonged contact with unrefined mineral oils and mildly refined distilled oils may even cause cancer.

Safer alternatives are available and should be used, so check the product safety data sheets (available direct from manufacturers and often posted on their websites).

Protective gloves often cannot be worn because they increase the likelihood of trapping the operator's hand in a machine's moving parts.

*continued opposite*

### Power presses and guillotines

The major risk is that of fingers or hands being severed or crushed if the press or guillotine operates unexpectedly.

### Safe working practices

1. Presses and guillotines require interlocking guards and a shrouded footpedal, both of which prevent the machine being operated by accident. The interlocking guard is linked to the power supply, so that the machine will only operate when the guard is fully closed. Guillotines should have a rear interlocking guard and a front opening small enough to prevent the operator's fingers from entering. Presses should have front and rear interlocking guards.

2. Guillotines should have in-built lighting and a marker to enable the cutting line to be seen, together with a sloped discharge chute to allow work pieces to be retrieved without having to open the guard.

3. Excessive noise from the impact of the operation of the press or guillotine, or from air ejection, can be minimised by enclosing the machine as much as possible with sound-absorbent linings. Ear defenders may also be needed.

4. Power presses and guillotines are often used in repetitive batch production work. In such cases, it is important to assess the workstation and seating to minimise twisting and turning when lifting and lowering heavy components. Chairs should be fully adjustable.

5. Use chromed leather gloves to reduce cuts when handling sharp and/or heavy work pieces from a guillotine.

**Shrouded footpedal**

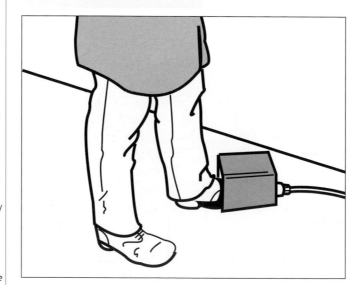

**Metal-cutting saws**

The major risk is of contact with the running saw blade. Metal-cutting saws can also be excessively noisy.

**Safe working practices**

1. Fit fixed adjustable guards. Work pieces should be fed through openings small enough to prevent access to the blade; alternatively, fit a linkage-operated moving guard to prevent contact with the blade in the raised position and exposure of the blade during cutting.

2. Gravity-operated guards should only be operated with power controls that have to be held in the 'on' position for the machine to operate (hold-to-run controls).

**Noise reduction – saws**

- Clamp the work securely.
- Use noise-absorbent material on the feed table.
- Use saw blades that are damped and in good condition.
- Enclose the cutting head.
- Provide ear defenders.

**Metal-cutting saw showing guards**

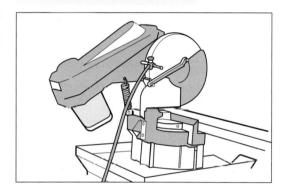

**Three-roll bending machines**

The major risk is of hands being drawn into the rollers.

**Safe working practices**

1. Do not wear gloves, which increase the risk of trapping hands in the rollers.

2. Do not wear loose clothing or ties, and tie back long hair, all of which may get trapped in the rollers.

3. Use controls that have to be constantly held down in order to run the machine, and which return to stop after release.

4. Install trip devices at both sides of the machine. Doing so will ensure that if someone gets trapped they can activate a device and free themselves.

5. Fit an emergency stop button that uses power brakes, which will stop the rollers in a matter of seconds.

6. Do not grip work pieces too close to the rolls; instead, use feed tables and rollers.

**Key health risk** *continued*

In order to use fluids and oils safely:

- only use fluids and oils recommended by the machine manufacturer. Follow suppliers' guidance on their use

- keep weekly records of visual sump inspections, leaks, and concentration, pH and bacteria dip-slide measurements, as recommended by the manufacturer

- keep machines, pipe work and sumps clean, especially before re-filling

- fluids and oils that are in poor condition smell unpleasant, indicating that bacteria are present; fluids and oils that are breathed in via a vapour mist are a health risk. Biocides can be used to reduce this risk, but too much biocide is also hazardous to health

- train employees in the hazards and safeguards of machine operation, including personal hygiene

- enclose sources of emissions and aerosols, and provide local exhaust ventilation where these are significant

- maintain recommended fluid or oil flow at correct volumes and pressures

- do not allow fluids or oils to overheat or stagnate, as this increases the risk of biological contamination

- do not use air lines to blow components clean; instead, use a vacuum cleaner.

### Computer-controlled machines

These machines can present additional hazards because they work faster than manual machines and to a set programme that does not necessarily depend on action by the operator. If an accident occurs the machine may carry on working. Computer controls that have been retrofitted to a manual machine can create greater risks, as the degree of guarding on the manual machine may be insufficient.

### Safe working practices

1. Fixed and interlocking guards must be fitted to prevent access to all machine movements, not just those involving metal-cutting. Work zone enclosures may be necessary to prevent unauthorised personnel approaching the machine.

2. Use the guards to reduce noise and control emissions of mists, fume and vapour, either from metalworking fluids or from the material being machined.

3. Manual machines that have been retrofitted with computer controls should be risk assessed. In general, a high standard of interlocking guards will have to be fitted, equal to those found on a new machine.

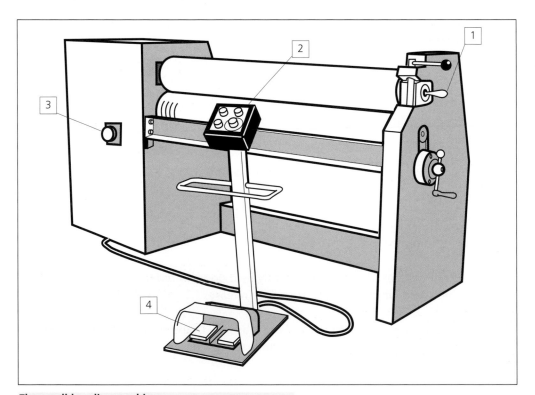

**Three-roll bending machine**
1. Trip device
2. Hold-to-run controls (positioned away from the machine)
3. Emergency stop button
4. Shrouded foot controls

# Cleaning and degreasing

The purpose of cleaning and degreasing is to remove all trace of oils, metalworking fluids or other unwanted residues that are produced in the manufacturing process. It is one of the most hazardous activities in the workshop as it uses solvents that pose serious health risks or which are easily ignited. At its simplest, cleaning of work pieces is done using rags that are dipped in or sprayed with solvent.

Vapour degreasing tanks are used to clean complex or multiple work pieces using a process similar to that used to dry clean clothes – indeed, the same chemicals are often used.

Also read...

Chapter 9 – Dry cleaning

**Follow this flow chart to decide how to deal with cleaning and degreasing in the workshop**

- Reduce the need for cleaning by using well-maintained machines and good workshop practice

- Find the least harmful cleaner that will do the job, by consulting manufacturers' data sheets
- Carry out a COSHH (Control of Substances Hazardous to Health) assessment and record it
- Consider flammability

- When using liquids to clean by dipping, wiping or spraying, avoid chlorinated solvents such as trichloroethylene (trike), perchloroethylene (perc) and methylene chloride, unless used in specialist facilities that are enclosed and provided with extraction
- Use the least flammable (flashpoint above 45°C) hydrocarbon solvents such as petroleum distillates, turpentine and alcohols
- Minimise contact with acid and alkali solutions, and their fumes and vapours

Also read...

Chapter 6 – Hazardous substances

Appendix A – Hazardous substance assessment

- Avoid spills by using pipe work or pumps, rather than pouring solvents from containers
- Keep lids on containers
- Store correctly
- Label properly

- Draw up a plan to deal with spillages. This should include bunded storage areas and the provision of clean-up materials

- Avoid work in confined spaces, such as the inside of metal fabrications

- If unavoidable, a risk assessment must be carried out and special precautions provided such as breathing apparatus, safety harness and rescue equipment, with a second person standing by
- Use a permit to work procedure
- Seek specialist advice

- Once all of the above have been considered, provide personal protective equipment such as respirators, gloves, overalls, eye protection and boots to eliminate any residual hazard

### Vapour degreasing tanks

Exposure to the vapours can cause drowsiness, unconsciousness or even death. Direct contact with fluids can cause dermatitis.

### Safe working practices

1. To minimise exposure, position the tank in an area that is free from draughts and use covers when the tank is not in use. Stack components so that they can drain, and allow them to dry fully before removing them. Do not load or remove components too quickly so that vapour is pushed or dragged out.

2. To prevent the build up of residues, maintain the tank properly. Correctly balance heating and cooling systems, and repair leaks. Pump in new fluid below the existing liquid level.

3. Treat pits (in which degreasing tanks are set) as part of the tank.

4. Many fatal accidents occur in degreasing tanks, so post a sign prohibiting entry. Arrange to drain off residues or pump dirty solvent directly into a container for recovery. If entry cannot be avoided, use a specialist contractor and provide full written details of the chemicals used. In return, insist on seeing a written safe system of work that includes a permit to work, as well as breathing apparatus, safety harness and line, rescue tripod, spare breathing apparatus and back-up personnel, oxygen resuscitation equipment, and full solvent-resistant protective clothing. Specialist advice is required.

Also read...

Chapter 13 – Confined spaces

### Welding and flame-cutting

Most workshops carry out welding and flame-cutting activities that can be hazardous to welders and others in the vicinity. Accidents occur as a result of:

Also read...

Chapter 5 – Storage of gas cylinders

Chapter 5 – Use of oxyacetylene (and propane) equipment

- Gas cylinders falling over. This could be a relatively minor accident, such as a cylinder falling onto someone's foot. More serious accidents can occur if the valve assembly is knocked off the cylinder, as the escaping compressed gas can turn the cylinder into a missile.

- Electric shocks from arc-welding equipment.

Also read...

Appendix B – Arc welding

- Fires started by sparks or hot material produced by welding or cutting.

- Fingers being crushed between the electrodes of fixed-resistance welding machines.

- Particles from the welding operation entering unprotected eyes. This is most likely to happen during the process of 'chipping' the weld or removing unwanted material.

Also read...

Chapter 6 – Manual handling

Chapter 6 – Hazardous substances

Chapter 6 – Noise

Chapter 6 – Hand–arm vibration

- Manual handling problems as a result of using loose cylinders.

- Inhalation of harmful welding fume.

- Noise and vibration during grinding for weld preparation.

- Looking directly at the electric welding arc, which can cause the painful condition known as 'arc eye'.

### Safe working practices

1. Welding and cutting inside tanks and other confined spaces are very hazardous activities. You need expert advice and a full, written risk assessment.

2. Never apply heat or a naked flame to containers, tanks or drums. They may contain, or may previously have contained, flammable or explosive liquids or gases. They must first be cleaned thoroughly, and a risk assessment carried out before cutting.

3. Welding on large structures needs a risk assessment, and the provision of a proper working platform.

### Key health risk

**Welding fume**

Welding, arc-welding, flame-cutting, brazing and burning produce different types of fume, all of which can be harmful. One of the main risks is contracting metal fume fever, an acute flu-like illness. Early symptoms include a dry throat, coughing and breathing difficulties. Ultimately, poisoning can cause long-term lung damage.

The greatest dangers occur when working with metallic coatings such as cadmium or zinc plating, and chromium, manganese, cobalt or nickel surfaces. Mechanised flame-cutting and frequent manual metal arc-welding also produce hazardous welding fume.

To control and minimise risks:

- ensure the workshop has plenty of fresh air
- avoid welding materials that are plated; instead, use alternative bonding techniques or plate after welding
- provide local exhaust ventilation, set up and maintained by a specialist supplier
- as a last resort, or for occasional use, provide welders with specialist respirators
- do not weld within 10m of cleaning processes that use chlorinated solvents, as the heat and arc from welding may break down the solvents into more harmful substances.

## Painting

The main risks associated with paint spraying are:

- breathing in the vapours, especially in confined spaces or unventilated open workshops (the most hazardous paints contain toxic materials such as lead or isocyanates)

- getting paint on the skin, in the eyes, or swallowing it

- fire or explosion from the ignition of flammable vapour, particularly vapour from oil-based paints.

### Safe working practices

1. Use the least hazardous paint, such as water-based paints.

2. Treat confined spaces with extreme caution and follow a similar procedure to that used for vapour tank degreasing (see earlier in this chapter).

3. Set up a dedicated spray booth with air extraction and filtration.

4. Keep no more than 50 litres of flammable paint at the spray booth, and enclose in a steel cupboard or box. Larger stocks should be kept in a bunded fire-resistant store that has good ventilation.

5. Ensure that there is adequate ventilation where paints are mixed. Breathing protection may also be needed.

6. Take care when disposing of empty containers. Paint residues can be flammable, toxic or harmful in other respects.

7. Obtain data sheets for all paints used and carry out an assessment of the risks. Brief painters on the results and make the data sheets and risk assessments available at the workplace.

8. If painting with isocyanates or powder coatings, expert advice is essential and a full, written risk assessment is required. Isocyanates and powder coatings can cause an allergic reaction, often leading to asthma. In both cases, an occupational health specialist should be consulted.

Also read...

Chapter 13 – Confined spaces

Also read...

Chapter 6 – Hazardous substances

Appendix A – Hazardous substance assessment

**Setting up a spray painting booth**

- When setting up or maintaining a spray booth, ensure that an air velocity of 0.7m/s is achieved at the front of the booth (0.5m/s inside an enclosure), and that filtration is provided.

- Ensure that the air is extracted to a safe place, away from people and sources of ignition. The extraction motor should be isolated and extend to the spray booth.

- Check booths and enclosures regularly for leaks, and employ a testing company to examine and test them every 14 months.

- Ensure that there is no source of ignition inside the booth, such as unprotected electrical equipment. Lighting is best shone into the booth from outside, behind a heat-resistant, wired-glass screen. Alternatively, use intrinsically safe light fittings, which are fully enclosed to prevent sparks from igniting a fire.

Also read...

Appendix B – Paint spraying

### Also read...

Appendix B – Woodworking

# Woodworking

## Circular saw benches

Circular saw benches must be:

- fitted with a suitable riving knife and saw guard

- fully enclosed beneath the table

- fitted with an emergency stop button that activates a braking device, bringing the blade to a stop within 10 seconds

- marked with the smallest blade diameter that can be used safely (small blades have a slower perimeter velocity for a given speed of revolution, and therefore cut slower, less efficiently and less safely at the cutting edge)

- fitted with local exhaust ventilation, both above and below the table, to control wood dust.

Portable saw benches are now commonplace. They have a smaller table and are less stable than fixed installations. The use of portable benches must be monitored daily. The same standards apply to both fixed and portable bench use.

**Circular saw**

1. Exhaust outlet
2. Extension table
3. Saw guard
4. Table
5. Rip fence
6. Cross-cut fence
7. Push stick

**Riving knife fixing (guard removed for clarity)**

1. Riving knife
2. Gap not to exceed 8mm

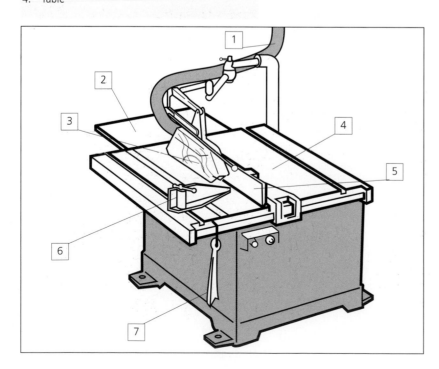

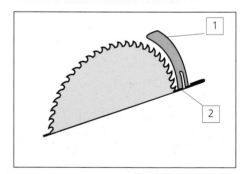

### Safe working practices

1. Use a rip fence or cross-cut fence to give adequate work piece support during cutting. A low position fence must be used for shallow or angled work.

2. A push stick must always be used to prevent hands coming within 300mm of the blade and to remove the cut piece, unless the cut piece is more than 150mm wide.

3. A riving knife must always be used. It should be rigid and set accurately in line with the saw. It should have a chamfered edge and be thicker than the body of the saw blade, but slightly thinner than the thickness of the saw cut.

4. The saw guard must be strong and easily adjustable without the use of tools, and kept as close as possible to the surface of the work piece.

5. Use sharp and clean blades, otherwise they will cut inefficiently and unsafely.

6. At all times, the teeth of the saw blade should project through the material – select the correct blade size.

7. Do not stand directly in line with the saw blade.

8. Never clean the blade while it is fixed to the machine.

### Setting of the saw guard

Saw guard must be as close to the work piece as possible

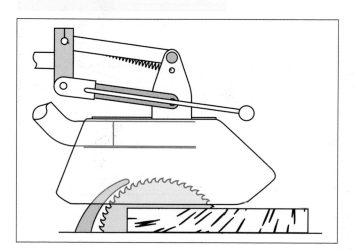

### Normal fence position for ripping

1. Push stick

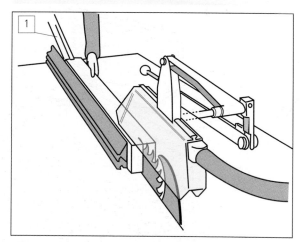

### Hard facts

Fifty-one per cent of workshop accidents occur in small premises that employ less than 25 people. In these premises, 56 per cent of those injured have received 'on-the-job' training only.

### Planing machines

A two-knife cutter block on a planing machine makes 10,000 cuts per minute. If a machinist's fingers are in contact for only a tenth of a second, 16 slices will be removed. To prevent this there are two main safeguards:

- a bridge guard

- a braking device that will stop the cutter block within 10 seconds (older machines must be retrofitted by December 2005).

The bridge guard must be strong and rigid, made from a material such as wood or aluminium so that, in the event of contact, neither the guard nor cutter block will shatter. The guard must cover the whole table gap, and be easily adjustable both horizontally and vertically without the use of a tool. The cutters must not project above the table more than 1.1mm, and the gap between the table and the drum must be 3mm±2mm. The gap between the bridge guard and the work piece must be as small as possible, and push blocks must be used when planing short pieces.

### Basic safeguarding of a planing machine
1. Full-width bridge guard attached to fence
2. Fence
3. Work piece
4. Guarded drive mechanism
5. Adjustable bridge guard

### Adjustment of the bridge guard – edging
1. Gap as close as possible
2. Fence
3. Bridge guard
4. Work piece
5. Table

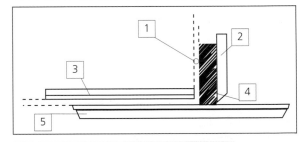

### Adjustment of the bridge guard – flatting

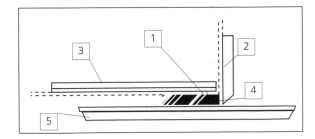

## Guarding of other machines

### Narrow band saw showing the use of adjustable guard, fence and guide block in straight cutting

1. Adjustable guard
2. Work piece
3. Fence
4. Push stick
5. Guide block

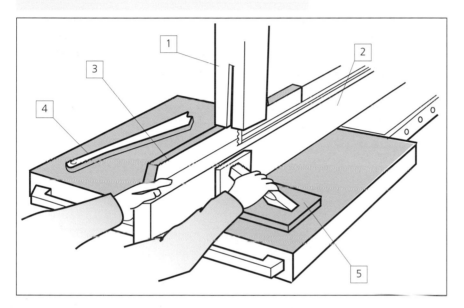

### Vertical-spindle moulding machine fitted with two guards, forming a tunnel and backed by a false fence. The false fence greatly reduces exposure to dangerous parts

1. Guard covers top of spindle and back of cutters
2. False fence
3. Work piece

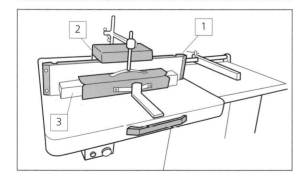

### Manually operated cross-cut saw

1. Dust extractor
2. Fixed top guard
3. Nose guard
4. Saw housing with extractor

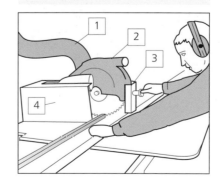

## Key health risk

### Wood dust

All wood dust is hazardous to health. It can cause:

- skin disorders
- respiratory disease
- nasal cancer
- general ill health effects.

Hardwood dust is classified as a carcinogen and health surveillance (medicals, questionnaires, enhanced training, protective equipment and long term record-keeping) is needed where workers are exposed to it. Softwood dust is not presently classified as carcinogenic, although there is mounting evidence that it too can cause ill health.

There is a legal requirement to reduce wood dust exposure to a minimum. The best way to do this is to provide local exhaust ventilation at woodworking machines. Many machines require this extraction equipment in order to operate effectively, so it is likely to be installed in any sizeable workshop.

Where the measures taken to reduce exposure to air-borne dust are inadequate, additional personal respiratory protective equipment must be provided and used. Disposable respirators to EN149 FFP2 are suitable for general use, but full-face masks to EN136 with a filter to EN143-P3 are necessary for entry to dust collection rooms and other very dusty atmospheres. Ordinary 'nuisance' dust masks are not suitable.

## Workshop health and safety
Engineering and woodworking

www.protect.org.uk

PDF 14

| Question | Yes or no | Action required and timescale |
|---|---|---|
| **Your people** | | |
| Are your machinists formally trained? | | |
| Are your machinists properly instructed on the specific equipment? | | |
| Have you authorised your machinists in writing? (Only operators who have been authorised as properly trained and competent should be allowed to operate machines.) | | |
| Has there been recent refresher training? | | |
| Is the person chosen to do a job confident, reliable and experienced? | | |
| Is the right machine being used for the job? | | |
| Have the risks been formally identified and discussed with the workforce via toolbox talks? | | |
| **A safe workplace** | | |
| Is the workplace clean and tidy? | | |
| Are gangways marked and kept clear? | | |
| Is there good lighting for the task? | | |
| Is there a canteen where food can be eaten outside of the working area? | | |
| Do employees wear safe clothing (with no loose items that could be caught in machinery), remove jewellery, and tie back long hair? | | |

| Question | Yes or no | Action required and timescale |
|---|---|---|
| **Handling and stacking** | | |
| Are there designated traffic or pedestrian routes, and are they kept clear so that pedestrians are not in danger of being run over by vehicles? | | |
| Are people prohibited from riding on forklift trucks or using them for access to heights? | | |
| Are trained and certificated operators the only personnel allowed to drive forklift trucks or other similar vehicles? | | |
| Are there designated storage areas? | | |
| Are stacks of materials low enough so that they remain stable? | | |
| Are people instructed in manual handling techniques and in the use of any handling aids? | | |
| **A healthy workplace** | | |
| Is dust extraction equipment provided? | | |
| Are dust masks and/or other respiratory protective equipment provided and used? | | |
| Are dry sweeping and the use of air lines to clean up dust prohibited? Are vacuum cleaners provided? | | |
| Have all hazardous substances been identified, data sheets obtained, assessments made, preventive measures taken, protective equipment provided, and employees trained? | | List substances identified: |
| Are metalworking oils properly maintained? | | |
| Is noise properly controlled (ie below 85 dB(A)) and/or hearing protection provided? | | |
| Are sound-reducing enclosures used on very noisy machines? | | |

# Workshop health and safety
### Engineering and woodworking (continued)

www.protect.org.uk

PDF 14

| Question | Yes or no | Action required and timescale |
|---|---|---|
| **Fire safety** | | |
| Are there adequate numbers of appropriate fire extinguishers and are they maintained? | | |
| Do fire drills take place regularly? | | |
| Are all fire exits clear and fire detectors working? | | |
| If you have any flammable liquids, is the total volume in the workshop no more than 50 litres, and are they kept locked in a steel cupboard or box? | | |
| Are the lids always replaced on cans of flammable liquids? | | |
| Are wood dust and other flammable waste prevented from accumulating? | | |
| Are walls, ceilings, ledges and other surfaces free from dust? (A build up of dust increases the risk of a fire.) Use vacuum equipment to remove dust, not air lines or sweeping. | | |
| Is the dust-collection hopper (connected to extraction equipment) emptied regularly, thereby preventing a build up of dust and the potential for an explosion? | | |
| Is there a smoking ban in the area of any flammable liquids and wood dust? Is this enforced? | | |
| **Machine safety** | | |
| Are all guards available and in place on every machine? | | |
| Are all guards set to the lowest practical position? | | |
| Are the guards inspected on a daily basis? | | |
| Do all machines have emergency stop buttons that bring the saw blade or cutter to a halt within 10 seconds? | | |
| Do machinists ever use their hands to remove waste? | | |
| Who sets up the machines and changes cutters? Are they fully trained and experienced? | | |
| Do all machinists use safe working practices? | | |

**The bottom line**

By law, as a minimum you must carry out risk assessments and put in place control measures for the following:

- handling and stacking materials
- transport and vehicle movements, inside the workshop and in the surrounding work yard
- metalworking fluids and oils
- cleaning and degreasing solvents
- wood dust created by wood machining
- machinery operation, setting and maintenance
- welding processes and materials
- paint spraying
- processes that create noise
- vibrating equipment.

Specific industries are subject to other risks in addition to those listed above.

## Introduction

This chapter is designed to provide hotel and restaurant managers, even managers of staff canteens, with an overview of the health and safety essentials that apply to their activities. Work practices in kitchens can directly affect public health, therefore the management of hotels and restaurants requires a high degree of expertise, part of which is a good knowledge of health, safety and food hygiene.

## Hotels

In terms of health and safety, the five elements of hotel management that are of primary concern are:

- fire precautions

- housekeeping, laundry and dry cleaning

- food and drink service

- kitchens and food preparation

- maintenance and facilities management (see Chapter 13).

### Fire precautions

Hotels are often complex buildings with many rooms. Fires can start anywhere in a hotel, and when they do they can quickly entrap guests and staff. Guests are in particular danger because they are unfamiliar with the building layout and means of escape. This lack of familiarity is aggravated by disorientation if a fire starts when guests are awoken from sleep. For these reasons alone, fire precautions are a matter of the highest priority.

By law, hotels have always required a fire certificate and now must carry out a fire risk assessment. The following fire precautions will be necessary:

**Also read...**

Chapter 5 – Fire risk assessments and fire certificates

- good means of escape, with short travel distances between rooms and a place of safety (such as a fire protected corridor or fire exit)

- an automatic fire detection and alarm system

- good access to the building for emergency services

- fire hydrants for the use of the fire service

- other general precautions (as described in Chapter 5).

In some cases, sprinkler protection should also be installed.

In a hotel it is important that the automatic fire detection and alarm system is linked to a central control point, so that the exact location of a fire can be established. The system should also be able to provide information on matters such as false alarms and sprinkler activation, and be capable of producing a log of events, which should be reviewed by management on a weekly basis. The control centre should be staffed on a

24-hour basis or, in the case of smaller premises, be linked directly to the local fire service.

It is crucial that a thorough emergency plan is written up and training provided to all staff on how to cope with fire (as well as other emergencies). Staff must also take care of guests, who must be accounted for and segregated from arriving fire appliances. For this reason, clearly signposted fire assembly points must be established, and a management system set up so that, in the event of a fire, an up-to-date list of guests can be produced and used as the basis for a roll call. A fire drill should be implemented that can be practised by staff without the involvement of guests, and should be rehearsed every three months.

'Fire assembly point' sign

In hotels there is constant activity, and therefore the ever-present possibility of a fire exit becoming blocked or new hazards being created. To guard against this, patrols of all corridors and exits should be carried out using an accompanying checklist. The patrols must ensure that:

- fire escape doors can be opened and are not blocked

- corridors are not blocked

- fire doors are closed and not held open with wedges or fire extinguishers

- fire extinguishers are in place and are not overdue for testing

- lighting and emergency lighting is in good working order throughout

- there are no dangerous accumulations of rubbish (which can provide fuel for a fire).

These simple but important checks should be carried out on a daily basis. The supervisor should review completed checklists once a week.

### Housekeeping

An important housekeeping matter is that of the storage and movement of food and other raw materials into the hotel (and similar considerations with regard to waste). This involves the use of a loading bay and the handling of materials from the loading bay to many locations within the hotel. In the hotel situation, the main housekeeping hazard is lack of space, which has implications for vehicle congestion and segregating vehicles from pedestrians. To prevent pedestrians from being trapped in a loading bay, separate pedestrian access should be provided.

Materials in the loading bay are usually transported manually into the hotel using trolleys. For this reason it is necessary to pay particular attention to the condition of the flooring in the loading bay area. In the loading bay and in corridors that are frequently used to transport materials, anti-slip flooring should be used, particularly if flooring is likely to get wet. The flooring should be replaced whenever it becomes worn or broken. A manual handling assessment should also be carried out.

**Also read...**

Chapter 4 – Outside your buildings

Chapter 4 – Loading bays

**Also read...**

Chapter 6 – Manual handling

Appendix A – Manual handling assessment

Chapter 12 – Slips, trips and falls

Chapter 6 – Upper limb disorders

### Laundry

Typically, laundry workers handle over 2 tonnes of laundry each working day. The work involves highly repetitive reaching and stretching, exposing workers to the risk of upper limb disorders (ULDs).

The specific tasks involved are:

*   collecting the laundry, often from beneath a laundry chute, and separating the different items into deep bins

*   filling bins with up to 25kg of dry laundry, pushing or pulling the bins to the washer, and loading the washer

*   after washing, filling bins with up to 50kg of wet laundry from the washer, pushing or pulling the bins to the dryer, and loading the dryer

*   removing towels from the dryer, folding and stacking them, or folding sheets from the rolling dryer, and pushing the finished laundry to its storage room and stacking it.

**Sorting laundry**

**Loading the washer**

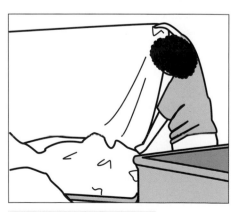

**Spreading out a sheet to put into the rolling dryer**

# 9 Hotels, restaurants and catering

### Practical ways of reducing risk

An awareness of the manual handling issues involved in laundry operations is the first step to reducing the risk of injury. While some manual handling is inevitable, the process should be examined to see if the amount could be reduced. One way of reducing injury is to use a chute to get bedclothes and towels down to the laundry. Another is to prevent piles of laundry from accumulating, thereby making the task of sorting so much easier. Other ways of reducing the amount of bending and stretching, and hence the risk of injury, include:

- training workers to handle no more than 8kg of laundry at one time

- ensuring that the bases of laundry bins are at least 400mm off the ground

- using carts with spring-loaded bottoms no less than 400mm off the ground, so that clothes are raised as the cart is unloaded (carts could also have a side-opening panel to reduce stretching distances and stress on the back and shoulders)

- using the lightest available bins or carts with wheels designed for hard floors, and ensuring that the bins, carts and wheels are maintained regularly

- providing employees with shoes that provide good cushioning (to lessen the stress on the feet and lower back)

- covering floors with closed-cell silicone floor mats that are at least 10mm thick and have a bevelled edge (to reduce the risk of leg fatigue and trips)

- providing suitable platforms to stand on at equipment (to reduce the amount of stretching)

- mounting washing machines and tumble dryers at a height, and instructing workers to collect partially folded sheets as they come out of a dryer, complete the folding operation on a conveniently placed counter, and place the items in a basket (to reduce the need for bending)

- using irons that are held by a suspension or counterbalancing device (to reduce the weight that the presser has to lift), and locating hand-ironing platforms near pressers (to reduce excessive reaching)

- providing seating, or sit-and-stand devices wherever practicable, and vertically adjustable bagging poles that employ a hydraulic pedal control system (to reduce the amount of stretching required to put a garment on the line)

- introducing job rotation and encouraging teamwork (to reduce the repetitiveness of the work and maximise job satisfaction).

### Dry cleaning

Dry cleaning is a generic name given to any cleaning process that does not use water to dissolve soiling from fabrics. However, dry cleaning does involve washing in a liquid solvent, with detergent added to make a washing solution. Water is also added to remove water-soluble soiling from the fabric.

In the dry cleaning process, the contents of the machine are agitated for a period of time, allowing the solution to remove soiling. Next, the clothes are spun at a high speed to extract the solvent, and are then tumbled dry. The drying process may occur in the same machine or a different one, depending on the system used. Garments are then pressed.

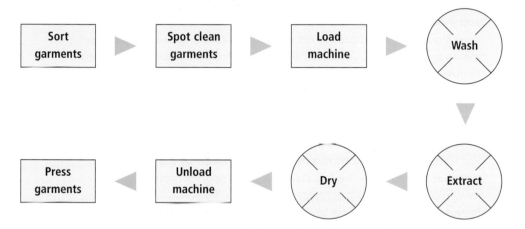

### The dry cleaning process

Perchloroethylene ('perc') is the most commonly used dry cleaning solvent. It is a hazardous chemical that, if inhaled, can damage the central nervous system, liver and kidneys; impair memory; cause confusion, dizziness, headaches and drowsiness; and irritate the eyes, nose and throat. Eye contact is particularly serious, and repeated skin contact may result in dermatitis. Perc is also thought by some to cause cancer.

Alternatives to perc include petroleum-based solvents. These were in use before the advent of perc, and were the cause of many fires and explosions. However, modern machines are available that use these solvents in an inert gas such as nitrogen, which greatly improves safety. There is also a water-based dry cleaning process. While neither is a substitute for perc in terms of cleaning ability, their use improves safety by reducing the total amount of perc used in the hotel. Where petroleum-based solvents are used, sprinkler protection should be provided and a 'no smoking' policy enforced.

### Practical ways of reducing risk

- Isolate the dry cleaning machines as much as possible from the rest of the laundry to limit the effect of any perc fumes.

- Use modern machines that have integrated washing and drying, a refrigerated condenser and carbon absorber, and adequate capacity. Loading and unloading the dry cleaning machine is by far the greatest source of exposure to perc, and modern machines remove most of the perc residue from the drum.

- Maintain machines by following manufacturers' recommendations to the letter. Proper maintenance is vital in reducing solvent exposures, and includes ensuring that vapour recovery systems are in good working order, and checking for liquid and vapour leaks on equipment piping and ductwork, and on the machine. Any leaks must be repaired immediately, otherwise the machine should be put out of use. Workers should wear proper personal protective equipment (gloves, goggles and respirators) to reduce exposure to perc during maintenance activities, which must always be carried out when the machine is out of operation and cold. This also applies to daily cleaning of button and lint traps. Solvents and hazardous waste produced by maintenance activities should never be left standing in an open container.

- Provide proper ventilation to dilute the effects of any perc leaking from the drum or off clothes. Local ventilation should be used to reduce exposure during machine loading and unloading and while performing maintenance. General ventilation should be used to add fresh air or remove air to dilute background perc concentration; a complete air change should occur in the workroom every five minutes. Ventilation must always be turned on when the machine is running.

- Instruct operators not to open the door of the dry cleaning machine while it is running. There should be an electro-mechanical interlock to prevent this from happening. The drying time should not be cut short or the machine overloaded, as this increases the likelihood of perc being left in the drum when the door is opened. Operators should also be advised not to put their heads into the machine and stay as far away as possible from the door during loading and unloading. A tool with a long handle should be used to retrieve items at the back of the drum. Doors should be opened only for as long as it is necessary to load or unload the drum, and be kept closed when not in use.

- Monitor drying times and temperatures, as well as solvent use, to check that the machine is working properly and efficiently.

### Fire risks in the laundry

Extract ductwork from dryers, dry cleaning machines and ventilation systems can easily become blocked by the build up of lint at filter points. This poses a serious fire risk. Filters must be checked and cleaned on a weekly basis, or more often if the conditions indicate a fast accumulation of lint or any other material.

## Food and drink service

Temporary or agency staff, and young people, are often employed as waiters and waitresses. It is the responsibility of the waiting supervisor to carry out a risk assessment to identify any hazards, and take steps to eliminate them. All staff must be advised of the risks and given appropriate training. This includes temporary staff and young people, whose inexperience and lack of familiarity increases their exposure to risks. This process is particularly important for outside functions or one-off events where normal routine may well be disrupted.

The risk assessment checklist on the following two pages is a useful basis for training employees in waiting and serving food.

## Waiting and food serving

www.protect.org.uk

PDF 15

| Activity | Hazard | Risk? Yes or no |
|---|---|---|
| Preparing for work: dressing appropriately | Slips, trips and falls; scalding; fire | |
| Cleaning, storing and carrying cutlery | Chemicals for cleaning silverware; cuts from knives | |
| Cleaning, storing and carrying crockery and service dishes | Stacking plates too high, causing overloading of shelves; carrying heavy loads | |
| Cleaning, storing and carrying glassware | Breakages | |
| Carrying trays and plates | Spillages; dropping trays | |
| Opening sparkling wine | Injury from flying corks | |
| Serving customers | Spillages at the table | |
| Clearing the table | Dropping items | |
| End of service | Fire | |

## Practical ways to reduce the risk

- Make sure that footwear is solid and stable, and entirely covers the feet (to prevent scalding from hot spillages)
- Do not wear loose clothing, which could become caught or, when working close to candles, catch fire
- Tie back long hair to avoid getting it in food, tangled in guests' jewellery, or coming into contact with candles or other naked flames

- Wear gloves at all times
- Do not leave cutlery in the sink
- Wipe cutlery on the blunt side
- Store and carry cutlery in baskets, with handles uppermost

- Mark the maximum stack height allowed
- Carry only the weight that feels safe and comfortable
- Get assistance with heavy loads

- Handle rims with care
- Use purpose-designed baskets or trays to transport items
- Pick up glasses by the stem or foot, and handle with care

- Go through swing doors sideways or backwards so that trays are protected
- Place hot foods and liquids in the centre of trays to contain spills
- Do not overfill containers
- Take particular care when negotiating stairs
- Carry only the weight that feels safe and comfortable
- Clear up spillages immediately

- After removing foil, keep pressure on the cork with the cloth or thumb while removing the wire clip. Then cover with the cloth and ease out slowly by turning the bottle, not the cork

- Warn customers if plates are hot
- Be aware that customers may move suddenly as you are about to serve them
- If space is tight, ask the customer to move to one side if they can
- Watch out for items on the floor
- Know how to deal with drunk or aggressive customers

- Never use broken trays
- Place heavy items at the centre of trays
- Carry only the weight that feels safe and comfortable
- Stack trays sensibly
- Use separate trays for glasses

- Make sure that all candles, cigarettes and food warmers are extinguished
- Switch off electrical equipment
- Make sure that fire exits are clear
- Do not stack chairs above chest height

**Also read...**

Appendix B – Kitchen hygiene

Appendix B – Knives and machines in kitchens

Appendix B – Cooking equipment in kitchens

# Kitchens and food preparation

This section is concerned with basic food hygiene and health and safety in the kitchen.

### Kitchen design

### Layout

Kitchens should be designed in a way that allows easy and thorough cleaning. If necessary, windows, doors and ventilation grilles should be fitted with screens to keep out flies, rats and other pests.

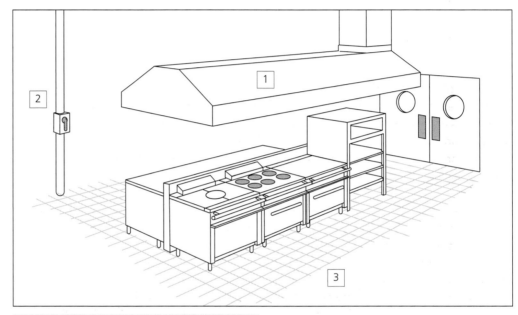

**Typical cooking layout with ventilation hood**
1. Ventilation hood with removable filter
2. On/off switch for ventilation fan in roof
3. Slip-resistant flooring

Kitchens should be large enough to allow sufficient space for personnel to circulate, and allow sufficient working space in front of cookers and food preparation areas. Unfortunately, this aspect is often neglected, leading to unpleasant and unsafe working conditions, inadequate ventilation, and excessive wear on floors, causing them to become slippery. In turn, this leads to additional maintenance demands, including the renewal of the floor covering on a regular basis.

There must be room for staff to move trolleys and carry trays safely, particularly in the vicinity of hot and exposed surfaces such as the griddle top, and where staff are using knives or cutting machines. To avoid staff bumping into each other, provide separate, clearly marked 'in' and 'out' doors to the dining room. If this is not practicable, vision panels must be provided.

Floor coverings should be of a seamless non-slip type, maintained to a high standard, and renewed whenever the non-slip property is eroded or the covering starts to fragment. Annual renewal is not unusual in a busy restaurant kitchen. Adequate drains should be provided to carry away water, steam drips and waste from tilting kettles, brat pans and other equipment.

Lighting

Lighting must be evenly distributed throughout the working area and there should be no glare or shadows. Good lighting is essential so that hazardous tasks can be performed safely, trips and slips prevented, and to facilitate thorough cleaning. The following minimum illumination levels are recommended by the HSE:

- preparation and cutting rooms – 540 lux

- kitchens – 300 lux

- passages and store rooms – 150 lux.

Ventilation

Good ventilation is required to introduce clean, cool air and remove excess hot air so that kitchen staff can breathe adequately and remain comfortable. Stressful working conditions are caused if this is not achieved, leading to sickness, absence and poor working practice. The general ventilation must provide sufficient air for complete combustion of gas-burning appliances, to dilute and remove the products of combustion, and to remove odours and steam.

Most air extraction in kitchens is carried out by cooker hoods and canopies. Canopies should overhang cooking appliances by 250mm to 300mm all round (150mm at the ends of wall-mounted canopies). To calculate the capacity required of the canopy extraction system, the air velocities over the hood face specified for individual items of equipment should be added up to give the total air movement. If this information is not available, allow an airflow rate of 0.4m per second × the total hood area (0.25m per second for light cooking and 0.5m per second for heavy cooking).

Cooker hoods must be provided with filters that collect grease, and be easily inspected and cleaned as necessary. The extract ductwork must also be cleaned periodically, at least once a year.

There must be a source of fresh air to replace that extracted and used by combustion. In large kitchens, mechanical ventilation provides most of this, with the balance coming from adjoining areas. This arrangement keeps the kitchen under negative pressure to prevent the escape of cooking odours. In smaller kitchens, sufficient replacement air may be drawn in through ventilation grilles, but care must be taken to ensure that the air is clean. Air from a restaurant where smoking is allowed, for example, is not suitable.

Ventilation systems need to be inspected and maintained on an annual basis and certificates of inspection kept. A maintenance contract is recommended.

Free-standing fans are a tripping hazard and should not be used. Fixed fans can be used but are not considered to be good practice as they do not provide fresh air and can help air-borne bacteria to spread.

### Washing facilities

It is very important that kitchen staff have good hand washing facilities, with hot and cold running water, soap, disposable towels and back-up hot-air dryers. Four separate sinks are required to accommodate:

- hand washing in the food preparation area

- food washing in the food preparation area

- the washing of floors, walls, equipment and utensils in the food preparation area

- hand washing in the washroom (personnel must not wash their hands in the other sinks after using the toilet, as germs could be brought into the food preparation area).

Signs should be placed above washbasins and sinks in food areas to indicate what they should be used for – washing hands, cleaning or washing food.

### Warning notices

Warning notices should be placed next to each piece of hazardous equipment, and after floors have been cleaned and are still wet.

### Kitchen equipment specification and maintenance

Gas-fired catering equipment, particularly ovens, must be fitted with flame-failure safeguards. A thermo-electric valve applies a source of ignition when the gas is turned on, so that it is not possible for gas to build up and an explosion to occur. Any equipment that does not have this safeguard must be replaced.

Deep-fat fryers are a source of many hazards in the kitchen. They should not be sited next to a sink because of the risk of water getting into the hot oil, causing an explosive reaction. The thermostat and controls should be checked on a regular basis and kept very clean, as a sticking thermostat could easily cause a fire, endangering the entire facility. An automatic fire protection system should be fitted in the hood over the deep-fat fryer and cooking range.

All new equipment supplied after 1 January 1995 must carry the CE mark, which indicates the manufacturer's declaration that it complies with the relevant harmonised European Product Safety Directives.

By law, pressure systems – such as steam jacket pans – require a safe operating pressure to be set and a written scheme of inspection carried out by a certifying body. Gas appliances and installations need to be inspected and maintained on an annual basis and certificates of inspection kept. Likewise, portable electrical appliances should be inspected at least annually, and tested every one to two years depending on use. With all of these regular maintenance and inspection items, a maintenance contract is recommended.

# Food hygiene

Poor hygiene can put both customers and staff at risk of food poisoning, which in severe cases can be fatal. The very young, very old, and those with an illness are most vulnerable. Even where a case of food poisoning is short-lived, damage to the reputation of the restaurant or hotel can be devastating. Good hygiene is required by law, and is enforced by the environmental health department of the local authority.

**The impact of temperature on bacteria**
- 60°C (140°F) and above – bacteria are killed

- 20°C to 50°C (68°F to 122°F) – optimal conditions for bacteria to grow

- 8°C (46°F) and below – bacteria do not grow

The introduction, growth and spread of bacteria causes food poisoning. Bacteria are present in raw food and are killed when the food is cooked to the correct temperature. If the food is not stored at a sufficiently low temperature, then bacteria can multiply or toxins (poisons) can form. Inadequate cooking allows bacteria to survive, whereas poor personal hygiene can introduce bacteria and germs, and cross-contaminate foods.

**Hard facts**

There are an estimated 4.5 million bouts of food poisoning in the UK each year – and approximately 60 people die. Each case is thought to cost up to £80 to the economy and health service when treatment and time off work is taken into consideration. This adds up to an annual bill of £350 million for the UK.

**The objectives of food hygiene**

**Maintain good standards of personal hygiene**

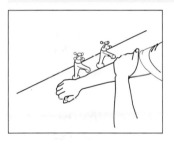

**Keep food areas clean**

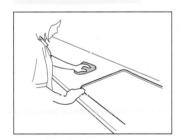

**Cool and store foods at the correct temperature**

8°C (46°F )
maximum

**Cook foods thoroughly**

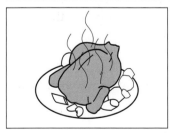

70°C (158°F)
minimum

**Prevent cross-contamination**

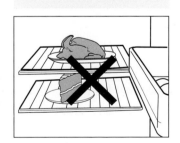

### Cleaning

Clean and disinfect all work surfaces, equipment, walls, floors and drains on a daily basis to a prescribed schedule. Follow the advice of cleaning product manufacturers and select the most effective cleaners that are the least harmful to the people doing the cleaning. Management should ensure that staff understand how and what to clean, and the high standards expected of them.

Cooker hoods and filters require regular cleaning. The associated extract ducting must also be cleaned periodically to remove accumulations of fats, which are unhygienic and pose a severe fire risk.

Waste must not be allowed to build up in food areas and should be removed on a regular basis. The waste storage area should be cleaned regularly, including the inside of bins.

A cleaning checklist is provided later in this chapter.

### Cooking, displaying and serving meat

Meat must be thoroughly cooked in order to kill dangerous bacteria such as salmonella, E.coli and listeria. The minimum cooking temperature and time for meat is 70°C for two minutes (see below for alternative temperatures and times). Probe thermometers can be used to check the temperature at the centre of meat, but these bring their own risks of cross-contamination and must be cleaned thoroughly and disinfected after each use.

| Minimum cooking times for meat | | |
|---|---|---|
| The centre of the meat should reach one of these temperatures for at least the time shown | 60°C – 45 minutes<br><br>65°C – 10 minutes<br><br>70°C – 2 minutes<br><br>75°C – 30 seconds<br><br>80°C – 6 seconds | |
| The only time that these rules need not be observed is when cooking whole cuts or joints of meat that are served pink or rare at the customer's request. Any form of minced or skewered meat, sausages or burgers, must always be thoroughly cooked in accordance with these times. Inspect meat to make sure it is thoroughly cooked, ie check that it is piping hot all the way through and that the juices have run clear. | | |

| Displaying and serving hot food | |
|---|---|
| Once food is cooked it should be served immediately, or kept hot (63°C and above) until serving. When serving or displaying hot food, it can be kept below 63°C for a single period of up to two hours, after which it must be either chilled quickly or thrown away. By law, hot food that is on display for more than two hours must be kept above 63°C (145°F) for the entire period. | **63°C (145°F)** |

### Chilling and storing food

Prepared ready-to-eat food, smoked meat or fish, ready-to-eat salads, certain dairy products and any food with a 'use by date' must be kept chilled. Food that has been cooked should be allowed to cool as quickly as possible before it is put in a refrigerator. Large quantities of cooked foods can be cooled quicker in several shallow dishes. The time between cooking food and chilling it should be no longer than two hours and preferably less than one hour. Keep chilled food out of the fridge for the shortest time possible during preparation, and do not overload the fridge.

| Storing and serving chilled food | |
|---|---|
| By law, chilled food must be kept below 8°C.<br><br>When serving or displaying chilled food, it can be kept above 8°C for a single period of up to four hours, after which time it must be chilled or thrown away.<br><br>Fix 'use by' labels on all packages of stored chilled foods. Best practice is to dispose of prepared but unsold chilled foods at the end of each working day, particularly sauces containing eggs.<br><br>Use a fridge thermometer to check the temperature of fridges and freezers. The coldest part of a fridge should be between 0°C (32°F) and 5°C (41°F). Monitor the temperature of all refrigerators and freezers three times each day and record the results. Take action if there are significant variations. | 8°C (46°F)<br><br>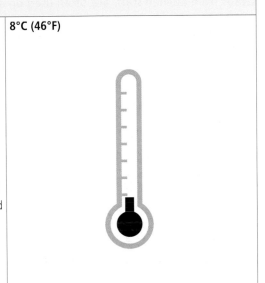 |

### Preventing cross-contamination

When one food touches another, bacteria are transferred. This causes cross-contamination, a major source of food poisoning. This is especially dangerous when raw food such as meat drips onto a food that will not be cooked before serving, eg a cake or salad. The three most common causes of cross-contamination are:

- storing raw and ready-to-eat food together

- not washing hands after touching raw food, or after using the toilet

- using the same chopping board or knife for raw and ready-to-eat food.

Best practice is to use separate refrigerators for raw meat, raw fish, cooked meats, ice cream, milk, and fruit and vegetables. If this is not practicable, then store raw meat in sealed containers at the bottom of the fridge, so that it cannot drip on or touch ready-to-eat food. Remove the outer packaging of foods that are to be stored in fridges, as packaging may introduce bacteria and be unsuitable for the damp conditions in the fridge. Observe the 'first in, first out' rule of stock rotation and ensure that nothing is used beyond its 'use by' date. Dried foods, such as cereals and vegetables, should be stored in sealed containers and off the floor to protect them from pests that may get into dry storage cupboards.

Check food delivery vehicles to see if appropriate standards of hygiene and temperature are being maintained. All of the rules mentioned above regarding separation and temperature apply to delivery vehicles and food processing plants.

The best way to prevent cross-contamination when preparing food is to use different chopping boards and different knives for raw and ready-to-eat food. People preparing fresh foods must wash their hands between each type of food being prepared.

Microbiological examination of kitchen work surfaces and prepared foods, and nasal swabs from kitchen staff, are often used on a routine basis to provide active monitoring of the effectiveness of hygiene arrangements. Such practices are recommended.

### Personal hygiene, supervision and training

Before staff start any work that involves the handling of food, they should receive induction training in the workplace to make them aware of food hygiene and personal hygiene issues. Staff will also need further instruction suited to the type of work they do. By law, restaurant staff must be supervised to ensure that they follow good food hygiene and health and safety practice (see toolbox talk on 'Kitchen hygiene' in Appendix B).

Everyone who works in a restaurant should wash and dry their hands regularly when handling food, to ensure that they do not contaminate it. Hands should be washed before starting work, before handling ready-to-eat food, after touching raw food (particularly raw meat or poultry), after using the toilet, and after work breaks.

Staff working in kitchens should wear clean aprons and hair coverings; cover cuts or sores with clean waterproof dressings; not touch their face or hair; not smoke, cough or sneeze over food; and not wear jewellery or false nails, which may fall into food.

Staff with symptoms of food poisoning, such as diarrhoea, vomiting or stomach pains, must not be allowed to work in the restaurant. Other illnesses and skin conditions should be checked with a doctor or the environmental health officer, as they may also pose a risk of contamination.

### Safety in the kitchen

Food preparation involves the use of knives and machinery, and cooking involves the use of a variety of ovens and hobs, grills, deep-fat fryers and pans. All are hazardous. Safe ways of using the equipment are given in the toolbox talks in Appendix B.

## The bottom line

**By law, hotels and restaurants must:**

- carry out a fire risk assessment and implement appropriate fire precautions, such as protected corridors and escape routes, automatic fire detection and alarm systems, and good fire-fighting access
- devise and implement an emergency plan
- monitor fire precautions on a regular basis
- devise housekeeping and laundry operations so that they comply with manual handling regulations
- establish dry cleaning facilities that prevent or minimise the exposure of workers to hazardous dry cleaning solvents
- train waiting staff in the risks involved in their job and the correct methods to be used to minimise these risks
- design kitchens so that they comply with statutory standards, including those that relate to layout, ventilation and lighting
- provide adequate washing and hygiene facilities
- ensure that food is cooked, displayed, chilled and stored in accordance with statutory standards
- promote personal hygiene
- provide supervision and training in all areas.

## Kitchen hygiene and safety

www.protect.org.uk

PDF 16

| Item | Yes | No | Action |
|---|---|---|---|
| Are there separate fridges for raw meat, poultry and fish? | | | |
| Is there a separate fridge for cooked foods? | | | |
| Where raw meat, poultry and fish cannot be segregated from cooked food by using separate fridges, is raw food stored in sealed containers below the cooked food in the fridge? | | | |
| Are milk, fruit and vegetables kept separate? | | | |
| Is there a separate fridge for ice cream? | | | |
| Are shelves labelled with the planned contents? | | | |
| Are fridge and freezer temperatures recorded three times per day and action taken where necessary? | | | |
| Are fridge and freezer temperature records displayed near the fridge or freezer? | | | |
| Does ready-to-use food have a 'use by' date, including food prepared in the kitchen? | | | |
| Are all prepared sauces disposed of at the end of the day? | | | |
| Are pre-cooked meals such as stews disposed of at the end of the day? | | | |
| Are cartons and packing materials removed before the food is put into the fridge? | | | |
| Are there any boxes of cereals or other foods stored on the cupboard floor in the kitchen? | | | |
| Are separate knives and chopping boards used for each food preparation process? | | | |

| Item | Yes | No | Action |
|---|---|---|---|
| Is there a hand washbasin with warm water and paper towels in the food preparation area? | | | |
| Is the emergency exit clear on the inside and outside? | | | |
| Is there a first aid kit with a list of contents? | | | |
| Is there a suitable number of $CO_2$ or dry powder extinguishers readily available? | | | |
| Are there fire blankets readily available near hot plates and fat fryers? | | | |
| Is there a pedal-operated rubbish bin that is emptied daily? | | | |
| Do chefs wear clean aprons? | | | |
| Do chefs wear hats or other forms of hair covering? | | | |
| Do kitchen staff remove watches, rings and so on? | | | |
| Are you satisfied with the cleanliness of the kitchen? | | | |
| Is the kitchen ventilation acceptable? | | | |
| Is the kitchen flooring adequately non-slip? | | | |
| Have all of the staff been inducted in hygiene and how to carry out their tasks safely? | | | |
| Is there microbiological sample testing of prepared food, work surfaces, and staff nasal swabs? | | | |
| **Signature of supervising chef** | **Date** | | |

## Kitchen cleaning (daily checks)

Quality grade – A: Very good
                 B: Good
                 C: Average (clean again)
                 D: Poor (clean again rigorously)

www.protect.org.uk

PDF 17

| Item | Quality | Action required |
| --- | --- | --- |
| Hand washbasins clean and complete with soap, nailbrush and paper towels | | |
| Worktops clean both top and bottom | | |
| Specified disinfectant products available and being used | | |
| Floor clean | | |
| Specified floor cleaning products available and being used | | |
| Waste bins and containers clean, inside and outside kitchen (daily clean required) | | |
| Gullies and drainage points clean (daily clean required) | | |
| Pots and pans clean inside and out and in good condition | | |
| Chopping boards clean, with different boards used for different purposes | | |
| Kitchen knives clean (must be cleaned after each use) | | |
| Small utensils clean and in good condition | | |
| Hot plates clean | | |
| Griddle clean | | |
| Ovens and ranges clean | | |
| Boiling pans, brat pans and bains-marie clean | | |
| Deep-fat fryer clean | | |
| Extract filters in good condition, not requiring changing | | |

| Item | Quality | Action required |
|---|---|---|
| Extract hood and ductwork clean, inside and out | | |
| Meat mincer clean and in good condition | | |
| Food processor clean and in good condition | | |
| Meat slicer clean (must be cleaned after each use) | | |
| Food mixer clean | | |
| Can opener clean | | |
| Fridge and freezer (shelving, floor, ventilator, lights) clean and working | | |
| Service trolleys clean | | |
| Heated trolley clean and working properly | | |
| Sink for washing vegetables and fish is available | | |
| Kitchen doors in good condition, including door closers | | |
| Walls, ceilings and tiles clean and in good condition | | |
| Display and serving cabinets clean and working properly | | |
| Dishwasher in good working order and filters cleaned | | |
| Cutlery clean | | |
| Plates and glasses clean | | |
| Lighting and fly-killing lamps in good condition, with all lamps working | | |
| Cleaning cloths clean and in good condition | | |
| **Signature of supervising steward** | **Date** | |

## Introduction

This chapter addresses events and exhibitions held at purpose-built exhibition halls, theatres, cinemas and other dedicated buildings.

Organisers of events and exhibitions often have to deal with large numbers of people in a restricted space, and crowds typically react unpredictably to unforeseen situations. A factor that greatly complicates many events is the large number of organisations that are brought together for a temporary show. These include the venue owner, the organiser, the exhibitors or performers, and numerous contractors.

There are three stages to an event – build up, the show or exhibition, and break down. There are different risks at each stage that should be considered when planning. This chapter aims to clarify the responsibilities of each party and provide some practical guidance on how to manage the risks at each stage.

## Structure and responsibilities

The typical structure of an exhibition held at a permanent venue is contained in the following diagram.

| **Mandatory services provided by in-house staff or term contractors, eg:** |
| --- |
| • special rigging |
| • power and gas connections to stands |
| • fire and emergency cover |
| • first aid |

| **Venue owner** |
| --- |
| • Holds annual public entertainment licence |
| • Reviews organisers' plans and compliance with licence |
| • Holds contract with the organiser that specifies licence and venue conditions |

| **Optional services provided by in-house staff or term contractors, eg:** |
| --- |
| • catering |
| • stand wiring |
| • supply and erection of demountable stands |
| • supply of stand furnishings |

| **Organiser** |
| --- |
| • Arranges exhibitors |
| • Holds contracts with the exhibitors that specify licence and venue conditions |

| **May employ contractors to organise:** |
| --- |
| • catering |
| • theming |
| • security and logistics |

| **Exhibitors/Performance manager** |
| --- |
| • Employ contractors to build stands |
| • Staff stands during the event |

| **Contractors** |
| --- |
| • Build stands |
| • Employ subcontractors |

### Responsibilities of the venue owner

The venue owner – as the holder of an annual public entertainment licence issued by the local authority – takes the lead in matters of public safety. For example, special rigging involves suspending heavy items from the roof, which may affect the roof structure. Arranging access to the roof void requires a knowledge of the specific hazards involved. By restricting access to in-house staff or a term contractor, the risks can be controlled more readily.

Power and gas connections are organised by the venue owner. This gives the owner control over the total load applied to the installations, and the ability to check the stand contractor's wiring and gas installation prior to connection.

Fire and emergency arrangements are key considerations at any public entertainment or exhibition venue. A large exhibition hall will have a dedicated control room, CCTV monitoring, zoned fire alarm system, and probably its own professional fire-fighting team.

### Responsibilities of the organiser

All parties have responsibility for the health and safety of events. By law, the organiser has the same responsibilities for public and employee health and safety as the venue owner, and must be satisfied that adequate measures are in place to control the risks. The organiser has a contractual link with the exhibitors and/or performers in a show. The contract must contain a clause that enforces licensing and venue health and safety standards on the exhibitors and/or performers.

In practical terms, the organiser is responsible for planning the show layout and submitting this to the venue for approval. A drawing will be produced showing the position of all the stands or, in the case of a music or other performance event, the stage and seating. This drawing must clearly show the position of all points of exit and entry in the venue. Signage will also be shown.

The organiser should produce a risk assessment for the event, including escape routes, fire and emergency provision, the adequacy and strength of barriers for crowd control, and the risk of overloading any part of the existing or temporary structure. The risk assessment must demonstrate the adequacy of these in relation to the numbers expected to attend.

In the case of temporary venues, such as a street carnival or a music festival in a public park, the organiser has overall responsibility for the health and safety of the public and performers.

### Responsibilities of the exhibitor or performance manager

Exhibition stands, or stages for pop concerts or shows, can be large and complex structures. These structures, including temporary seating, require formal structural design and erection by contractors who are competent in such work. It is the responsibility of the exhibitor or performance manager to appoint competent contractors. The structural designs will be submitted for approval through the organiser to the venue and licensing authority.

Also read...

Chapter 14 – How to select
a good contractor

### Responsibilities of contractors

Exhibition contractors have to comply with relevant health and safety law. This includes
the requirement to produce risk assessments, erect proper working platforms and,
where necessary, to ensure that personal protective equipment (PPE) is worn.
Unfortunately, the industry's record is poor in terms of enforcement, particularly as the
direct employers – the exhibitors and/or organiser – are often absent when stands are
being erected. The monitoring and enforcement role, therefore, has to be taken by the
venue owner, who retains responsibility for activities within the premises.

### Events that require a licence

Permanent venues usually have an annual entertainment licence, granted by the local
authority, with specific conditions attached to different types of events. There will be
on-going liaison between the venue and the authorities, including the local fire
authority. This includes a specific review of each major event, and on-site monitoring.

Events may be 'one off' affairs, held in a local park, shopping centre, school or street. In
cases where there is no clearly defined venue operator, the organiser assumes overall
responsibility for the event, and for obtaining any required licences and ensuring that
their terms are fulfilled.

Events that require a licence from the local authority or licensing magistrate include:

- concerts, discos and clubs

- theatres

- cinemas

- sports grounds (local authorities issue and enforce specific safety
  certificates for sports grounds)

- other forms of public entertainment.

Licences are required for these types of event even where the venue is not designed for
the purpose, such as a park. Organisers are advised to consult with their local authority
and fire authority at an early stage in order to obtain guidance for particular events.
Licences are also required for gambling and the consumption of alcohol.

## Event risk assessment

The organiser should carry out an event risk assessment. This involves considering the following issues as a minimum, but also being prepared for any unforeseen hazards.

### Managing the crowd

- Capacity of the venue and the risk of excess numbers turning up for the event.

- Means of crowd limitation and control, including police and stewarding.

- The risk of visitors being crushed against barriers, being trampled underfoot, of the crowd surging or swaying, and aggressive or dangerous behaviour.

- Circulation routes, including the risks arising from bottlenecks.

- Obstructions due to queuing or stalls sited in walkways and the risk to crowd movement.

- Entrances and exits, and the means of escape in an emergency.

- Emergency escape signage.

- Public address system to be used in directing crowds.

- Provision for people with special needs.

- Facilities such as toilets and information points.

- Provision for adverse weather conditions.

- Does the nature of the crowd present any special risk?

### Managing the venue

- How to ensure that all planned escape doors are unlocked on the day.

- How to ensure that all escape routes are free from obstruction on the day.

- Adequate lighting in all areas.

- Walkways free of slipping or tripping hazards.

- Venue maintenance, and equipment in good order, eg escalators and turnstiles.

- Temporary seating and the risk of loading being exceeded.

- Parts of the structure that will not take the anticipated crowd loading with an adequate margin of safety (assess balconies and boxes, any cantilevered structures, any lightweight elevated walkways or bridges, guardrails, fences and crowd barriers).

- Cooking equipment and the risk of fire.

- Removal of rubbish and fire/public health risks.

- Segregation of delivery vehicles from pedestrians.

- Access to first aid facilities.

- Means of access for the emergency services.

- Segregation of any construction or maintenance activities.

- Does the nature of the venue present any special risks?

## Event build up

### Temporary seating stands

There has been more than one disaster caused by the collapse of temporary stands or crowd control barriers during sporting events and pop concerts. As a consequence, the effects of a swaying crowd on a barrier, or rhythmic swaying or dancing on a stand, have been researched and loading standards upgraded.

There is an inherent conflict in the systems used to erect temporary stands. On the one hand, economics demands a fast build up and break down of the stand using lightweight systems. On the other hand, structural engineers prefer heavy duty components with plenty of safety built in. The structural analysis of temporary stands under dynamic crowd loading is notoriously difficult, and there is the possible fatigue of components to take into account as well.

There are a number of steps that the venue owner and organiser can take to control the risks associated with erecting temporary seating stands and other structures. These are:

1.  Select a system specifically designed for the type of event, supplied by a contractor who is known to be competent and who carries adequate public and employers' liability insurance. Brief the contractor as to the exact requirements, including all of the items to be checked by the structural engineer.

2.  Employ a structural engineer to:

    ○ specify the loading

    ○ check that the system proposed by the seating contractor is an engineered system

Also read...

Chapter 14 – How to select a good contractor

- check the calculations produced by the seating contractor

- check the drawings produced by the seating contractor

- check the fatigue testing of the proposed system (5 per cent of components should undergo a yearly radiological examination)

- check the installed stand(s) before use, including a random selection of components using a spanner to verify tightness

- issue a certificate of acceptance, or permit to load the stand(s).

The structural engineer's brief should mention in writing that these seven checks must be carried out. Cases have occurred where, due to a misunderstanding, the structural engineer carried out a visual inspection only and no design check, with disastrous results. Use only a structural engineering firm of standing that has sufficient professional indemnity insurance to deal with the consequences of a collapse.

3. Finally, a member of the venue owner's or organiser's own staff should inspect the stand before and during the event, particularly if the crowd is likely to jump up and down or sway, imposing extra loading on the seating stand structure.

### Rigging

Rigging involves the suspension of lights, signs and banners, stage canopies and pieces of heavy equipment from the roof structure or tall masts. The use of high-level rigging is in decline because of the risks faced by riggers, who in previous times climbed freestyle along high girders, carrying wire ropes and tools used to suspend equipment, lights and banners.

Rigging can be performed safely using rope access techniques, with attachment points situated every few metres along the girder. A drawback is the need to test each anchorage on an annual basis. At lower levels, rigging can be carried out from the safety of a mobile elevating work platform.

Where objects are hung from the roof structure, an evaluation of the loading is required. Often relatively flimsy attachment points are used to tie off the wire ropes, such as a catwalk handrail. A structural engineer should check these. A good plan is to commission a structural appraisal of the roof or other structure, so that predetermined anchorage points can be provided with designated loadings.

Finally, a risk assessment should be made of every special rigging task. The question to be asked is: Is this task really necessary, or is there a better way to complete it?

### Permanent structures

Many disasters involve the collapse of permanent elevated walkways, balconies and similar vulnerable structures. Before any such structure is used in a show, a structural engineer should determine its maximum loading capacity. As a general policy, crowds should be prevented from gaining access to elevated structures, especially if they are

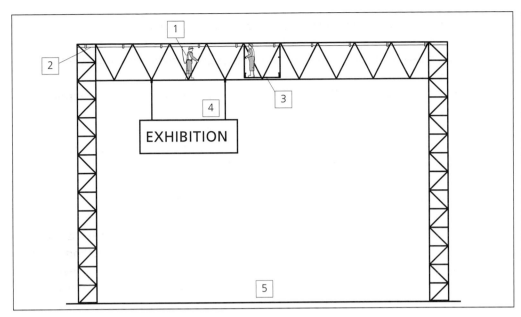

likely to be jumped up and down on, eg in time to music or at some moment of drama at a sporting event.

## Stand construction

One of the most exciting times during an exhibition is when the construction of the stands is underway. Exhibition halls are hired by the day, which includes the days taken to build up and break down the event. Consequently, the time spent to set up and break down is kept to an absolute minimum.

The exhibitor employs a contractor to construct the stand, and invariably all stands are in construction at the same time. Generally, stand contractors are highly efficient, and travel with the stand to each event, both erecting and dismantling it.

## Logistics and other matters

Because of tight timescales, there are many logistic issues associated with stand construction, not least the traffic management of incoming materials and exhibits. Good traffic management requires detailed planning of deliveries, which should be closely timed and segregated. Often, a holding park is established away from, but close to, the venue. Pedestrians must also be kept away from the materials and exhibits being delivered. This is done by providing separate entrance and exit points for pedestrians and delivery vehicles. Logistical issues should be incorporated into the risk assessment and planning for the event.

The venue owner must control the materials used in the stand construction in order to minimise the fire load and comply with the licensing requirements. All timber and flammable board materials should be treated to provide a 'Class 1' spread of flame (board that is in accordance with BS 476, Part 7), or as specified in the licence. Highly flammable products such as untreated polystyrene should not be used. Packaging materials should be kept tidy and removed on a daily basis to a secure and protected compactor or loading bay, ready for disposal.

As controller of the premises and the event, the venue owner and organiser should monitor all contractors to ensure that they meet current safety standards for construction activities. In terms of PPE, hard hats, high visibility vests and safety footwear should be worn as a minimum.

## Safe management of crowds

Safe management of a crowd depends on good planning, an assessment of the risks, adequate staffing to control the crowd, thorough emergency procedures, and good communication and monitoring during the event.

### Planning and risk assessment

The first step in planning the event is to determine the suitability of the venue for the expected numbers and nature of the crowd. Clearly people attending a large scale pop concert over two days will require more space than those attending a football match.

The first thing to do is establish the maximum capacity of the venue with reference to four factors:

- the time it takes to get into the venue

- the time it takes to get out of the venue

- the emergency evacuation time

- the accommodation capacity.

The safe capacity is the lowest of the four. Once established, the crowd should be limited to this number. This may entail a police presence to deter gatecrashers, making the event all-ticket, or displaying signs outside the event indicating that all tickets are sold. If the event is an all-ticket affair, make this clear in any advertising. Be sure to liaise with the police and transport authorities well ahead of the event and follow their expert guidance.

Carry out a risk assessment for the event and record it. This is a legal requirement, so you need to be able to produce a document. The risk assessment document should incorporate all of the information required in order to obtain a licence, including the information described earlier in this chapter under 'Event risk assessment'. There should be a scale drawing of the venue with the event layout superimposed, indicating all of the key features such as the location of each stand, access routes, escape doors or routes, and emergency signage.

### Crowd management

Research shows that crowds react best when they are given clear information and instructions on how to act. This includes which doors are entrances and which are exits, walking directions, where people can and cannot park, and where they can and cannot smoke or drink. Without such direction, crowds follow the example of those who appear to know what to do, which can lead to disastrous consequences. Good use of signs and public address systems is therefore extremely important, and vital during an emergency.

People are more likely to react favourably if they find the event well organised and the stewards courteous. An event that is not excessively overcrowded, and has adequate numbers of toilets and food and drink outlets, and good information, will please its audience. As a result, happy customers will be more likely to comply with any directions from the stewards.

An adequate number of well-briefed stewards are needed to manage crowds effectively. At a large event there will be a chief steward and a number of supervisors. The stewards' duties are to:

- assist the public

- point out entrances and exits, and the location of toilets and first aid posts

- manage and direct the crowd so that overcrowding does not occur

- check emergency exits before opening time to ensure that they have been unlocked and are not blocked

- inspect stands to ensure that they comply with the venue's safety rules

- keep gangways and exits clear

- deal firmly with unruly behaviour

- make sure that litter does not accumulate

- monitor the performance of temporary seating during a show

- monitor crowds at key points such as turnstiles

- control parking and traffic

- understand the emergency arrangements and assist in any evacuation.

### Emergency procedures

The emergency procedures that should be put in place by the venue owner and organiser depend on the types of risk faced. The largest exhibition halls employ full-time fire and emergency personnel, who are supplemented during events. No matter how large or small, every event should designate a fire and emergency co-ordinator and deputy, whose task is to liaise with the emergency services, obtain and implement their advice, and control operations in the event of an emergency. The co-ordinator and deputy must be given the authority to stop the event if necessary.

Once an emergency is identified, such as a bomb threat or fire, then the co-ordinator must call the relevant emergency services immediately and seek their advice. The evacuation of a major show is never undertaken lightly, but where this is necessary it is essential that the stewards remain calm in order to avoid panic.

The arrangements for coping with an emergency should be written down in an emergency plan, and include:

Also read...

Chapter 5 – Step 4. Making emergency plans

- appointment of co-ordinator and deputy

- duties of co-ordinator and deputy

- duties of stewards

- how to inform the emergency services, including exact address and location of the event

- communications, including mobile phone numbers and portable walkie-talkie radio channels for the venue owner, organiser, exhibitors, performance managers, and fire, security, police and first aid services

- communication with the public

- evacuation procedure

- assembly areas

- re-opening the venue.

### Communication and monitoring

Communication and monitoring should be organised from a control centre or manager's office, depending on the scale of the event. Communications are usually well established in a permanent venue, but a street carnival, for example, would need a special communications network to be set up. CCTV is an excellent aid to the monitoring of events, and can be used to direct stewards to potential trouble spots. However, there is always a strong case for experienced managers to take to the floor during an exhibition or show to see for themselves how smoothly the event is running.

The size of the crowd should be monitored to ensure that the planned safe numbers are not exceeded. Where there are turnstiles, this is a relatively easy process. Where this means is not available, make an estimate based on a head count of the number of people in a defined area, and the rate of flow into or out of an area (the number of people passing a particular feature). The estimate can then be scaled up to provide an assessment of the total number of people in attendance. The crowd should also be observed for any signs of distress, such as pushing and surging, shouting, bad temper or fighting, and action taken swiftly to remedy the situation.

## Event break down

The event break down is the least observed part of the whole process. At this stage, the public, exhibitors and/or performers have all left, as may have the organiser, and the contractors who erected the stands and stages will return to dismantle or demolish them.

Yet there are still risks, eg work at height, work with electricity and gas, demolition, multiple lorries and vans removing materials, and multiple contractors in the restricted show space. The venue owner retains responsibility for the safety of the premises, including the risk of fire, which is high at this stage because of the volume of waste generated. The organiser has a duty to co-ordinate the contractors so that they work together safely. Contractors have a duty to their employees and others affected by their activities to ensure safe working practice.

During the break down stage, the opportunity should be taken to review the event and its management. This presents an opportunity to learn lessons for the future.

### The bottom line

- Events and exhibitions are dynamic and fast-moving affairs that blend construction with show business. They are often located in high profile buildings that present their own particular sets of challenges.
- Good health and safety in such circumstances demands leadership and a clear vision. Tight timescales may produce good safety if the event is planned well. But if the degree of planning is inadequate, then chaos and disaster may result.
- The scale of responsibility for public safety is enormous. Because of this the response in terms of health and safety planning and control should be proportionate.
- By law, systems and plans must be documented and risk assessments recorded; training must be given; specialists must be employed to take care of major concerns, eg the safety of crowd barriers and seating; and local authorities, the fire service, the police and public transport operators must be consulted at every stage.

## Introduction

This chapter outlines the hazards inherent in the management and maintenance of golf courses, parks and the grounds surrounding premises such as offices and hotels. Practical guidance is provided on the safe use of machinery and chemicals, and the health issues are explored. Even businesses with small grounds will find something of use.

There are five main aspects:

- management

- hazards of the location

- machinery

- chemicals

- other health issues.

## Management

Most accidents are caused by the use of heavy machinery such as tractors, mowers, brush cutters and chainsaws, or by the use of chemicals. These accidents are more frequent than is generally realised, and can be very serious or even fatal. Managers responsible for grounds maintenance face all of the same responsibilities as those who are responsible for other parts of the business, and so must carry out risk assessments, develop safe systems of work, train staff in safe working practices, monitor and review the working practices, and organise effective communication.

The use of tractors and cutting machines is hazardous, so operators must be competent. Competency involves both training and experience. Those who have received training but have no experience must be closely supervised by a competent operator. Training is also required in manual handling and the safe use of pesticides, as well as in other health issues.

## Hazards of the location

When considering a large facility such as a park or golf course, the entire working environment needs to be examined. There may be workshops, offices, shops and restaurants, the health and safety aspects of which are examined in other chapters. There may also be serious hazards to consider, such as overhead power lines, underground services, roads, lakes or rivers.

### Overhead power lines

Grounds staff working with items such as ladders, pole pruners, irrigation pipes, tipper lorries or tractors with elevating equipment are in particular danger when working near overhead power lines. If any of these items touches or comes close enough to overhead power lines to cause arcing, the operator could be burned or electrocuted. Equally, anyone who is in the vicinity of equipment that becomes live is also at risk. The danger of burns and electrocution is increased if cranes or mobile elevating work platforms are used to erect temporary stands, flagpoles, lighting masts or other facilities. Any manager faced with such a hazard should contact the electricity company that is responsible for the power lines and ask for advice on the safe approach distance. Unless the electricity company indicates otherwise, it is essential to keep all activity at least:

- 15m from power lines on steel supports

- 9m from power lines on timber supports.

If such hazards are present, specialist advice will be needed. It may even be necessary to arrange for power lines to be diverted, or fencing or goalposts to be erected to prohibit access.

### Underground services

Underground power lines present a danger to anyone digging or using an excavator nearby. Gas, water or telephone services may also be present and they too are a source of risk. The utility companies that are responsible for providing them must be asked to supply plans of all buried services before any excavation takes place, even for post holes or sprinkler pipes.

Where excavation is to be carried out near to buried electricity cables, the first step is to check their location on the electricity company's plans. Following this, use a cable locater, which identifies their location by measuring the magnetic field around them. The next step is to create trial holes using hand tools such as spades and shovels, carefully exposing the cables. Power tools, picks and forks should not be used because of the danger of causing damage, and mechanical excavators should be used only where it is known that there are no underground services. Where road or car park surfaces have to be excavated in the vicinity of buried services, a specialist contractor should carry out the work.

Where gas, water or telecommunication lines are expected to be present, a cable locater will be unable to find them. In such cases, use drawing plans produced by the utility companies to trace lines and locate manholes and access points, then use trial holes as outlined above.

### Roads, footpaths and public rights of way

The presence of roads, footpaths and public rights of way introduces a danger to the public from grounds maintenance activities. In such cases, signage advising the public of any risks should be posted at each entrance to the property. In addition, grounds staff should be advised of the caution needed when working close to public access areas. In terms of the way in which this impacts on golf courses, for example, there should be signs warning of the risk of wayward golf balls. Grounds staff must show consideration to golfers and be mindful of their own safety, organising their work to minimise interference with play.

### Lakes and rivers

Lakes, rivers and other watercourses pose a risk of drowning and of contracting illnesses such as Weil's disease (leptospirosis). Lifebelts should be available in the vicinity of lakes or rivers where work takes place or the public have access.

Also read...

Chapter 13 – Weil's disease

Appendix B – Sewers and watercourses

# Machinery

## Maintenance

It is essential to maintain machinery in accordance with manufacturers' recommendations. In a large undertaking, a workshop will be required for this purpose. It is particularly important to maintain safety devices, guards, brakes, tyre pressures, and steering and starting systems. Machines must not be left running while unattended, and must be kept free of grass and debris around the engine to minimise the risk of fire.

| Also read... |
| --- |
| Chapter 13 |

### Features of a well-run grounds maintenance workshop

- A system based on routine maintenance rather than just the repair of breakdowns.

- A manual for every type of machine that is in use.

- Every machine marked with a unique number that corresponds to its maintenance record.

- A record-keeping system with a different file for each machine.

- A computer system that automatically advises the workshop supervisor when machines need servicing.

- Modern tools and equipment with proper guards and emergency stop buttons.

- An automatic, fully guarded, blade-sharpening machine for lawn mowers.

- A lift that allows lawn mowers to be raised to waist level for maintenance.

- A good stock of spare parts.

- A clean and tidy work area.

## Battery charging

Golf buggies and other similar modes of transport that are powered by electric storage batteries need to have their batteries recharged on a regular basis. However, the charging of batteries, even those that are described as maintenance-free, gives off flammable hydrogen gas. If the gas accumulates and a flame or spark is introduced, then the gas and battery will explode. Common injuries include acid burns to the face, eyes and hands.

| Also read... |
| --- |
| Appendix B – Battery charging |

Charging should take place in a dedicated facility that is well ventilated, away from sources of flame or spark (such as a kitchen), and fuel such as petrol. When battery leads are connected or disconnected, a spark can occur, igniting any hydrogen gas that may be present. Smoking must be prohibited and the person doing the charging should wear goggles. The electrical power supply, charger and battery should be in good condition. The public and untrained staff should not be allowed in the charging room.

### Mowers

There is a large selection of grass mowers available, ranging from tractor-pulled gang mowers and self-propelled mowers, to pedestrian-controlled mowers and hover mowers. They all have their specific applications and all can be dangerous if used inappropriately or if poorly maintained.

The most important maintenance issue is that trained and competent personnel should change the blades at specified intervals. If blades are not changed regularly they can become detached and cause serious injury. Accidents often happen on older machines when the operator tries to clear a blockage while the blade is still turning. On newer machines the blade rotation and drive mechanism are disengaged as soon as the throttle is released.

New ride-on mowers are fitted with a spring-loaded safety seat, so that the machine will only operate when someone is sitting on the seat. Older machines will keep running even if the operator alights or falls off. The best action that management can take in relation to mowers is to ensure that operators use only modern equipment with these safety features incorporated, and that the machines are well maintained.

Hover mowers are often used to cut steep banks. However, if the operator slips, the feet, arms or other parts of the body can slide under the mower and come into contact with the rotating blade. Therefore, steep banks should not be cut with a rigid-blade rotary mower; instead, a grass trimmer should be used. When working on banks, steel toe-capped boots with a good grip should be worn, and the work carried out in dry conditions.

**Brush cutters, brush saws and grass trimmers**

Brush cutters are used to clear undergrowth and to fell large weeds, reeds and bushes, using thermoplastic or steel blades, or heavy-duty nylon line. Brush saws are fitted with a circular saw blade and are used to trim bushes and thin small trees. Grass trimmers use a rotating nylon line to cut grass and small weeds growing around obstacles.

Blades are guarded to prevent material being thrown out and injuring the operator. For this reason, other people should be kept at least 10m away. The safe use of brush saws and cutters in particular requires skill and experience, although training is necessary for all of the machines, and operators should wear hearing and eye protection, protective trousers and sturdy footwear. Maintenance and sharpening by a competent person is essential, and any blade that shows signs of cracking or overheating should be replaced. There is such a variety of equipment available that skill and knowledge are required to ensure that the right blade and guard are fitted on the machine. Therefore, the changing of blades and guards should be restricted to a competent person, usually a supervisor, who is trained to perform the task.

**Brush cutter showing guards and PPE**

Image based on Stihl product photography

## Tractors

Tractors are used for large-scale grass-cutting operations, rolling, spiking, fertiliser spreading and other similar work, using attachments that are towed or which are driven through a power take-off (PTO).

Tractors can overturn on slopes, when working on uneven ground, or near ditches and lakes. Certain ground types and features can cause particular problems, such as gravel, grass and potholes. Therefore, it is essential that:

- tractors are fitted with a roll bar or reinforced safety cab

- operators are trained both in the tractor controls and the risks of the location

- brakes and steering are properly maintained

- tyres are correctly inflated.

Every year people are killed or seriously injured in accidents involving PTO and PTO shafts. These are usually at the rear of the machine, but some also have a mid-mounted PTO drive facility. A drive shaft is used to couple the rotating tractor PTO to the power input on the attachment. There are flexible couplings that allow a degree of movement between the tractor and the attachment. The rotating drive shaft presents a serious hazard, as the operator's hands, arms, hair or clothing can become entangled in the rotating shaft.

A number of safeguards must be in place:

- by law, the PTO and shaft must be completely guarded by purpose-made guards (home-made guards are not appropriate); a supervisor must check that guards are fitted correctly before the machine is started

- guards, quick-release yokes and drive shafts should be lubricated on a weekly basis

- inspection for damage should be carried out on a daily basis (broken, damaged or badly fitting guards can be just as dangerous as having no guard at all)

- the PTO drive should be interlocked with the driving seat, so that someone has to sit on the driving seat before the machine can be driven (the interlock must be given particular attention during maintenance).

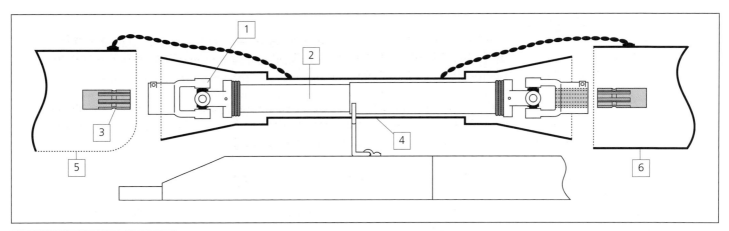

**Power take-off**
1. Flexible coupling
2. PTO shaft
3. PTO drive
4. Guard fully enclosing PTO shaft
5. Tractor
6. Attachment

### Tractor-towed equipment

Turf groomers, scarifiers, slitters, spikers and fertiliser spreaders are all towed by tractor. They each have their own characteristics and safety requirements, but the following should be noted:

- the attachment will affect the handling of the tractor, especially on slopes

- no-one but the operator must be in the vicinity while the machine is in use

- each machine has specific guards that must be fitted and used

- before attempting any maintenance on the machine or guards, the power must be disconnected and all moving parts must have stopped

- careful maintenance of hydraulic controls is essential.

### Hard facts

Chainsaw accidents are typically the result of a lack of training or protective equipment:

- Three partners in a farming company were prosecuted under the Provision and Use of Work Equipment Regulations and Reporting of Injuries, Diseases and Dangerous Occurrences Regulations following an accident to a farm worker who was using a chainsaw. The partners, fined £5,040, had failed to ensure that the employee had been adequately trained in using a chainsaw, to report the accident and to ensure that the saw was maintained.

- A contractor was prosecuted and fined £1,500 under the Provision and Use of Work Equipment Regulations and the Personal Protective Equipment at Work Regulations following an accident to an employee who was injured when the chainsaw he was using kicked back into his face during tree work, causing injuries to his face and eyes. Adequate protective equipment had not been provided.

### Chainsaws

Chainsaws are dangerous even when properly maintained and equipped with all of the safety devices. Only trained and experienced tree surgeons should carry out tree felling and limbing. An occasional user will not have the necessary experience even if training has been provided. Safety in the use of chainsaws depends on the saw, the operator's technique, and the use of personal protective equipment (PPE).

Some key points to consider when using chainsaws have been included in a toolbox talk in Appendix B. Only modern chainsaws with all of the safety features noted in this toolbox talk should be used. Anyone using a chainsaw for even a short period must wear full protective equipment, ie:

- safety helmet

- face visor

- ear defenders (noise levels are typically 115 dB(A))

- close-fitting clothes

- chainsaw operator's protective gloves

- chainsaw operator's protective trousers (with material that can stop a chainsaw cut); two types are available: full-leg protection for occasional users and tree surgeons, and front-of-leg protection for professional loggers

- chainsaw operator's safety boots (not ordinary safety boots)

- chainsaw operator's jacket (for use by trainees).

**Chainsaw operator with protective equipment**

Image based on Stihl product photography

## Chemicals

The main chemicals used in grounds management are fertilisers, pesticides, cleaning agents, oils and greases, paints and battery acids. Many chemicals are hazardous and fall within the scope of the Control of Substances Hazardous to Health (COSHH) Regulations. If the label on the container indicates that the substance is toxic, corrosive, harmful or an irritant, then COSHH applies and written assessments must be carried out.

Pesticides include fungicides, herbicides, insecticides, pest control chemicals, rodenticides and wood preservatives. Only approved pesticides that have been allocated a government registration number should be used. The conditions of use are printed on the product label and must be followed to the letter. Full data sheets should be obtained from the manufacturer and toolbox talks developed with which to brief those working with the pesticide. Workers must also be competent.

PPE will be required, and may include disposable overalls, boots, gloves and appropriate respirators. When making an assessment of chemicals spread by mechanical means, such as a tractor, the risk of wind drift onto the operator and others should be assessed and protective equipment (eg respirators and disposable overalls) used accordingly.

Some pesticides approved for agricultural use require the operator to have been formally trained and to hold a certificate of competence. The supplier can provide further information. Pesticides that are not clearly labelled must be disposed of properly, using a licensed carrier to take them to an appropriate hazardous waste site.

Pesticides must be stored securely in locked metal bins capable of resisting fire for 30 minutes, and reasonable impact damage or vandalism. The store should contain bunding or a sump to contain the entire contents of the store plus a further 10 per cent. It should be kept away from staff accommodation, and be waterproof if kept outside. 'No smoking' signs and cautionary warning signs, indicating the type of contents, should be posted. A notice should also be displayed indicating that only those trained and authorised may enter and mix the pesticides. Best practice is to post the data sheet and assessment for each product on a notice board near the store.

Fertilisers should also be kept secure in a store that has a fire resistance of at least 30 minutes and contains no flammable materials. Entry should be restricted to authorised personnel, and a smoking ban strictly enforced because of the flammable nature of fertilisers. Again, 'no smoking' and warning signs should be posted.

Also read...

Chapter 6 – Hazardous substances

Appendix A – Hazardous substance assessment

## Other health issues

Apart from exposure to pesticides, the main health issues are manual handling, noise and vibration. Assessments are required for the main hazards in these categories and should be written down. Training should then be developed from these assessments, normally in the form of toolbox talks (see Appendix B).

The checklist below sets out some typical health risks and possible courses of action.

www.protect.org.uk

PDF 18

| Activity | Hazard | Risk? Yes or no |
|---|---|---|
| Use of pedestrian-controlled mowers | • Heavy to control when mowing, and to lift when transporting or in a workshop | |
| Use of brush cutters and brush saws | • Heavy and awkward to use<br>• Twisting action when using equipment<br>• Exposure to noise and vibration when cutting trees and brush | |
| Use of chainsaws | • Exposure to noise and vibration when cutting trees and brush | |
| Use of workshop grinding wheels and other power tools | • Exposure to noise and vibration when sharpening mower blades and tools | |
| Use of pesticides | • Exposure to pesticide spray, either to operators or passers-by<br>• Mixing pesticides | |
| Clearing and working in ditches and watercourses, and other similar heavy manual work | • Exposure to rats' urine, which can cause Weil's disease (leptospirosis)<br>• Heavy manual work with hand tools, and dragging and lifting debris out of ditches | |

Also read...

Chapter 13 – Weil's disease

Appendix B – Sewers and watercourses

## Practical ways to reduce the risk

- Use drive-on mowers for all but the lightest tasks
- Use a mower lift in the workshop so that mowers can be worked on at waist level and do not have to be lifted manually

---

- Use personnel who have adequate physical strength
- Provide training in cutting techniques
- Wear ear defenders capable of reducing the noise exposure from 115 dB(A) to below 90 dB(A) (on their own, earplugs are not sufficient)

---

- Operators must be formally trained and certificated
- Wear ear defenders capable of reducing the noise exposure from 115 dB(A) to below 90 dB(A) (on their own, earplugs are not sufficient)

---

- Use a modern, automated, mower-blade sharpening machine
- Limit daily exposures by introducing job rotation

---

- Make an assessment based on information provided on the label and on data sheets
- Select the least harmful product
- Provide information and training
- Provide full PPE and supervise personnel to ensure that it is being used
- Ensure that only essential personnel are present in the work area

---

- Introduce a vermin eradication programme
- Maintain ditches regularly to keep the build up of debris to a minimum; this will make the task more frequent but the work lighter
- Provide wet suits
- Provide training and an information card regarding Weil's disease
- Monitor health

## 11 Grounds maintenance, parks and golf courses

**The bottom line**

**To ensure legal compliance, a high degree of management control must be exercised by:**

- making a risk assessment of the facility and location to identify specific hazards
- carrying out preventive maintenance on all machinery and vehicles
- ensuring that personnel who use machinery are trained and competent
- ensuring that hazardous equipment, such as tractor power take-offs and chainsaws, is inspected daily, before use, and kept in good condition
- ensuring that personnel understand the need for, and wear, the appropriate PPE
- assessing the health and fire risks arising from the use of chemicals, and putting in place adequate precautions, training and PPE.

# Introduction

This chapter looks at the health and safety issues surrounding work activities in offices, shops and warehouses. Previous chapters have examined a number of health and safety aspects of buildings and need not be repeated here.

In this chapter we are concerned with the following work activities and issues:

- Offices and shops

  - the use of computers and workstations

  - stress

  - slips, trips and falls

  - filing cabinets

  - employment of young people in retail establishments

- Warehousing

  - storage systems

  - forklift trucks

  - operation of road vehicles.

**What is...** ?

**DSE?**

DSE stands for 'display screen equipment', a technical term that describes all equipment that is used in a work environment to display words, numbers and images on a screen. To most of us this means our computer monitor, but it also covers other items such as microfiche readers. TV sets showing films are not regarded as DSE. DSE includes computer software, which can have an important influence on health as it can govern the size and clarity of text, and the rate of keying. In most office environments, computer monitors are known as VDUs or 'visual display units'.

# Offices and shops

### The use of computers and workstations

Regulations governing the use of computers and workstations at work state that employers must carry out a risk assessment, provide properly designed workstations and equipment, as well as training, and offer eyesight tests to those considered to be 'users'.

### Workstation hazards

If you carry out a risk assessment by spending 15 minutes with each member of your office staff, you will probably discover a wide range of problems such as broken chairs, defective keyboards, glare on the screen, lack of space on the desk, draughty windows, poor lighting, and inadequate or excessive heating. In addition, staff members may have health complaints such as headaches, arm and wrist pains, and eye strain. Many managers know about such problems and complaints, yet avoid the risk assessment exercise for fear of having to sort them out. At the same time, office workers are often reluctant to complain, not realising that there are potentially serious health risks involved.

However, it is worth bearing in mind that a significant number of people who work in offices in the UK needlessly suffer injuries or stress in their jobs, and that proper attention to the working environment can reduce or eliminate them.

### Hard facts

In the UK, around one in five employees believe that they are suffering from work-related stress.

### Also read...

Chapter 6 – Upper limb disorders

### The main health hazards

- **Repetitive strain injury (RSI)**
  RSI is a form of upper limb disorder (ULD). The effects can range from temporary soreness to serious conditions that prevent the user continuing to work with the equipment. The onset of any disorder depends on a number of factors, including sitting in a poor position, awkward positioning of the hands and wrists as a result of lack of space or sitting at the wrong height, or a continual high workload combined with tight deadlines. All of these factors can be eliminated by using properly designed equipment, furniture and software, and work planning that allows for breaks and variety.

- **Eye fatigue**
  Eye fatigue is caused by staying in the same position and concentrating for a long time; poor positioning of the screen; poor legibility of characters; glare and reflection; and a drifting or flickering image. Temporary symptoms such as red or sore eyes and headaches, if not addressed, can lead to visual problems. Visual problems will continue as long as the causes remain, resulting in discomfort for the employee, and other impacts such as reduced efficiency, errors and absenteeism. Eye fatigue can be reduced by regular breaks, by rotating activities so that DSE work is combined with other activities, and by exercising the eyes by looking out of a window. For this reason, it is bad practice to site DSE workers in windowless basements and the like.

- **Fatigue and stress**
  Fatigue and stress are found in all work environments, and in particular affect those in jobs requiring high-speed repetitive actions, or where errors can be catastrophic, such as in air traffic control and stock market trading.

Most experts discount the suggestion that there is a link between radiation emission from VDUs and miscarriage and birth defects among pregnant women. In addition, current evidence indicates that looking at most work-related software programs on monitors does not trigger epilepsy.

### Risk assessment

A risk assessment of the entire workforce should be carried out to identify who is a DSE user and who is not. Following that, each user's workstation and DSE should be assessed individually using a structured checklist, such as the one included in Appendix A. Training is best given at the same time, by sitting down with users, observing them at work, and then discussing the issues as the checklist is completed. Generally, specialist expertise is not required in order to carry out an assessment, although outside help will be needed for eye testing and any medical investigation of serious aches and pains. Following the guidance in this book should be sufficient for most office environments.

### Training

Topics covered in DSE user training should include:

- risks from DSE work

- the importance of good posture and changing position

- how to adjust the chair to achieve good posture

- how to arrange the keyboard, VDU, document holder, mouse and phone to avoid awkward or repeated stretching

- the importance of having a non-reflective, glare-free screen

- how to adjust and clean the screen

- the importance of taking breaks from DSE work by doing other types of work such as filing, or using a central printer rather than a personal printer

- the importance of exercising the eyes by blinking and looking at distant objects

- the legal right to an eyesight test

- the importance of reporting any problems.

### Eyesight tests

DSE users have a legal right to a sight test on request, paid for by the employer. If the optician decides that spectacles are needed as a result of DSE work, the employer must provide basic spectacles free of charge. The employer must also pay for repeat tests.

People who are self-employed have to pay for their own eyesight tests and spectacles.

### Information

Employers are required to provide users with information on:

- health and safety relating to their workstations

- workstation assessment and steps taken to reduce risks

- breaks and changes of activity

- eye and eyesight tests.

**What is...**

**A 'DSE user'?**

Part of the risk assessment process is to decide who is a DSE user. Many organisations consider that people who work with a VDU for two hours or more per day are users, however more factors should be taken into account.

Typically, a user is someone who:

- is dependent on DSE to do their job
- has little or no discretion as to when to work on DSE
- requires significant training in DSE use
- uses DSE daily, for periods of more than one hour
- needs a fast transfer of information
- knows that errors may be critical.

Examples of users include:

- word processing and data input staff
- secretaries
- journalists and sub-editors
- telesales and call centre workers
- air traffic controllers
- financial dealers
- graphic designers and computer-aided design operators
- librarians.

People not considered to be users include senior managers who use DSE largely to send and read emails, and receptionists who use DSE infrequently and can do so at their own discretion.

### Home workers

Employers have the same obligations to those employees who use DSE for home working as they do to those who work in the office. Unfortunately, many home workstations fall well below the required standard, and even if the employee has provided the workstation the employer will still be held liable for any health problems that result as a consequence of its use. Therefore, training and assessment are still required and an adequate standard of workstation and equipment must be ensured.

### Working as a consultant or seconded person in another employer's office

In cases such as these, the third party must provide:

- a fully assessed and compliant workstation

- a reasonable daily routine, including breaks

- site-specific training and information about the workstation and task.

The employer is still responsible for:

- basic training

- free eyesight tests and, if necessary, basic spectacles.

**Seating and posture for typical office tasks**

1. Screen height and angle allow a comfortable head position
2. Wrists flat and level, without strain
3. Forearms approximately horizontal
4. Sufficient space in front of the keyboard to support hands and wrists during pauses in typing
5. No excess pressure on the underside of the thighs or backs of knees
6. Good lumbar support
7. Adjustable seat back
8. Adjustable seat height
9. Space to move, with no obstacles under the desk
10. Foot support if needed
11. Stable chair with five-star base

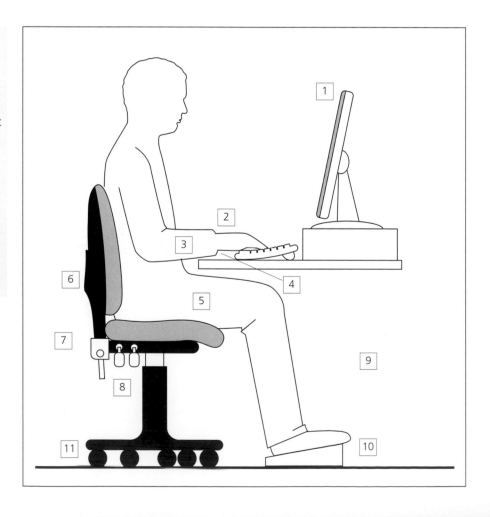

### Elements of a good office environment

1.  Adequate lighting
2.  Adequate contrast, with no glare or distracting reflections
3.  Window blinds
4.  Monitor screen that is clean, has a stable image, and is adjustable, readable, and glare- and reflection-free
5.  Software that is appropriate to the task, adapted to the user, and provides feedback on system status. Software must not be used to monitor the user, eg speed of keying, unless the user has been told that this is taking place
6.  Keyboard that is usable, adjustable and detachable, with legible characters
7.  Work surface that allows flexible arrangements and is spacious and glare-free
8.  Distracting noise kept to a minimum
9.  Chair that is adjustable
10. Room to move under the desk
11. Footrest

### How to organise the desk and avoid unnecessary twisting and stretching

1.  No clutter
2.  Comfortable viewing distance between the eyes and the monitor screen
3.  Document holder close to the screen, in a central position if possible
4.  Phone and mouse close to the keyboard
5.  Space between the keyboard and the front of the desk to rest hands and wrists

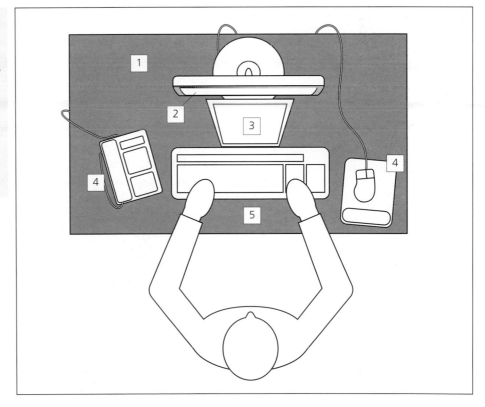

### Hard facts

*Stress cases have attracted high settlement bills. A further education lecturer was awarded £80,000 after receiving stress-related injuries at work. The out-of-court settlement followed her nervous breakdown while working at college. The lecturer had previously been asked to undertake a management role while retaining a heavy teaching load. She had also been given responsibility for expanding the college's adult education provision, and had been asked to take responsibility for quality control in a key curriculum area. Her working hours often exceeded 70 per week. The college did not assess the risk of damage to the lecturer's mental health.*

### Self-employed people

Self-employed people are responsible for their own training, daily routine (including breaks), eyesight tests and provision of spectacles. The organisation paying the self-employed person is still responsible for providing:

- a fully assessed and compliant workstation

- site-specific information about the workstation and task.

### Stress

There is no legislation in the UK at present that directly addresses work-related stress. Guidance has been published, and research continues in order to formulate standards of good management practice on which to base any future legislation.

Office workers are considered to be one of the groups of employees most susceptible to stress. The causes include:

- being treated with indifference or contempt by managers

- constant routine and repetitive work

- work pressure brought on by under-staffing

- having no control over the job in hand, eg personal pressure from management to get a job done, yet unable to do so because of having to rely on someone else to fulfil their role first

- inadequate breaks (often associated with VDU work) and long working hours

- conflict, eg sexual harassment or bullying.

### Hard facts

*A recent survey found that 44 per cent of UK employees had been bullied in the workplace, and that 21 per cent of respondents were still experiencing it. Bullying can lead to stress and increased levels of staff absence, and ultimately reduced productivity. The effects of workplace bullying are estimated to be responsible for between one third to a half of all stress-related illnesses.*

Stress as a health and safety issue is not yet fully accepted by all employers, but there is little doubt that anyone who is subject to any of the causes mentioned above will suffer. Stress can lead to ill health, absenteeism, aggressive behaviour and reduced work performance, so it makes good business sense to recognise the issue and strive for better management.

### Slips, trips and falls

Some managers in offices, shops, supermarkets and warehouses are unaware that injuries caused by slips, trips and falls are so commonplace. Some don't even know where the accident book is kept!

A fundamental part of the management process in these types of premises is to gather together whatever data are available and conduct regular reviews. There should be one accident book, kept by a first aider, and everyone should be encouraged to report accidents and record them in the book.

The prevention of slips, trips and falls depends on good housekeeping, in particular:

- maintaining good levels of lighting

- maintaining all walkways, and ensuring that they are free from obstructions such as rubbish, old filing cabinets, or trolleys containing food or other items

- no trailing cables (where unavoidable, use cable covers fixed to the floor)

- developing a culture of holding the handrail when going up and down stairs, and paying particular attention to the condition of the stair treads and carpets

- repairing or replacing torn or worn out carpets and floor coverings

- using anti-slip floor coverings in warehouse areas and shop entrances

- cleaning up spillages promptly

- storing files and materials within easy reach

- suitable footwear.

**Hard facts**

In the UK, slips, trips and falls account for some 50 per cent of all major workplace injuries, and more than 25 per cent of all reportable injuries.

### Filing cabinets

When more than one heavily loaded drawer in a free-standing filing cabinet or storage system is opened at the same time, there is a risk of the cabinet or storage system over-turning onto the user, resulting in serious injury. Filing cabinets should have interlocks that prevent more than one drawer being opened at once. In all cases, large units should be fixed to a wall, even if interlocks are fitted. Older filing cabinets without interlocks should be replaced, and instructions on not opening more than one drawer at a time should be given to users for as long as any older cabinets remain in use. Warning labels should also be attached to them.

**Also read...**

Chapter 3 – Young people at work

### Employment of young people in retail establishments

Many retail establishments, particularly supermarkets, make extensive use of young people on part-time employment contracts. For many this is their first taste of working life. However, young people invariably have little or no knowledge of employment rights or experience of health and safety practice. All too often they are bullied by more senior staff; persuaded to work through their breaks (often to cover for absentees); put to work in outdoor car parks without protective equipment; or asked to undertake manual handling without training.

Notwithstanding these breaches of health and safety law, it is the legal responsibility of management to provide extra training and management time to make sure that the health and safety needs of young people are addressed. There is a requirement to undertake a risk assessment of a young person's work activities while they are in employment. A safe system of work must be devised, taking into account the young person's inexperience and physique. The risk assessment and safe system must be recorded and provided both to the young person and his or her parents/guardian. Training must be given, normally in the form of a thorough induction process.

Senior management must ensure that company policies in respect of young people are actually implemented. Frontline supervisors need to be fully trained in the health, safety and welfare issues involved, and a system of audit should be put in place to monitor how this works in practice. In addition, a means of consultation should be established, providing young people with the opportunity to express any concerns they may have about the work tasks they are being asked to perform.

When a young person is allocated a new task, further training should be given on the risks and safe systems of work associated with that task. Even if the training had been given at the young person's initial induction, it will probably have been long forgotten and should be repeated.

# Warehousing

The warehousing aspects considered here are:

- storage systems, including racking and pallets

- forklift trucks

- operation of vehicles.

### Storage systems

#### Racking

Racking should be designed around the goods to be stored and the pallets used to transport them. Racking requires structural design, and safe working loads, heights, widths and equipment tolerances should be specified by the manufacturer. Racking is relatively lightweight and can therefore be damaged by a forklift truck driving into it. Any structural component that is damaged will have its safe working load considerably reduced, increasing the risk of collapsing the entire structure.

- Racking should be properly designed, erected on a structural floor and bolted down to the floor if forklift trucks are operating nearby. As a minimum, where the height-to-depth ratio of the racking does not exceed 6:1, the uprights adjacent to the aisles must be bolted down to the floor. Many consider it prudent to fix down all uprights. Where the height-to-depth ratio exceeds 6:1 but does not exceed 10:1, all uprights must be fixed to the floor. For ratios greater than 10:1, specialist advice and design is needed.

- The aisle widths should be adequate to allow forklift trucks to manoeuvre properly. Aisles should be properly marked on the floor.

- Where adjustable pallet racking is installed, beam connector locks should be used to prevent them from being dislodged by a forklift truck.

- The safe working load should be clearly marked on notices attached to the racking.

- Racking should never be altered without consulting the manufacturer.

- Bent or broken components should be replaced, not repaired.

- Pallet stops should not be used, as they increase the likelihood of the racking being overturned or damaged if the stop is hit too heavily. If the racking layout is correctly designed, allowing adequate clearance between pallets or loads, then a trained and competent driver will be able to deposit the load safely.

**Hard facts**

Following the death of a warehouseman, a logistics company was fined £7,500 and ordered to pay £15,000 costs for failing to meet the requirements of the Health and Safety at Work etc Act. The warehouseman died under racks of pallets that collapsed on top of him. He lay undiscovered for many hours.

### Racking maintenance

Where racking is likely to be struck by forklift trucks, it should be protected using renewable column guards or guide rails set away from the racking structure. Corner uprights are especially vulnerable and should be carefully protected and painted in a bright colour.

To ensure that a racking installation is maintained properly, regular planned inspections should be made and any defects corrected. Staff should be encouraged to report any damage, however minor, and to adhere to the safe working load notices. If there is any doubt about the stability of the racking, the manufacturer should be contacted for advice. A logbook should be kept to record inspections, damage and repairs. Where it is suspected that damage could affect the stability of a racking system, it should be off-loaded and put out of service.

### Pallets

Flat timber pallets form an essential part of handling systems in warehouses. Many accidents are directly attributable to these pallets because of:

- poor design

- poor construction

- the use of a pallet that is unsuitable for a particular load or racking system (most pallets are designed for a specific load and racking system, and it is unsafe to mix loads, pallets and racking systems)

- the continued use of a damaged pallet (a system should be put in place that checks the pallets before loading, and damaged pallets should be repaired to their original specification or destroyed)

- bad handling (empty pallets should be handled carefully and not dragged or thrown about).

**Pallet handling faults that damage the pallet**

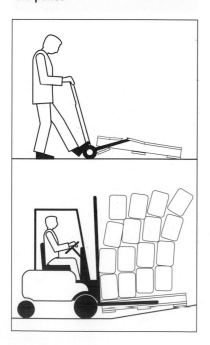

## Forklift trucks

Forklift trucks are more properly called 'lift trucks'. There are many different types, eg rough terrain, counterbalanced, pedestrian-controlled and telehandlers. While recognising that this is the term used by the HSE among others, because the term 'forklift truck' is still in common use, we have used it throughout.

Forklift trucks must carry a CE mark and the following information:

- manufacturer and truck type

- serial number

- unladen weight

- rated capacity

- load centre distance and maximum lift height

- tyre inflation pressures.

A forklift truck should be fitted with:

- brakes and handbrakes

- a removable key start

- a seat belt

- a horn

- an overhead guard that is strong enough to protect the operator from falling loads

- guards to prevent access to dangerous moving parts that are within the operator's reach when operating the machine (such as the lifting mechanism)

- rear view mirrors for reversing operations.

The following additional equipment may also be necessary:

- a load back rest (if to be used to move small objects that are liable to fall on top of the operator)

- lights (if to be used in poorly lit areas)

- a flashing or audible warning beacon (if to be used near other people).

**Hard facts**

On average, 10 people in the UK are killed each year as a result of accidents involving forklift trucks.

**Also read...**

Appendix B – Forklift trucks

**Counterbalanced forklift truck**

The load placed on the forks is counterbalanced by the weight of the vehicle.

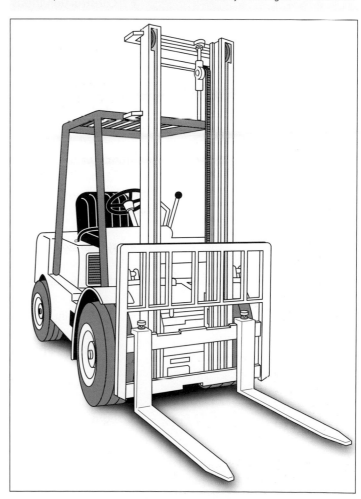

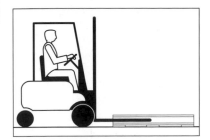

**Correct procedure for entering a
pallet using a forklift truck**

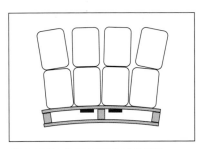

**Incorrect setting of fork spacing**

Forklift truck operators must:

- be trained, ie given basic training, specific job training, and
  familiarisation training in the workplace

- be competent

- be authorised in writing to use the vehicle

- be at least 18 years old

- have certain personal qualities – reliability; an ability to do the job; a
  sense of responsibility; and good physical fitness, eyesight and hearing.

Basic and specific job training may be combined but should always be off the job.

The Health and Safety Commission recognises the voluntary training accreditation
schemes operated by the following bodies:

- Agriculture Training Board

- Construction Industry Training Board

- Road Transport Industry Training Board

- Association of Industrial Truck Trainers.

Operators should be in possession of a certificate of training achievement (for a specific
type of truck) that is issued by one of these organisations.

### Maintenance
### Daily checks

Operators should check their forklift truck at the beginning of each shift to ensure
that:

- tyre pressures are correct

- the brake and handbrake work properly

- the flashing or audible warning beacon (if fitted) works properly

- fluid levels are correct and batteries are charged

- systems for lifting, tilting and manipulation are working properly

- lights (if fitted) are working

- the horn works.

### Weekly checks

Weekly checks must be recorded in a register and should include:

- all of the daily checks

- the operation of the steering gear, lifting gear and other working parts

- the condition of the battery

- the condition of the mast, forks, attachments, chains or ropes, hydraulic cylinders and hoses

- the security of the overhead guard and load back-rest extension.

### Six-monthly examination

A competent person such as an insurance company engineer should carry out a thorough examination of all working parts of a forklift truck every six months. A certificate should be issued stating that the vehicle is free from defects and is safe to use. If repairs are required they should be carried out and the truck re-examined before use. A similar examination should also be carried out after an accident or major repair following a breakdown or similar event.

### Refuelling and recharging

Refuelling must always take place outside the warehouse, regardless of whether the fuel is petrol, diesel or liquefied petroleum gas. The correct method of charging battery-powered vehicles is explained in Chapter 11.

> **Hard facts**
>
> In 2004, a DIY store group was fined £550,000 plus £250,000 costs following the death of a member of the public. The person in question, an elderly woman who was shopping at the store, was killed when a forklift truck driver reversed his vehicle into her, pinning her against a shelf and crushing her.

**Also read...**

Chapter 4 – Outside your buildings

## Operation of road vehicles

Many accidents in and around warehouses are associated with vehicles. The following are some of the main considerations:

- Provide an entry and exit road system that avoids reversing as far as possible (reversing lorries are a hazard to pedestrians).

- Specific routes across the yard should be provided for pedestrians (segregating them from vehicles).

- Only essential relevant employees should be allowed in the vehicle movement area.

- Provide pedestrian exits or escape points at loading docks so that the possibility of trapping by a reversing lorry is reduced.

- Guide vehicles back into loading docks.

- Prevent premature departure of the lorry (eg the lorry drives away while the forklift truck is still loading items onto it) by using vehicle restraints to anchor the trailer to the loading dock, and withholding the journey paperwork and vehicle keys until loading is complete.

- Maintain the stability of uncoupled trailers. Uncoupled trailers stand on 'landing legs' when the tractor unit is removed, and the legs can collapse if a forklift truck accidentally bumps into them when loading or unloading. These legs are not tested as part of a vehicle MOT, so in order to reduce the risk:

    ○ chock the wheels

    ○ use proprietary safety jacks or other suitable support

    ○ have the landing legs examined at regular intervals.

- Before loading, check the condition of the floor of the vehicle, maintain an even distribution of load, and secure the load fully.

- When loading or unloading a vehicle from one side, maintain the opposite curtain or side in position to prevent any imbalance tipping the load out.

- Before unloading, check the load for movement before removing ropes, tarpaulins or curtains; open container doors with caution as the load may have shifted.

- Loading or unloading should never be carried out on a significant gradient.

- The driver of the vehicle is responsible for ensuring that the load is secure. The driver should direct the forklift truck operator concerning the positioning of the load.

Also read...

Chapter 3 – Working time

**Safe driving time**

The rules are detailed and complex, but the basics for commercial vehicle drivers are as follows:

- Maximum driving time is 90 hours in a 2-week reference period.

- This driving time includes driving from home.

- There must be 11 hours daily rest and every third weekend off, as a minimum.

- Driving can be done for a maximum of 10 hours per day, with a 45-minute break after each 4½ hours. Alternatively, drivers should take a 15-minute break after each 1 hour driving.

- Driving time must be recorded on a tachograph and checked by the business.

Similar rules should be applied to business car and van drivers.

## The bottom line

**To comply with the law:**

- the users of DSE equipment must be identified and an assessment made of their workstation and working environment
- DSE users must be provided with information and training
- DSE users must be offered free eyesight tests, and basic spectacles if required
- all accidents must be reported in a statutory accident book
- workplaces must be kept in good working order to minimise injuries caused by slips, trips and falls
- specific risk assessments, information and training are required where young people are employed
- a logbook must be kept of the inspections, damage and repair of storage racking
- forklift truck operators must be trained and competent, at least 18 years of age, and be authorised in writing to use their vehicle
- forklift truck operators must make daily checks of their vehicles and maintain a weekly register of inspections
- forklift trucks require a six-monthly thorough examination by an authorised, competent person.

## Introduction

This chapter focuses on the health and safety aspects of building maintenance and facilities management. It covers all types of facilities from hotels to offices, workshops to shopping centres.

The role of maintenance error as a contributory cause of accidents and ill health is increasingly recognised. Maintenance is particularly liable to human error as hazards often cannot be seen, eg lack of oxygen in a confined space, asbestos hidden inside a fire door, Legionella bacteria in a cooling tower. Without a systematic approach, an unseen hazard can become a serious risk. Therefore, routine preventive maintenance and good record-keeping are essential.

The following topics will be dealt with in this chapter. They are not the exclusive domain of the maintenance engineer, and are also relevant to construction and refurbishment activities.

- Maintenance of essential services

- Electrical equipment and services

- Legionnaire's disease

- Asbestos

- Hot works

- Confined spaces

- Weil's disease

- Roof work

### Lone workers

In developing maintenance or other procedures, consideration must always be given to the issue of lone workers. A risk assessment should consider:

- the probability of a lone worker encountering health and safety hazards

- the lone worker's means of raising an alarm

- the means of rescue

- the means of escape in the event of fire.

If these issues cannot be addressed satisfactorily, then lone working should be avoided.

**Hard facts**

A mechanic's death in 2001 resulted in a coach firm being fined £18,000 plus costs after it admitted breaching the Health and Safety at Work etc Act. The firm had failed to assess the risks inherent in its vehicle recovery activity. The mechanic sustained crush injuries when he took up position underneath a bus being recovered to access its brakes. When he released the brakes the bus rolled back over him.

## Maintenance of essential services

There is a duty in law to maintain essential services in good working order and to provide for the health and safety of building occupants and, in some cases, the general public. Critical maintenance programmes are often contracted out to specialists who carry out inspections, correct defects and issue reports.

The frequency of maintenance, inspection and testing depends on manufacturers' recommendations and the age and condition of the equipment, although once every 12 months is normal for most typical equipment.

Facilities management and maintenance should be carried out in a systematic way, in order to prevent unforeseen events, implement preventive maintenance, work according to checklists, and keep well-filed auditable records.

Use the checklist below to identify the services in your premises and devise a plan for regular maintenance, inspection and testing.

www.protect.org.uk

PDF 19

| Maintenance of essential services | | | |
|---|---|---|---|
| Equipment | Is the equipment present? | Frequency of inspection and testing? | Who will provide maintenance? |
| Emergency lighting | | | |
| Fire detection systems, alarms and sprinklers | | | |
| Fire extinguishers | | | |
| Electrical systems and transformers | | | |
| Boilers and hot water storage systems | | | |
| Water storage tanks and water supply | | | |
| Air conditioning cooling towers, hot and cold water systems, fountains, shower heads and ice machines (checks required for Legionella bacteria) | | | |
| Cooker hood extraction systems, including cleaning ducts and fans, and the changing of filters | | | |

| Maintenance of essential services (continued) | | | |
| --- | --- | --- | --- |
| Equipment | Is the equipment present? | Frequency of inspection and testing? | Who will provide maintenance? |
| Gas installations in kitchens and other areas | | | |
| Filters and ductwork in laundries | | | |
| Cradles and fixed window cleaning equipment | | | |
| Window cleaner and other safety harness anchorage points | | | |
| Window opening limiters | | | |
| Machine guards | | | |
| Portable electrical equipment (see following section) | | | |
| Powered doors and gates | | | |
| Lifts and elevators | | | |
| Escalators and moving walkways | | | |
| Fuel tanks (checks required for leakages) | | | |
| Pest control | | | |
| Swimming pools and fountains (cleaning, maintaining and chlorinating pool water, and maintaining filters and pumps in good condition, including water quality analysis) | | | |
| Other | | | |

## Electrical equipment and services

Electrical equipment is a major cause of fires and fatal injuries at work, and good maintenance and testing play a significant role in preventing them. Hazards include:

- damaged insulation

- old rubber wiring

- inadequate fuses and circuit breakers

- overloaded circuits

- loose contacts and connectors

- inadequate earthing

- working on live circuits

- working without a permit to work or 'lock off' system (see below)

- using incompetent or unqualified electricians.

All electrical systems must be inspected and tested at regular intervals, normally annually, and a report on their condition should be provided by the inspecting organisation. Any deviations from the relevant standards should be rectified as a matter of priority. It is recommended that any defective elements be isolated until they have been replaced or repaired. The testing of the electrical installation should be in accordance with the standard laid down in the current edition of the Institution of Electrical Engineers (IEE) Wiring Regulations.

Companies who are members of the National Inspection Council for Electrical Installation Contractors (NICEIC) should undertake all electrical work and testing. Proof of an organisation's membership should be checked, together with the competency and qualifications of the electricians who will carry out the work.

All electrical installations must be in the charge of a nominated manager who has a duty to control any contractors or others who work on or test the equipment or circuits. The manager should keep records of the installation, any alterations, the defects reported and corrected, and liaise with electrical contractors.

**Also read...**

Chapter 14 – How to select a good contractor

The name and title of this person should be prominently displayed, close to the main circuit breaker. This person is the legal 'duty holder' of the facility, and must have sufficient training, knowledge and experience to carry out the role.

Live electrical circuits must not be worked on except under exceptional circumstances (circumstances beyond the scope of this book). Therefore, any circuit that is to be worked on must first be isolated. It is worth bearing in mind that electrocutions often occur when an electrician switches off a circuit breaker and someone else switches it back on without the electrician's knowledge. So, to ensure this doesn't happen, one or more of the following techniques may be employed:

- Use an isolator on or near to the equipment being worked on, so that the electrician can see it at all times. This will give the electrician direct control over the isolator.

- Use a permit to work system. The electrical contractor normally issues the permit, after consultation with the duty holder. The duty holder has the responsibility of ensuring that no-one else in the organisation can switch on the power. This is usually achieved by locking the room that contains the isolator. The duty holder will usually pass the room key to the contractor carrying out the work, who also has a duty holder with technical responsibility for the installation work. Problems can arise if there is a second or third key in circulation. In this case the duty holder is responsible for ensuring that the key holders know that work is being carried out and that they do not interfere. In view of the potential consequences of failure, such information and instruction should be in writing and acknowledged by way of signature of those briefed.

- Use a 'lock off' system. This is appropriate in critical high-voltage situations in complex buildings. The procedure begins when a clasp is secured to the equipment containing the isolators, to which two or more padlocks are attached. The electrician carrying out the work controls one padlock, and other duty holders have their own padlocks and keys. All key holders therefore have to be brought together to remove the clasp and energise the circuit.

**Hard facts**

A pet food manufacturer was fined £600,000 following the death of a worker. The death happened when two technicians went into a silo to repair a stirrer. In the course of this work one of them was electrocuted. This was caused by the worker coming into contact with the live parts of the welding electrode. The voltage was above the threshold where precautions were required to be taken when work was carried out in a confined or conductive location, or in damp or wet conditions. There was no system for warning technicians of the inherent risks. No proper risk assessment had been undertaken and no steps had been taken to avoid the risks.

### What is...

**An RCD?**

A residual current device (RCD) is an electro-mechanical device that trips when, due to a fault, the current flowing into a machine or tool is different from that flowing out. This difference in current is the tripping current, which should be 30mA.

The RCD should be installed at the distribution board or at a fixed mains supply socket. In this way it will protect the extension lead as well as the tool.

RCDs do not protect from every type of electric shock and do not warn the user if they are faulty. For this reason, it is preferable to use low voltage, rechargeable power tools.

### Portable appliance testing (PAT)

PAT is a legal requirement. The table below gives suggested intervals for inspecting and testing electrical equipment.

| Equipment/application | Voltage | Formal inspection and test |
|---|---|---|
| • Low voltage rechargeable power tools<br>• Torches | 25v maximum | Not required |
| • Portable and hand-held tools<br>• Extension leads<br>• Lighting | 110v maximum, as used on construction sites | Before first use, then every three months |
| • Portable and hand-held tools<br>• Extension leads<br>• Lighting | 230v through an RCD (30mA); RCD must be used | Before first use, then every three months; include a test of the RCD |
| • Fixed equipment<br>• Woodworking machines<br>• Lifts<br>• Hoists<br>• Floodlighting | 230v | Before first use, then annually |
| • Office and IT equipment, including photocopiers and printers | 230v | Before first use, when moved, then every three years (one year for construction site offices) |
| • Earthed equipment, eg electric kettles, fires<br>• Certain floor cleaners | 230v | Before first use, then annually |

If appliances do not rely on earthing for their safety, only visual inspections are required, although the cable and plug may need to be checked. If appliances do rely on earthing, combined examination and testing is required.

In addition to formal testing, users are expected to check equipment visually on a monthly basis (weekly for hand tools) and ensure that any defects are repaired. Users should also check the effectiveness of RCDs by operating the test button daily. Experience gained when operating the maintenance system over time, and the faults found, should be used to review the frequency of inspection and testing.

## Legionnaire's disease

Legionnaire's disease is a pneumonia-like condition caused by the bacterium *Legionella pneumophila*. Up to 30 per cent of those who contract the disease die. People of any age can contract it, although normally it affects middle-aged and older people.

Typically, outbreaks occur when people breathe in water-borne bacteria in the form of water mists or sprays. The source of contamination is normally an air conditioning cooling tower, whirlpool spa or shower.

Legionella bacteria are widely distributed in water systems. It is important to remember that any water system can be a source of disease if the water is subject to conditions that promote growth of the Legionella bacteria.

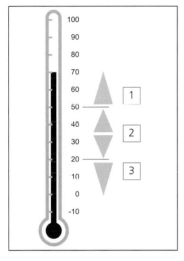

**Optimal temperature range for growth of Legionella (20°C to 50°C)**
1. Bacteria are killed
2. Bacteria grow
3. Too cold for bacteria to grow

### Water conditions

Water conditions that tend to promote the growth of the bacteria include:

- stagnation

- temperatures between 20°C and 50°C (68°F and 122°F)

- pH between 5.0 and 8.5.

Sediment and micro-organisms such as algae supply the essential nutrients for bacterial growth and therefore present a hazard if the conditions for growth of the bacteria are present.

### Water sources

Water sources that provide optimal conditions for growth of the organisms include:

- air conditioning systems

- cold water systems

- hot water systems.

# 13 Maintenance and facilities management

The maintenance of each system in relation to the prevention of Legionnaire's disease is outlined below.

### Air conditioning systems

Cooling towers, evaporative condensers and fluid coolers remove heat through evaporation and should be monitored and maintained according to manufacturers' recommendations to prevent build up of scale, sediment, algae and other impurities. Visual inspection, quarterly testing and periodic maintenance of the system are the best ways to control the growth of Legionella bacteria and related organisms, together with the following actions:

- Use chemical biocides and rust inhibitors to treat circulating water for control of micro-organisms, scale and corrosion. Obtain information on the appropriate biocide selection and use from the equipment manufacturer. Alternatively, use a specialist organisation to carry out the treatment. In general, inspect equipment for organic matter on a monthly basis.

- Clean and disinfect cooling towers with a biocide at least twice a year. This should be done before initial start up at the beginning of the cooling season and after shut down in the autumn.

- Maintain sump water at a low temperature.

- Carry out weekly dip slide tests to monitor the make up of cooling water. Depending on the results, biocide dosing should be adjusted accordingly.

- Provide procedures for proper operation and maintenance of the system.

- On the basis of a risk assessment, produce a documented scheme for the control of Legionella bacteria. The scheme should cover cleaning, monitoring and testing regimes, the personnel responsible for these activities, and a diagram of the system.

- Document operations and maintenance in a log book. Log books should list dates of inspection and cleaning, water-quality test results, follow up actions where Legionella bacteria have been detected, and routine maintenance.

- Seek specialist advice, and consult the relevant HSE guidance (see Appendix C).

### Cold water systems

Cold water systems that are a potential source of Legionella bacteria include ice machines with cold water lines near heat sources, water tanks that allow water to remain stagnant for long periods, cross-contamination of a domestic cold water system with process water, and emergency water systems. Emergency water systems include fire sprinklers, safety showers and eyewash stations. These systems experience little water flow and can be subject to periods of high temperatures. In addition, operation of these devices produces a breathable water mist.

Maintaining cold water lines below 20°C limits the potential for bacteria to grow. Other methods include:

- chlorination of the water supply

- frequent flushing of the system by running water through the taps

- replacing stagnant tanks and 'dead leg' pipe sections

- insulating cold water lines that are close to hot water lines or exposed to sunlight or heating

- fitting non-return valves to protect connections to process water

- flushing safety showers and emergency eyewash stations at least once per month.

### Hot water systems

Maintaining hot water lines above 60°C (140°F) limits the potential for bacteria to grow. Keep domestic water heaters at 60°C and water delivered to taps at a minimum of 50°C . Where these temperatures cannot be maintained, other methods must be used, including:

- Insulating hot water lines and heat-tracing specific pipes, helping to maintain distribution and delivery temperatures.

- Frequent flushing of the pipes in order to clean rubber or silicone gaskets, which can be a source of nutrients for the bacteria.

- Periodically chlorinating the system at the tank to produce 10 parts per million free residual chlorine and flushing all taps and showers until a distinct odour of chlorine is evident. Control of the pH in the range of 6.8 to 7.0 is extremely important to ensure that there is adequate residual chlorine in the system.

- Cleaning shower heads.

- Periodically draining hot water tanks to remove scale and sediment and cleaning with chlorine solution if possible. The tank must be thoroughly rinsed to remove excess chlorine before re-use.

- Testing the domestic hot or warm water system for Legionella bacteria every three months, or more frequently if the results indicate the presence of the bacteria.

- Where a closed system is adequately chlorinated and the temperature controlled above 60°C, dip slide testing is not required. However, if this is not the case, monitoring is required (seek specialist advice).

## 13 Maintenance and facilities management

## Asbestos

Many buildings contain asbestos, and employers have a legal duty to protect their employees and the public from the dangers associated with it. Breathing in asbestos dust is extremely dangerous and can cause cancers of the chest and lungs, including asbestosis and mesothelioma. The effects are not immediate, but take between 15 to 60 years to prove fatal. During this time, if a source of asbestos dust is not removed, many more people can be exposed.

There is a duty of care here, even if you are not the owner of the building you occupy. It may be a landlord's responsibility to carry out surveys or remedial work, but as an employer you must ensure that it is done in order to protect your staff and others, eg contractors who carry out work on your behalf.

You must find out if your building contains asbestos, and if it does you must decide what to do about it. Maintenance workers are at particular risk. For example, they may disturb asbestos dust in an asbestos ceiling when changing a light fitting, or drill through asbestos fire protection in a door or doorframe. And those operating or maintaining boilers and associated pipe work may be exposed to asbestos dust from crumbling insulation.

It might be assumed that because asbestos is so dangerous it will already have been removed from most buildings. This is not the case. There is no legal requirement to remove asbestos materials from buildings, and to do so would prove ruinously expensive for many organisations. The legal duty is to prevent people breathing in asbestos dust, and it is generally accepted that undisturbed asbestos in good condition poses little risk.

### Types of asbestos

There are three main types of asbestos:

- blue or crocidolite (the most hazardous type)

- brown or amosite

- white or chrysotile (the least hazardous type but still very dangerous).

### Management strategy

If your building was constructed or refurbished between 1950 and 1980 and you do not have conclusive information that it is asbestos-free, then by law you must have a survey carried out to determine if asbestos is present. Be aware that between 1950 and 1980 older buildings may have had new boilers installed or some other refurbishment that contains asbestos. Following the survey, you must either remove the asbestos or maintain it in such a way that it does not pose a threat to employees or the public. In order to inform your decision, follow through this checklist of actions.

- A laboratory or contractor accredited by the United Kingdom Accreditation Service (UKAS – t +44 (0)208 917 8400, www.ukas.com) must be used to obtain and analyse samples. The taking of samples for analysis does not require a licence.

- The analyst's report should indicate:

- the precise location of the asbestos

- the form of the asbestos (lagging, ceiling tiles, partition board and so on)

- the condition of the asbestos

- the type of asbestos

- the recommended remedial action, such as sealing, encapsulating or removal.

- The decision to remove depends on the condition of the asbestos and the future likelihood of it being disturbed by building work or damaged by maintenance workers or others. Clearly, blue asbestos pipe lagging in poor condition should be removed, while ceiling tiles containing white asbestos in good condition can be sealed safely using PVA adhesive followed by two coats of paint.

- Any asbestos that remains in a building must be indicated by drawings and, by law, be recorded in a register. The location of the asbestos should also be labelled to make sure that maintenance and other workers are aware of the hazard.

- A competent person should inspect any asbestos remaining in the building on a quarterly basis to ensure that it remains undamaged. Record the inspection findings with the results of the observations.

### Asbestos removal

All forms of asbestos must be removed by a licensed asbestos removal contractor. All contractors who work with asbestos should be members of the Asbestos Removal Contractors Association (ARCA). References must be taken up to check whether the contractor is competent and that they are members of ARCA (t +44 (0)1245 259744, www.arca.org.uk).

All work with asbestos must be notified to the enforcing authority at least 14 days prior to any works or associated works commencing. The removal contractor will complete the appropriate form.

Safe removal of asbestos is carried out behind polythene enclosures by a trained specialist workforce using respirators and disposable overalls. It is necessary to evacuate the area while this is happening. An analyst must take clearance readings before the enclosure is removed and staff are allowed to return.

Asbestos must be removed cold. Where asbestos has to be removed from a boiler or associated pipe work, the boiler must first be closed down. This is because working conditions in enclosures, in protective suits and breathing apparatus, and in excessive heat, is intolerable. Consequently, the employer should co-operate with any request from the specialist contractor to turn off heating appliances.

Under no circumstances should you allow your staff to enter asbestos enclosures or respirator zones established by a licensed asbestos removal contractor.

All waste that contains asbestos must be sealed in double plastic sacks and be appropriately labelled. The waste is classified as special waste and must be removed by a licensed carrier to a licensed tip. This will be organised by the removal contractor.

### Where is asbestos found?

Asbestos was used extensively in buildings because of its fire resistance and insulation properties, and its ability to bind and strengthen other materials such as cement. The forms most likely to be in a state of deterioration include sprayed asbestos used to insulate pipe work and provide fire breaks in ceiling voids. These materials are particularly dangerous as they often contain blue or brown asbestos and give off fibres easily.

Insulating boards and ceiling or floor tiles are less likely to release fibres if they are not disturbed, but will do so if they are drilled or cut, perhaps for new light fittings or to route computer cabling.

Asbestos cement products are considered to be the least hazardous provided that they are treated with care and are not smashed or broken up. This is because the fibres are bound within a cement matrix and comprise about 10 to 15 per cent of the total product. Asbestos cement roof sheets in the open air can therefore be dismantled carefully without the use of special equipment such as enclosures or respirators, although they must not be broken up before they are double wrapped for disposal.

| Location of asbestos in buildings | | |
|---|---|---|
| **Location** | **Form** | **Risk** |
| Fire breaks in ceiling voids | Sprayed and loose-packed asbestos | **Highest** |
| Boiler and pipe lagging | Moulded or pre-formed units and sprayed coatings of asbestos | |
| Fire protection in shafts and voids, fire breaks, panels, partitions, soffit boards, ceiling panels, and around structural steel members | Sprayed coatings of asbestos mixed with hydrated asbestos cement | |
| General fire protection, thermal insulation and partitions | Insulating boards | |
| Ceiling and floor tiles | Tiles used in retail units | |
| Insulation of electrical equipment, and as a fireproof facing on wood fibre board | Asbestos paper | |
| Corrugated sheets used extensively as roofing and wall cladding, gutters, rainwater pipes and water tanks | Asbestos cement products | |
| Coating materials | Textured coatings | **Lowest** |

## Hot works

Hot works include flame-cutting and welding, the use of blow torches and hot air guns by plumbers and decorators, soldering and brazing, and the use of bitumen heating equipment by roofers. Disc cutters that produce showers of sparks are also considered to be hot works. They all have the potential to cause fires, particularly in a maintenance situation. For this reason, all hot works should be under the control of a hot works permit to work issued by the facilities manager.

Also read...

Appendix A – Hot works permit to work

**Before undertaking hot works:**

- check that the area is safe to work

- remove all combustible material from the area, including those items below and on the other side of the wall where work is to take place

- protect timber floors with non-combustible material

- provide a non-combustible screen for welding and cutting operations

- ensure that sparks cannot fall onto areas below or onto flammable material

- provide suitable fire extinguishers (foam or powder) near hot works

- in high risk areas, provide a fire-watcher, ie someone whose job it is to check that nothing catches fire

- use a hot works permit to work.

**During the hot works:**

- carry out regular inspections

- provide a metal bucket of water for welding rods

- fit flashback arresters to oxygen and acetylene tanks, or any other gases that are mixed for cutting and welding operations.

**After the hot works ceases:**

- remain in the area for 15 minutes to check for fire, then check again after 30 minutes and one hour. In critical cases, make a further check after two hours. Ideally, these checks should be made in normal working hours by finishing the hot works early

- security guards should be made aware of hot works areas by way of a copy of the permit, and be required to check for fire at intervals throughout the night.

Blow lamps must not be used for paint stripping; they are notorious for causing fires. They may be used for small repairs of existing thermoplastic tiles, provided they have a holding stand and are not left unattended. Hot air paint strippers must be unplugged when no longer in use.

## Confined spaces

Some confined spaces are fairly obvious, such as closed tanks and chambers, manholes, sewers, ducts, vats, silos, pits, trenches, pipes, flues and wells. However, less obvious confined spaces can also present equally dangerous risks. These include deep excavations, excavations in chalk, open-topped tanks, and unventilated rooms in which dangerous gases can build up because of restricted air circulation.

Manholes and sewers must always be classed as confined spaces, even if no water is running through them.

Temporary confined spaces can also be created by maintenance activities, and construction activities such as the spray application of paints or the use of volatile adhesives.

**Risks associated with confined spaces**

- Lack of oxygen

  Normally, the atmosphere contains 21 per cent oxygen. Oxygen reduction to 17 per cent causes clouding of judgment and poor physical co-ordination.

  Dangerous oxygen-deficient situations can be caused by:

  ○ purging tanks with an inert gas to remove hazardous vapours or gas

  ○ heavy corrosion of a steel tank (the rusting process uses up oxygen)

  ○ chalk ground that comes into contact with rain water (this can then poison anyone who enters the trench).

- Too much oxygen, or the presence of flammable gas

  Both of these create a risk of explosion.

  ○ Oxygen enrichment of the atmosphere can be caused by operations that use oxygen, eg flame-cutting, or by a leaking oxygen cylinder.

  ○ Flammable gas such as methane is often present in landfill sites. If a trench is dug through this ground, it could become a confined space filled with explosive gas. Methane also displaces oxygen, creating a further hazard.

- Toxic gas fumes or vapours

  These can be naturally occurring, such as hydrogen sulphide in sewers, or created by the work activity, such as using cleaning chemicals inside a tank. Sources of gases and vapours can arise from both within and outside the confined space, eg:

  ○ gases and fumes from works that are being carried out in the confined space, eg welding, flame-cutting, cleaning and painting

  ○ gas or vapour from an earlier process

  ○ gas or vapour entering from adjoining plant that has not been isolated. For example, effluent still passing through a sewer, or exhaust from compressors or vehicles standing next to an open manhole

- fumes emitted from sludge, deposits or other substances in the confined space, or generated by them when disturbed, eg when walking along a live sewer or cleaning a tank.

- Other hazards

  - The presence of high levels of dust/fine particles.

  - Being trapped by a free-flowing solid such as grain in a silo.

  - Drowning, eg when unexpected storm water flows down a sewer.

  - The presence of excessive heat, leading to exhaustion.

The level of risk created by these situations may be significantly increased where entry and exit are difficult.

The law states that if an activity can be carried out using a method that does not require entering the confined space, then that method must be used. Where there is no option but to enter, there must be a written safe system of work that incorporates rescue arrangements. This requires a permit to work system that is clearly understood by all involved.

### Procedures
Only trained personnel with adequate protective and rescue equipment must enter a confined space and only after a safe system of work has been established and approved. All confined space work must be under a permit to work system.

### Risk assessment
Before any work commences, a risk assessment must be undertaken. The following should be established:

- that it is not reasonably practicable to carry out the work without entry into the confined space

- the nature of substances and gases present (samples should be taken and tested where necessary, including soils if excavation is required)

- the likelihood of gases and vapours entering

- the type and concentration of any gases/vapours likely to be generated by the work activity

- the likelihood of flooding

- the nature of the work to be carried out

- the methods used to ventilate the space

- air monitoring of the atmosphere in the space

- the means (and ease) of access and egress

- the plant and materials to be used

- the type of personal protective equipment required

- supervision and specific inspections

- the method of communication

- emergency procedures and equipment, raising the alarm, safety of rescuers, calling emergency services, first aid and so on (see next section on safety equipment)

- training for normal work, supervision and rescue

- the competence and fitness of those carrying out the work.

### Safety equipment

The following are the minimum levels of safety equipment needed for working in sewers, manholes and tanks. The final decision on the procedure and equipment necessary must be made after risk assessment of the specific situation. Ensure that there are enough trained people present to operate the required safety equipment.

**Permit to work system**

A permit to work system must be used for all confined space entries. Even if contractors make the entry, the facility manager should control the permit. This is because it is only the facility manager who will know the contents of the confined space, the processes involved, and when the confined space has been isolated.

Also read...

Appendix A – Confined space entry permit to work

| Location/conditions | Safety equipment |
| --- | --- |
| • Normal manholes less than 1.5m deep | • Atmospheric monitor (to check for oxygen, explosive and toxic gas)<br>• Intrinsically safe lamps<br>• Boots, overalls, gloves, helmet |
| • Normal manholes 1.5 to 3.0m deep, where there are no indicators of adverse weather or other risks<br>• Other chambers of 1.5 to 3.0m deep on dry foul or surface water sewers, where access is straightforward, rescue can be effected easily, and there are no indicators of adverse weather or other risks<br>• Normal surface water manholes and other straightforward chambers deeper than 3.0m, where there are no indicators of adverse weather or other risks<br>• Surface water sewers where there are no indicators of adverse weather or other risks | • Atmospheric monitor (to check for oxygen, explosive and toxic gas)<br>• Harness for each entrant<br>• Lifelines<br>• Winch (or adequate number of people on the surface to pull out entrant)<br>• Intrinsically safe lamps<br>• Boots, overalls, gloves, helmet |
| • All entry into live foul sewers and manholes that are more than 1.5m deep<br>• Entry into sewers and manholes on foul and surface water systems, where entry conditions are complicated and/or there are indicators of adverse weather | • Atmospheric monitor (to check for oxygen, explosive and toxic gas)<br>• Harness for each entrant<br>• Lifelines<br>• Winch<br>• Escape breathing apparatus<br>• Rescue breathing apparatus<br>• Means of communication<br>• Intrinsically safe lamps<br>• Waders, overalls, gloves, helmet |
| • All entry into enclosed tanks or chambers for the purpose of cleaning or repair, where sludge and contamination are present, or where toxic chemicals are to be applied. If reasonably practicable, these tanks must be cleaned without having to enter. Those who do enter must wear breathing apparatus. Inflows into these tanks must be locked off to prevent the accidental opening of valves by a third party | • Atmospheric monitor (to check for oxygen, explosive and toxic gas)<br>• Harness for each entrant<br>• Lifelines<br>• Winch<br>• Personal breathing apparatus<br>• Rescue breathing apparatus<br>• Means of communication<br>• Intrinsically safe lamps<br>• Waders, overalls, gloves, helmet |

# 13 Maintenance and facilities management

There is a fundamental duty in law for the facility manager to be a part of the process, to ensure that all of the risks have been assessed, and that nothing done or which happens outside of the confined space affects the people inside. Typically, the process works as follows:

- Part 1 of the permit to work is completed by the facility manager.

- Part 2 is completed by the supervisor of the works (either contractor or employee) and then signed by the facility manager to authorise commencement of the works. The entrants' supervisor keeps the original of the permit, and a copy is kept in the facility office.

- Part 3 is completed by the supervisor on completion of the works and the original permit is handed back to the facility manager.

- The facility manager completes Part 4 and files the permit.

- Work must stop immediately if a condition in the working environment changes and causes increased danger. The permit is withdrawn and not renewed until a further risk assessment has been carried out and a fresh method statement drawn up.

**Typical safe working procedures**
In the office

- Carry out risk assessment.

- Check plans and records where available.

- Check for known engineering defects and local hazards.

- Obtain information about local weather conditions, eg do not proceed if heavy rain or other adverse weather is forecast.

- Check that the method statement written by the supervisor is adequate.

- Ensure that the supervisor briefs members of the workforce on the method statement and emergency procedures.

- Ensure that the supervisor checks and tests safety equipment for serviceability and quantity.

Before entry

- No naked flames or smoking on site.

- Secure site by use of barriers and signs.

- Prevent entry of fumes, isolate pumped flows and so on.

- Lift as many covers as are necessary to execute the work and ventilate the confined space, and erect safety barriers.

- Use a four-gas monitor to detect oxygen deficiency, flammable gas, hydrogen sulphide and carbon monoxide. Specific monitors are available for special situations. Allow a full five minutes for the monitor to give an accurate reading.

- Ventilate for two to four hours depending on monitor readings.

- Check for unusual smells.

- Visually check condition of ladders, step irons, platforms and so on.

- If possible from surface, check depth and velocity of flow where appropriate.

- Test atmosphere at all entry and exit points.

- If atmosphere test indicates hazard, continue ventilation and re-test the atmosphere. Continue until clear readings are obtained.

- Set out, prepare and check rescue equipment (breathing apparatus, rescue lines, winch and so on).

- Check the workforce's personal safety equipment.

- Re-brief working party.

- Check that walkie-talkie radios are working.

- Raise permit to work.

- Sign part 2 of permit.

Entry

- Brief as many top, intermediate and bottom workers as may be necessary.

- First person to descend on safety line, with winch in position.

- If first person down discovers any defect on descent, inform person at top.

- On arriving at landing or benching, stand clear of ladder and call next person down.

- Only one person on a ladder or step irons at a time.

- Fix safety chains and or barriers within the confined space.

**Confined space entry**
Worker with full breathing apparatus, wearing a safety harness with a lanyard connected to a winch. In an emergency, the worker can be lifted to the surface without others having to enter the manhole

Once inside

- Monitor atmosphere continuously.

- Check atmosphere monitor(s) at regular intervals.

- Inform top person when working party is ready to move off.

- Members of working party to keep together.

- Maintain continuous contact with top person.

- Walk slowly and carefully, taking care not to disturb any sludge that may be present.

- Before answering any call from top person, check each working party member and atmosphere monitors before answering.

- On arrival at benching of exit manhole, inform top person.

Emergency procedures

- If atmosphere monitors sound the alarm, put on escape breathing apparatus (if in use) and evacuate immediately.

- If depth or velocity of flow increases, evacuate immediately.

- If top person calls for working party to leave, evacuate immediately.

- Do not waste time recovering working equipment.

Accident procedures

- If a working party member collapses, put on escape breathing apparatus, take all reasonable steps to place collapsed worker in a safe position and evacuate immediately.

- Do not attempt to recover collapsed worker unless rescue breathing apparatus is available.

- Top person must raise the alarm and obtain support from colleagues with rescue breathing apparatus, and provide the emergency services and facilities manager with details of the accident.

Exit

- Members of working party who are not required for recovery of working equipment should leave. Fix safety chains or barriers.

- Ascend ladder or step irons one person at a time.

- Top person calls out each worker when exit is clear.

- Do not stand at bottom of ladder or step irons while any worker is ascending.

- When all workers have exited, conduct a headcount.

- Restore connections that were isolated prior to starting work.

- Complete, sign and return permit to the appointed person.

### Weil's disease

Weil's disease (leptospirosis) is an infectious disease caused by rats' urine. The main source of infection is sewers, but it is also found in water and land around canals and docklands, railway stations, disused sites and other locations where rats are or have been present. Infection can be fatal.

It is essential that all employees exposed to the risk of Weil's disease are made aware of the risks and the hygiene precautions necessary. People working in sewers must be given individual training, written information and, in case of illness, a card containing information required by doctors to enable them to diagnose the disease correctly.

A briefing and a card format are contained in a toolbox talk in Appendix B.

Also read...

Chapter 7 – Fragile roofs and roof lights

Appendix B – Roofs

### Roof work

The maintenance of roofs presents many risks, particularly from fragile roof lights and old roofs made of asbestos cement.

- All roof lights must be assumed to be fragile. Only specialist contractors should carry out work on or near them.

- All roofs that do not have a 1.1m high parapet should have a fall arrest system installed to protect roofers when carrying out maintenance. Specialist contractors can readily fix these to most roofs.

- All asbestos cement and other fragile roofs must have signs attached to them indicating that they are fragile, and other signs prohibiting access.

- Edge protection is required for large works, eg replacement of roof sheets.

### The bottom line

**By law, you must:**

- maintain essential services in good working order, including electrical systems, emergency lighting, air conditioning systems, water supply systems, gas installations, lifts, escalators, powered doors and gates
- organise annual checks and inspections of fire extinguishers, heat/smoke detectors and sprinklers
- arrange annual checks and inspections of cradles, fixed window cleaning equipment, and window cleaning and other safety harness anchorage points
- carry out testing of portable electrical appliances
- maintain air conditioning and hot and cold water supply systems to prevent the growth of Legionella bacteria
- establish whether asbestos is present in your premises, and decide if you need to have it removed; if it is to stay, you must maintain it in good condition, label it clearly, and maintain a register of the type and location of asbestos on the premises
- carry out risk assessments in relation to hot works, confined space entry and roof work; in the case of confined spaces, you must avoid entry if at all practicable
- use permits to work to control confined space entry, hot works and electrical works
- provide sewer and river workers with information and training in relation to Weil's disease and require them to carry a card containing relevant information needed by doctors in the event of illness.

## Introduction

The chapters on construction and demolition and maintenance and facilities management highlight the importance of using specialist contractors to carry out activities that are not within an organisation's competence. The range and complexity of technologies and risks in the workplace make the use of contractors imperative for most organisations, and those that do not use them to the full extent often neglect essential health and safety activities. This chapter shows you how to acquire good contractors and make them an asset, not a liability.

## Shared responsibility

One of the most difficult concepts for many managers to grasp is that by using a contractor you are not divesting yourself of all health and safety responsibility for an activity. This is a fact that has been demonstrated in court many times. As the employer, client and occupier of the premises, you are still liable in law. You can contract out the work, but not the overall responsibility for what happens.

As a general rule, the client or employing organisation has a shared responsibility in law with the contractor in the following circumstances:

- where something done by the contractor affects the health and safety of the client's workforce or the public

- where something done by the client organisation affects the health and safety of the contractor's employees or the general public

- where the employing organisation is the 'expert' and the contractor is told by the employer how to proceed

- where the client fails to inform the contractor of all the risks that they know about

- where the client appoints an incompetent contractor or a contractor who has inadequate resources

Of course, in the event of actions brought before a court of law, each case is decided on its own merits, and the list above can only act as a guide. To be on the right side of the law, therefore, employers should monitor contractors to ensure that they meet the standards required by law and the employing organisation.

A simple example illustrates the concept of shared responsibility. A food manufacturer's production line is in a building that has an asbestos cement roof. As the roof is in poor condition, the manufacturer decides to have it replaced by contractors. The production line is to be kept running, and therefore any asbestos dust that falls from the roof will land on the production line and contaminate the food.

Here the food manufacturer, as the employer of the contractor, has made a key decision that has created a hazard. Having created the hazard, the employer must ensure that extensive measures are taken to isolate the roof works from the food production area.

The contractor has to be told about the risks before he/she prices the work, and the employer has to ensure that an adequate safe system of work is developed.

In this example of shared legal responsibility, it is reasonable to expect the employer to take steps to ensure that the roofer's activities do not contaminate the food. However, it is not reasonable to expect the employer to go up on the roof to check that the roofers are working safely and are not likely to fall and injure themselves. That is the responsibility of the contractor.

There are occasions, however, when the client or employer is responsible for the health and safety of contractors' personnel. This can occur when the client does something that may affect the health and safety of the contractor's staff, eg making live a power circuit that a contractor's electrician has first isolated before working on. There are also situations where the consequences of failure are so great that the client effectively has to supervise the work, eg some activities in chemical plants and oil refineries.

### Building work

Chapter 7 sets out the relationships between client, consultants and contractors in construction and demolition works. In practical terms, the client must ensure that the building works do not create hazards for the organisation's staff and premises, or the public. Examples of such 'interface' issues include:

- fencing the site to prevent unauthorised access (this includes both small and large sites or places of work)

- maintaining fire detectors, fire alarms and sprinklers, or substituting them with other measures

- maintaining all fire exits and fire escape routes, or substituting them with other measures

- erecting scaffolding safely in occupied areas, outside of normal working hours

- isolating asbestos removal, construction and demolition areas, including the labelling and removal of asbestos waste

- removing rubbish efficiently without blocking fire exits or causing a fire hazard

- segregating construction vehicles and lorries from public areas and pedestrians

- prohibiting the over-sailing of public areas by cranes, in case an item of material is dropped.

### Partnering

Partnering is the process of using a small list of selected contractors to carry out work, often to agreed rates of remuneration. This has much to commend it as it allows the contractor to build up knowledge of the facility or business and its risks. It also saves time for busy managers, as they do not have to keep briefing different companies. It allows a stable and trusted workforce to be established, which is by far the best way of achieving good health and safety performance.

There are many types of partnering. One type, the use of term contractors, involves the employer committing contractually to a selected contractor for a predetermined period, usually two or three years. In return, the contractor provides a stable and committed workforce, to agreed costs. Obviously, term contractors have to be chosen with care, whereas an informal partner can be dropped if they do not perform.

### How to select a good contractor

There are many health and safety considerations to be taken into account when selecting a contractor (alongside other matters, such as quality and service). Initially, it is best to use a formal process. This can then be supplemented by measures of performance as the initial contract is carried out, such as accident and incident statistics. This experience may then enable a simplification of the paper process for subsequent work, unless it is very different from the first contract. Working experience is always a better measure of a contractor than replies to questionnaires.

The process has four stages, as shown in the following diagram.

## The contractor procurement process

**Stage 1: Pre-qualification**
Send a questionnaire to a number of contractors, asking for answers to a set of health and safety questions. The questionnaire is reviewed and those with a satisfactory response are allowed to tender for work.

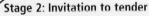

**Stage 2: Invitation to tender**
The smart way to procure contractors is to get this stage right. The tender documents should accurately describe the job, what will and will not be provided, and what the risks are. The aim is to get a quote from the contractor that covers everything that has cost implications. If the contractor allows for all costs, there should not be a problem in paying for them once the contract has started. But if items are inadvertently or deliberately left out of the equation, then health and safety will inevitably suffer.

**Stage 4: Pre-start meeting**
This is the final meeting after award of the contract but before work starts. At this meeting, detailed arrangements are discussed with the managers who will be overseeing the work. Part of the meeting should be devoted to presenting the method statement or safe system of work, and verifying the qualifications and skills of those who will actually carry out the work.

Further details on each of these stages, including samples of documents, are to be found at the end of this chapter.

**Stage 3: Mid-tender interview**
At this stage, the main health and safety considerations are competency and resources. Detailed questions are asked about the general competency of the contractor's workforce and supervision. In addition, resources are discussed, both human and physical, to make sure that the works can be executed safely within the agreed timescale.

### Also read...

Chapter 7 – Commissioning construction works

Chapter 7 – Construction phase health and safety plan

### Co-operation and co-ordination

At the outset, it is essential to establish that the contractor (or all contractors, where there are two or more) will co-operate with the client or employer, and allow their activities to be co-ordinated. For construction works, this is enshrined in law. Nothing leads to unsafe working conditions more quickly than a multitude of contractors all doing their own thing without regard for each other or for the main undertaking. Allowing it to happen is weak management and could lead to disaster.

The key to co-operation and co-ordination is to establish weekly meetings that include health and safety as an agenda item. If all contractors attend the meeting, everyone is given the opportunity to voice their opinions, and to hear at firsthand the decisions that are made. This meeting should be minuted, especially if dealing with safety critical issues where strict instructions must be followed.

A monthly meeting, attended by each contractor's director, can reinforce the weekly meeting and be a forum for contractors to present a monthly report that, among other things, covers health and safety.

### What is...

An inspection?
An inspection is a check of physical conditions and behaviour.

### Monitoring

Contractors should make health and safety inspections of their own works using an in-house or consultant health and safety specialist. Reports should be prepared and copies given to the employer, together with a note of any actions taken.

Depending on the risks and nature of the work, many clients commission their own health and safety inspections or audits – in addition to those carried out by the contractor – in order to verify that the works are proceeding safely. This is recommended good practice.

### What is...

An audit?
An audit is a detailed examination of the entire work process and includes safe systems of work and training records.

### Induction

It is standard practice for all contractors' personnel working in an employer's premises to be inducted before starting work on their first day. A format for an induction session is given in Appendix A. This induction can be carried out by the employer, or by the contractor to an agreed format that is monitored by the employer. It is essential that the induction includes information on the risks and the emergency arrangements on the premises.

### Also read...

Chapter 7 – Workforce information and training

### Information and training

All employees must be provided with information on the hazards and risks, and the safe system of work, as set out in method statements and operating manuals. The responsibility of the employer's facility manager is to make relevant risks known to the contractors and check that they take these into account in their method statements. It is the responsibility of contractors to communicate the safe system of work to their employees and any subcontractors they use, and to supervise the work, ensuring that the safe systems or method statements are followed.

## Stage 1

| Contractor's health and safety competency questionnaire | | |
|---|---|---|
| This questionnaire will be used to assess your competency regarding health and safety. Please take time to complete it carefully. | **Issuing company:** | |

www.protect.org.uk

PDF 20

For which contract is this form being completed?
Name of contractor/supplier
Trade or business
Address



Telephone                    Fax                         email

### 1. Health and safety policy

Do you have a health and safety policy?        Yes/No        Please enclose a copy. Attached?        Yes/No
Is it signed by a director?                    Yes/No

### 2. Health and safety advice

Do you have a person who provides you with health and safety advice?        Yes/No
Name                    Qualifications        Employer        Telephone

### 3. Employee training

| Do you provide any of the following training: | Employees | Subcontractors | |
|---|---|---|---|
| Induction? | Yes/No | Yes/No | n/a |
| Skills/trade? | Yes/No | Yes/No | n/a |
| Toolbox talks? | Yes/No | Yes/No | n/a |
| Abrasive wheels/cartridge tools/mobile towers? | Yes/No | Yes/No | n/a |
| Mobile plant? | Yes/No | Yes/No | n/a |
| First aid? | Yes/No | Yes/No | n/a |

### 4. Management/supervision training

| Do you provide any of the following training: | Employees | Subcontractors |
|---|---|---|
| Managers' five-day health and safety course? | Yes/No | Yes/No |
| Supervisors' five-day health and safety course? | Yes/No | Yes/No |
| Other managers'/supervisors' health and safety training course(s)? | Yes/No | Yes/No |

### 5. Monitoring

Do you carry out health and safety inspections of your activities?        Yes/No
Who does these inspections?
What is the frequency of inspections?
Are written reports prepared, and do they outline specific actions required?        Yes/No

### 6. Risk assessment

Do you carry out risk assessment of your activities?        Yes/No
Do you produce task-specific method statements?        Yes/No
How do you communicate these to your workforce?

### 7. Subcontractors

Do you employ subcontractors (including labour only)?        Yes/No
How do you check their health and safety competency?

## Stage 1 (continued)

**www.protect.org.uk**

PDF 20

### What are...

**Inspectors allowed to do?**
HSE and local authority inspectors can:
- gain access to premises at any time without a warrant
- use the police to assist their enquiries
- carry out investigations and take statements
- remove documents and equipment
- issue prohibition and improvement notices
- prosecute offenders.

### What is...

**A prohibition notice?**
A prohibition notice is the means by which an HSE or local authority inspector informs an employer that there is an imminent risk of serious injury. Work may not proceed until the notice has been acted on, otherwise prosecution will follow.

### What is...

**An improvement notice?**
An improvement notice indicates a contravention of regulations, but unlike the prohibition notice it allows a time period for the matter in question to be rectified. Failure to comply may lead to prosecution.

**8. Accident statistics for the past three years**

|  | Year 1 | | Year 2 | | Year 3 | |
|---|---|---|---|---|---|---|
|  | Employees | Subcontractors | Employees | Subcontractors | Employees | Subcontractors |
| **Average employed** |  |  |  |  |  |  |
| **Fatal injuries** |  |  |  |  |  |  |
| **Major injuries** |  |  |  |  |  |  |
| **Over-three-day injuries** |  |  |  |  |  |  |

**9. Enforcement action**
Please provide details of all HSE, Environment Agency or local authority prosecutions, prohibition or improvement notices in the past three years

**10. Membership of health and safety groups/trade associations**
Please provide details

Completed by (capitals)
Title
Signature                                    Date

Assessment:

## Stage 2

| Information to be provided by employer/client to contractors when tendering |
|---|

### 1. Standards

- Health and safety standards that apply, including site rules
- Arrangements for workforce induction
- Arrangements for co-ordination and communication between the employer and contractors, such as a meeting schedule or reporting requirements
- Information about the employer's/client's requirements for monitoring or supervision
- Welfare arrangements
- For a construction project, the pre-tender health and safety plan (see Chapter 7)

### 2. Methods

- Outline method statement as anticipated by the employer/client
- Information about facilities to be provided, such as scaffolding or other forms of access. Make clear who will be providing and inspecting/maintaining the facilities, so that the contractor can cost the works appropriately

### 3. Information on the risks

- Details of the relevant hazards and constraints within which the contractor must work
- Information about fire and emergency systems that must be maintained
- Information about the condition of the buildings and the presence of asbestos, fragile roofs or roof lights, contaminated land, unstable structures and so on
- Information about any process that may influence the health and safety of the contractor's personnel, such as the use of chemicals (in this particular case, data sheets must be provided)
- Any relevant information from consultants' reports, eg asbestos survey

*Note: the objective is to make the contractor as familiar with the facility and its risks as the employer's/client's own staff*

## Stage 3

www.protect.org.uk

PDF 22

| Specific checks of competency and resources during a tender interview |
| --- |

The facility or project team should assess the general competence of the contractor's personnel and the human and physical resources to be employed. The team must be satisfied that both the resources and standards of competence are adequate.

When asking the following questions, evidence need not be seen at this stage. However, advise the contractor that the answers will be minuted and that, should the contractor be successful, certification will be required before work starts and when personnel change during the contract.

### 1. Competency
**Managers**
- Are managers experienced in this work? Name similar appointments.
- Are managers appropriately qualified? Which qualifications?
- Are managers trained in health and safety? Which course(s)?
- Are there sufficient managers? Determine ratio and structure.

**Supervisors**
- Are supervisors experienced in this work? Name similar projects or roles.
- Are supervisors appropriately skills-certificated? (All supervisors should be.) Which schemes?
- Are supervisors trained in health and safety? Which course(s)?
- Are there sufficient supervisors? Determine ratio.

**Employees**
- Are employees experienced in this type of work? Name jobs.
- What percentage of tradesmen are skills-certificated? Which schemes?
- Are employees trained in health and safety? Which course(s) or training scheme(s)?

### 2. Resources
- Considering the scope of work and time allowed, is the size of the management/supervisory team and workforce adequate?
- Is the contractor proposing a method of work that minimises risks and the amount of manual labour needed, by using the latest equipment and technology? (There is a statutory duty to minimise risk in this way.)
- Has manual handling been eliminated, as far as is practicable, by the use of mechanised plant?
- How are the major hazards to be controlled, particularly fall protection, and what equipment will be used?
- Obtain a list of the contractor's subcontractors and ask how their competency and resources are checked. Are you satisfied with the proposed arrangements?

### 3. Documentation
Minute this meeting and the answers to these questions for future reference.

## Stage 4

| Information to be supplied by contractors prior to beginning work |
| --- |

www.protect.org.uk

PDF 23

### 1. Organisation

- Health and safety policy statement.
- Health and safety organisation chart.
- Name of site supervisor responsible for safety.
- Name of safety practitioner and visiting frequency.
- CVs of site manager, safety practitioner and any other key personnel.

### 2. Risk control

- Contractor's written risk assessments and method statements, including the safe system of work to control the hazards identified. Resources such as plant and equipment should equal those promised at tender.
- Noise assessments for plant and operations creating excessive noise.
- COSHH and manual handling assessments, where applicable.

### 3. Proof of competency

- Copies of managers', supervisors' and employees' health and safety training certificates.
- Copies of supervisors' and employees' skills certification certificates.
- Copies of plant operators' certificates of training achievement.

### 4. Proof of resources

- The numbers of managers and supervisors compared with those promised in the tender interview.
- Details of subcontracting by the contractor, ie names of subcontractors and details of their management, supervision, workforce numbers and competency.

---

### The bottom line

**By law, as an employer you must:**

- appoint competent contractors who have adequate resources to complete the task safely
- provide contractors with information on the hazards and risks that are known to the employer/client
- monitor the contractor's activities where they could cause a risk to the employer's/client's undertaking, workforce or the public
- provide co-ordination and secure co-operation and supervision where the employer's/client's activities could pose a danger to the contractor.

# Useful health and safety tools

## Assessments

www.protect.org.uk

PDF 24

### Risk assessment and method statement

Employer:

Title:

| Assessment no: | Date: | Revision: | Review date: | Assessor: |
|---|---|---|---|---|
| | | | | |

### Organisation

Location of work (include sketch plans where possible):

| Start date: | Duration: |
|---|---|

Sequence of work (include programme if reference made to it):

| Name of supervisor responsible: | List any subcontractors involved: |
|---|---|
| Number of persons involved: | |
| Plant and equipment to be used: | Materials to be used: |

### Method statement and task briefing

Keep sentences brief and to the point, and use sketches and drawings where possible. Refer to the control measures checklist later in this section. Use additional sheets if necessary. Fully describe the task and control measures to provide a method statement, and then carry out a risk assessment. Revise the method and control measures as required to minimise risk, using a new form if necessary. This should then be used to brief the workforce on the safe way to perform the task.

| Hazard identification checklist | Yes | No | | Yes | No |
|---|---|---|---|---|---|
| Work at height | | | Electrical | | |
| Fall of material | | | Lighting | | |
| Slips and trips | | | Fire | | |
| Machinery/lifting equipment | | | Hazardous substances | | |
| Vehicle–pedestrian segregation | | | Dust/fumes/vapours (state which) | | |
| Construction/demolition/excavations (state which) | | | Personal/environmental noise (state which) | | |
| Confined spaces | | | Vibration | | |
| Radiation/chemicals (state which) | | | Control of contractors | | |
| Manual handling | | | Other(s) (provide details) | | |
| **Who might be harmed?** | | | | | |
| Own personnel | | | Office staff/visitors | | |
| Trainees/young workers | | | Cleaners/maintenance workers/security guards | | |
| Contractors | | | Members of the public | | |

**Risk assessment**

| Severity of harm | | MAJOR – death, major injury, permanent environmental damage, incapacitating ill health or serious harm to reputation | SERIOUS – three-day-plus injury, temporary ill health or environmental damage, moderate harm to reputation | SLIGHT – less than three-day injury, minor health effect, no harm to reputation |
|---|---|---|---|---|
| | Tick box ▶ | | | |
| **Likelihood of occurrence** | | HIGH – near certain or large numbers exposed | MEDIUM – frequent or many people exposed | LOW – harm seldom occurs |
| | Tick box ▶ | | | |
| **Risk assessment** | INTOLERABLE – change method and re-assess | HIGH – improve control measures and re-assess | MEDIUM – review control measures for best practice | LOW – satisfactory |
| Tick box ▶ | | | | |

| Control measures checklist | | | | | |
|---|---|---|---|---|---|
| **Personal protective equipment needed** | Yes | No | | Yes | No |
| Safety helmet | | | Gloves | | |
| Protective footwear | | | Hearing protection | | |
| High-visibility clothing | | | Overalls | | |
| Eye protection | | | Body harness | | |
| Face respirator (specify type) | | | Other(s) (provide details) | | |
| **Training certificates required and to be checked** | | | | | |
| Scaffold | | | Mobile elevating work platform | | |
| Forklift/dumper | | | Mobile access tower | | |
| Excavator/crane/construction plant | | | Slinger/signaller | | |
| Abrasive wheels | | | Other(s) (provide details) | | |
| **Permits required** | | | **Assessments required (attach)** | | |
| Hot works | | | Hazardous substances | | |
| Electrical | | | Noise | | |
| Excavation | | | Manual handling | | |
| Confined space | | | Other(s) (provide details) | | |
| Other(s) (provide details) | | | | | |
| **Security/rescue measures required?** | | | **First aid measures required?** | | |
| Details: | | | Details: | | |
| Any alterations to existing systems (eg traffic re-routing, fire detection and alarm systems)? | | | Monitoring required? | | |
| | | | Task briefing | | |
| Details: | | | Control measures – frequency? Who will monitor? | | |
| | | | Lifting equipment certification | | |
| Signed (assessor): | | Print name: | | Date: | |

| Manual handling assessment | | www.protect.org.uk |  |
| --- | --- | --- | --- |
| | | PDF 25 | |

| Employer: |
| --- |
| Project/department: |
| Description of operation: |
| Names of persons affected: |

## Section 1

| Is there a risk of injury? | | | Yes | No |
| --- | --- | --- | --- | --- |
| Can the operation be: | avoided? | (If the answer to any of the questions is 'yes', proceed and check result is satisfactory. If the answer is 'no', go to Section 2.) | | |
| | mechanised? | | | |
| | automated? | | | |

## Section 2

| The tasks – do they involve: | Yes | No | Working environment – are there: | Yes | No |
| --- | --- | --- | --- | --- | --- |
| holding loads away from trunk? | | | constraints on posture? | | |
| twisting? | | | poor floors? | | |
| stooping? | | | slopes or steps? | | |
| reaching upwards? | | | hot, cold or humid conditions? | | |
| carrying loads long distances/up stairs? | | | strong air movements? | | |
| insufficient rest or recovery? | | | poor lighting conditions? | | |
| strenuous pushing or pulling? | | | **The loads – are they:** | | |
| unpredictable movement of loads? | | | heavy? (state weight) | | |
| repetitive handling? | | | bulky/unwieldy? | | |
| excessive work rate? | | | difficult to grasp? | | |
| **Individual capability – does the job process:** | | | unstable/unpredictable? | | |
| require unusual capability? | | | harmful, eg sharp or hot? | | |
| endanger those with a physical weakness? | | | **Is movement affected by:** | | |
| endanger those who are ill/pregnant? | | | clothing? | | |
| call for special information/training? | | | PPE? | | |

| Section 3 – Overall assessment of risk | | | | | | |
|---|---|---|---|---|---|---|
| Overall assessment of the risk of injury | Low | | Medium | | High | |

If 'low', the assessment need go no further. If 'medium' or 'high', go to Section 4.

| Section 4 – Measures to reduce the risk to 'low' |
|---|
| Method statement for safe handling: |

*Note: use additional sheets as required to describe fully the method of safe handling*

| Signed (assessor): | Print name: | Date: |
|---|---|---|

| **Hazardous substance assessment** | www.protect.org.uk <br> PDF 26 |  |
| --- | --- | --- |

Employer:

Substance:

Manufacturer:

Describe the process or tasks that result in exposure:

### Hazard identification (tick as appropriate)

| **Corrosive** | | **Toxic** | | **Harmful/Irritant** | | **Oxidising** | | **Explosive** | | **Flammable** | |
| --- | --- | --- | --- | --- | --- | --- | --- | --- | --- | --- | --- |
| Yes | No | Yes | No | Yes | No | Yes | No | Yes | No | Yes | No |
| | | | | | | | | | | | |

| **Exposure** | | **Engineering controls** | Yes | No |
| --- | --- | --- | --- | --- |
| What quantity is used? | | Can the process be isolated? | | |
| How often are people exposed? | | Can the process be enclosed? | | |
| What is the duration of exposure? | | Is ventilation/extraction needed? | | |

| **Hazard identification** | Yes | No | | Yes | No |
| --- | --- | --- | --- | --- | --- |
| Hazardous by inhalation (through breathing)? | | | Irritant to the skin – dermatitis? | | |
| Hazardous by ingestion (through eating)? | | | Irritant to the eyes? | | |
| Hazardous by absorption (through the skin)? | | | Asthma causing? | | |
| Hazardous by chemical burns? | | | Cancer causing? | | |

| **If the answer to any of the following questions is 'yes', attach relevant information to this form** | Yes | No |
| --- | --- | --- |
| 1.  Is manufacturer's hazard information sheet available and included? | | |
| 2.  Does the substance readily form a vapour? If so, describe how it affects health. | | |
| 3.  Does it have a workplace exposure limit? If so, state limits. | | |
| 4.  Will exposure monitoring (including biological monitoring) and/or control measures be required? | | |
| 5.  Is specific training required? | | |
| 6.  Will health surveillance be necessary? | | |
| 7.  Does substance need to be disposed of by an authorised waste disposal contractor? | | |
| 8.  Have storage requirements for the substance been provided or arranged with site? | | |

| Personal protective equipment (tick where necessary) | | | | | | | | | |
|---|---|---|---|---|---|---|---|---|---|
| Face mask/ respirator | | Eye protection | | Gloves | | Boots | | Overalls | |

Fully describe the safe method of use and highlight any additional precautions, actions or control measures required (attach additional sheets if necessary):

| Signed (assessor): | Print name: | Date: |
|---|---|---|

| Workstation assessment | | | www.protect.org.uk | |
|---|---|---|---|---|
| | | | PDF 27 |  |

Name:

Department:

Job:

Average time spent using DSE each day:

| 1. Display screen | Yes | No | Action |
|---|---|---|---|
| Is the screen clean? | | | |
| Is the screen large enough to see the characters clearly? Ask the user. | | | |
| Are there any reflections on the screen? If so, use a mirror to check where they are coming from. It is better to site monitors with their backs to windows to avoid reflections. If necessary, window blinds should be provided. | | | |
| Is there any glare on the screen? Glare may come from the wrong type of overhead lighting. If so, directional diffusers are required. | | | |
| Does the screen appear to flicker? If so, the monitor refresh rate may be too low or it may be that the room lighting frequency is too low and needs upgrading. | | | |
| Are the brightness and contrast correctly adjusted? | | | |
| Does the monitor swivel and tilt? The monitor must be able to swivel and tilt so that the user can adopt a comfortable working posture. | | | |
| Is the monitor propped up on books or similar? A monitor that is propped up on books is a sure sign of problems with the workstation, and if necessary a proper support should be provided. | | | |
| **2. Keyboard and mouse** | **Yes** | **No** | **Action** |
| Is the keyboard separate from the monitor? Note that laptops are not designed for extended daily use in an office environment. The screen and keyboard are too small and the user is forced to adopt a cramped posture. | | | |
| Where laptops are used, is a separate keyboard provided for more extensive use? | | | |
| Is the keyboard tiltable? | | | |
| Is it possible to rest the forearms on the chair or desk while using the keyboard and/or mouse, and without over-stretching or bending the wrists? | | | |
| Does the user hit the keys too hard? Hitting the keys too hard applies unnecessary force on the fingers. | | | |
| Is the keyboard in good condition and glare-free? | | | |
| Does the user make excessive use of the mouse? | | | |
| Is the mouse in good condition? Work with a mouse can tend to concentrate activity on one arm or even one finger. Intensive use can lead to problems in the fingers, hands, wrists, arms or shoulders. | | | |

| 3. Chair | Yes | No | Action |
|---|---|---|---|
| Is the chair stable, on casters, and in good condition? Having a chair that moves easily is a legal requirement. | | | |
| Is the seat height adjustable? Having adjustable seat height is a legal requirement. The arms should be horizontal and the eyes roughly at the same height as the top of the VDU casing. | | | |
| Is the seat back adjustable in terms of both height and tilt? Having adjustable seat back height and tilt is a legal requirement. | | | |
| Does the chair support the small of the back? | | | |
| Is the back straight, supported and relaxed, or is the user leaning forward? | | | |
| Do the arms of the chair (where fitted) prevent the user getting close enough to use the keyboard comfortably? | | | |
| Is the seat correctly adjusted for the user and does the user understand how to adjust the seat? | | | |
| With the chair adjusted to the correct height for the desk, is a footrest required? | | | |

| 4. Desk | Yes | No | Action |
|---|---|---|---|
| Is the desk large enough for its purpose? The monitor should be capable of being set back a reasonable distance from the keyboard and there should be enough space in front of the keyboard to rest the arms. With typical office furniture, there is often insufficient space for large monitors. However, the problem can be solved using flat panel monitors. | | | |
| Is there sufficient space on the desk for documents? A computer-aided design operator or magazine editor will require more desk space than a secretary, for example. | | | |
| Personal printers take up desk space – is a personal printer necessary? | | | |
| Is a document holder available? | | | |
| If a document holder is used, is it stable and adjustable (so as to minimise the need for uncomfortable head and eye movements)? | | | |
| Is the desk surface anti-reflective? | | | |

| 5. Environment | Yes | No | Action |
|---|---|---|---|
| Is there adequate space around the desk? | | | |
| Are the temperature and lighting comfortable? | | | |
| Is the area free from distracting equipment noise? A workstation sited next to a high volume photocopier, for example, would be an excessively noisy work environment. | | | |
| Does the work area have adequate ventilation, and is it free from draughts? | | | |
| Are the power cables properly managed and in good condition? | | | |
| Is the equipment positioned so as to ensure that it doesn't fall off the desk and cause injury/damage? | | | |
| Is the space under the desk free from an excessive number of power cables and multiple connectors, allowing the user freedom of movement? | | | |
| **6. Software** | Yes | No | Action |
| Is the software user-friendly and suitable for the task? | | | |
| Has the user had sufficient software training? Ask the user. | | | |
| Does the software force the work pace? It should not do so unless there is an agreement with the user. | | | |
| **7. Other issues** | Yes | No | Action |
| Has the user had an eyesight test? | | | |
| Is there evidence that an eyesight test would be appropriate? | | | |
| Are records kept of eyesight testing? | | | |
| Does the user require training on the use of the equipment? | | | |
| Is the user able to get away from the workstation on a regular basis? Breaks away from the workstation help to rest the eyes and body, which is necessary for good health. | | | |
| Has the user experienced any headaches, eyestrain or aches and pains that may be attributable to VDU use? | | | |
| Does the user wish to raise any other issues? | | | |

| Signed (assessor): | Print name: | Date: |
|---|---|---|

## Permits to work

www.protect.org.uk

PDF 28

| Hot works permit to work | | |
|---|---|---|
| Facility or project: | Permit number: | |
| Contractor/department carrying out the work: | | |
| Location of work: | | |
| Description of work and equipment used: | | |
| Date of permit (the supervisor responsible for the works must sign permits on the day specified – permits are only available for single shifts): | Day and date: | Time:<br>between<br>and |

**Precautions to be taken:**

- hot works must cease one hour before end of shift
- all gas cylinders must be transported and kept upright
- valves and hoses must be in good condition and all gas cylinders must be fitted with flashback arresters
- when not in use, gas cylinders must be shut off and returned to store
- gas cylinders must not be left in the building overnight without formal approval
- minimum radius of hot works from other workers must be 1.5m (screens should be erected where necessary)
- work areas to be kept tidy and free from combustible materials
- services affected must be isolated before work commences
- a suitable fire extinguisher must be available
- the supervisor must ensure that suitable personal protective equipment is provided and worn, and that there is a good working platform
- isolate smoke detectors in the vicinity of hot works
- spent welding rods must be immersed in a bucket of water.

**Employees must:**

- understand the fire and safety precautions and be in possession of a permit
- stop work if required to do so by an authorised person
- report immediately any hazard likely to affect the fire and safety precautions
- remain in the area for 15 minutes following completion of work to check that no fire starts.

**Confirmation by contractor or department supervisor**

I confirm that the precautions specified above will be maintained and I will ensure that the persons carrying out the work will comply with these precautions.

| Signed: | Print name: | Date: |
|---|---|---|
| | | |

**Authorisation by facility or project manager**

I certify that the above work can commence with the precautions listed above.

| Signed: | Print name: | Date: |
|---|---|---|
| | | |

**Cancellation by contractor or department supervisor**

I confirm that the work has been completed/stopped, and that the area has been checked by me and is safe.

| Signed: | Print name: | Date: |
|---|---|---|
| | | |

**Cancellation by facility or project manager**

I confirm that the work has been completed/stopped, and that the area has been checked by me and is safe.

| Signed: | Print name: | Date: |
|---|---|---|
| | | |

www.protect.org.uk

PDF 29

## Confined space entry permit to work

| Facility or project: | Permit number: |
|---|---|

Contractor/department carrying out work:

Location of work:

Description of work and equipment used:

| Date of permit (the supervisor responsible for the works must sign permits on the day specified – permits are only available for single shifts): | Day and date: | Time: between and |
|---|---|---|

Known hazards:

| Persons involved (whether or not they will enter space): | Number in gang: |
|---|---|

## Precautions (tick as applicable)

| | Yes | No | n/a | | Yes | No | n/a |
|---|---|---|---|---|---|---|---|
| Systems of work checked | | | | Warning signs/barriers | | | |
| Adequate supply of oxygen | | | | Watchers to be posted | | | |
| Breathing apparatus worn | | | | Radio communication link | | | |
| Atmosphere tested | | | | Flameproof/intrinsically safe lighting available | | | |
| Continuous monitoring in place | | | | Gaseous flows stopped/sealed | | | |
| Safety harness/lifeline available | | | | Liquid flows stopped/sealed | | | |
| Flood warning system in place | | | | Forced ventilation provided | | | |
| Dangerous deposits removed | | | | Protective clothing worn | | | |
| Adequate access/egress | | | | Emergency procedures and rescue equipment in place | | | |
| Free from toxic/ flammable substances | | | | First aider in attendance | | | |
| Safety equipment checked and working | | | | | | | |
| Nearest telephone located at: | | | | Emergency telephone nos: | | | |

| **Part 1 Authorisation by facility or project manager** | | |
| --- | --- | --- |
| This permit covers entry to the above confined space only. All work entailed in effecting entry must be covered with an approved method statement and risk assessment. | | |
| Method statement/risk assessment checked? | Yes/No | |
| Supervisor's confined space training checked? | Yes/No | |
| I certify that the above work can commence with the precautions listed above. | | |
| Signed: | Print name: | Date: |

| **Part 2 Confirmation by contractor or department supervisor** | | |
| --- | --- | --- |
| I confirm that the persons listed above have been made familiar with the safety and emergency arrangements, risk assessment and method statement, and are properly equipped. I am satisfied that the atmosphere within the confined space is safe to work in at present and will be monitored continuously. | | |
| Signed: | Print name: | Date: |
| Countersigned by facility or project manager: | Print name: | Date: |

**To be read to workforce by supervisor**

- At first sign of dizziness, eye irritation, headache, pulsating of the temples or nausea, vacate confined space at once.

- If you suspect that a colleague has been overcome, do not attempt to enter the confined space unless equipped with and trained in the use of suitable breathing apparatus. Summon effective help quickly.

- Any adverse changes in conditions in the confined space must be reported immediately to the facility manager.

- If for any reason work conditions change, work must stop immediately, the confined space must be evacuated, and the facility manager should be informed.

| **Part 3 Cancellation by contractor or department supervisor** | | |
| --- | --- | --- |
| The work detailed in this permit has been completed/stopped and all employees under my control have been withdrawn and warned that it is no longer safe to work in the confined space. I confirm that the site has been made safe and that equipment will be returned to store and any discrepancies reported. I have noted any changes that have occurred in the confined space. | | |
| Signed: | Print name: | Date: |

| **Part 4 Cancellation by facility or project manager** | | |
| --- | --- | --- |
| This permit is cancelled. I have noted any changes reported and taken the necessary action. | | |
| Signed: | Print name: | Date: |

# Reports

| Safety, health and welfare inspection report | |
|---|---|
| Facility or project: | Date: |
| To: Facility manager/project manager: | |
| Copy: | |
| Safety adviser: | |

www.protect.org.uk

PDF 30

**Safety performance indicators (decide on minimum scores for satisfactory performance and take action below this level, detailed in 'Description' box below)**

| Item | Scores out of 10 |
|---|---|
| Safety paperwork (policy, procedures, risk assessments and so on) | |
| Scaffold/edge protection | |
| Personal protective equipment | |
| Plant/equipment/lifting | |
| Access/ladders/towers | |
| Excavations/floor openings | |
| Public protection/traffic routes | |
| Fire safety | |
| Housekeeping/lighting | |
| Welfare | |

**Site inspection and advice given on future issues**

| Item | Description | Action required by (name and date) | Date rectified |
|---|---|---|---|
| | | | |
| | | | |
| | | | |
| | | | |
| | | | |
| | | | |
| | | | |

www.protect.org.uk

PDF 31

| Accident investigation report | Sheet no. 1 of 4 |
|---|---|

**Organisation name:**

**Name and address of the premises or site where the accident occurred:**

| Investigation date: | Report date: |
|---|---|
| Date of accident/near miss: | Time of accident: |

| Where on the premises/site did the accident happen? | Nature of work being undertaken: | Weather conditions: |
|---|---|---|

**Name of injured person:**

| Home address: | Age: |
|---|---|
| | Date of birth: |
| Postcode: | Job title: |
| Telephone: | Return to work date/expected return to work date: |

**Employer's name and address:**

Postcode:

Telephone:

| Was the injured person: | on work experience? | on a training scheme? | self-employed? | a member of the public? |
|---|---|---|---|---|
| Tick box ▶ | | | | |
| Hospital attended: | | | Detained? | |

| Accident investigation report (continued) | Sheet no. 2 of 4 |
|---|---|

**Injuries/damage**

What was the injury (eg fracture, cut)?

Which part of the body was injured?

| **Delete as appropriate** | Was the injury fatal/major/over-three-day/lost time (shift following the accident lost), and was property damaged? |
|---|---|
| | Did the injured person become unconscious/need resuscitation/remain in hospital for more than 24 hours/none of these? |
| | Was the accident a dangerous occurrence as defined in RIDDOR? If so, state type of dangerous occurrence |

**Witnesses**

| Name: | Name: |
|---|---|
| Address: | Address: |
| Telephone: | Telephone· |

**Contractual arrangements**

Where applicable, outline the relationship between the injured person's employer and the controller of the premises.

| Accident investigation report (continued) | Sheet no. 3 of 4 |
|---|---|

Organisation name:

Date of accident:

Name of injured person:

Investigation (give a full description of the incident):

Plant involved (state description of plant, identifying numbers, name of owner and details of any damage):

Contributory causes of the accident:

Management actions taken since the accident:

Additional measures recommended:

*Note. use additional sheets if necessary*

| Accident investigation report (continued) | Sheet no. 4 of 4 | | |
|---|---|---|---|
| Organisation name: | | | |
| Date of accident: | | | |
| Name of injured person: | | | |

| Enclosures<br>If available, enclose the following items: | Yes | No |
|---|---|---|
| 1. Copy of site incident/accident report | | |
| 2. Copy of entry in BI 510A accident book | | |
| 3. Copy of contractor's company accident book entry | | |
| 4. Copy of contractor's accident investigation report | | |
| 5. Copy of safety representative's investigation report | | |
| 6. Copy of first aider's report | | |
| 7. Copy of RIDDOR report to the HSE (F2508 rev) | | |
| 8. Any relevant prohibition or improvement notice, or letter from the HSE | | |
| 9. Minutes of health and safety committee meetings where this accident was discussed | | |
| 10. Photographs relevant to the accident | | |
| 11. Sketches/drawings relevant to the accident | | |
| 12. Copy of induction training register | | |
| 13. Copy of method statement explanation register | | |
| 14. Copy of toolbox talks register | | |
| 15. Copy of skills certificate(s), eg CITB | | |
| 16. Pre-accident risk assessment and method statement | | |
| 17. Post-accident risk assessment and method statement | | |
| 18. Health surveillance records (if appropriate) | | |
| 19. Plant and equipment records | | |
| 20. Manufacturer's instructions in relation to plant and equipment | | |
| 21. Details of hazard warning signs | | |
| 22. COSHH risk assessments | | |
| 23. Manual handling risk assessments | | |
| 24. Witness statements | | |
| **Signature of person investigating the accident/incident:** | | |

| Signed: | Print name: | Date: |
|---|---|---|
| Position: | | |

## A  Useful health and safety tools

### Induction, PPE and signage

**Standard induction/orientation training format**

Every individual working in the facility or on the site must be inducted before starting work. It is important that the induction is thorough and covers all of the headings shown below in a site-specific manner. Thirty minutes is considered to be the minimum appropriate time for the induction, which should be conducted by a competent member of the management team. More time may be required for a large and complex organisation. The content and delivery of the induction programme should be discussed and practised with your safety adviser.

**1. Introduction (1 min)**

- Introduce yourself

- What is induction?

- Reasons for induction – to keep you safe and make sure you remain a fit and healthy person, able to support your family and enjoy life

- The risks faced in the industry or sector

- Outline of facility/project

- Explain who the management team are, and the key employers or contractors

**2. Induction form (3 mins)**

An induction form should be distributed at this stage, completed by those being inducted, and discussed as necessary. The form should ask for disclosure of any health, fitness, drugs or alcohol problems that may affect safety; date of birth to identify young people; understanding and acceptance of the safety rules; previous skills and safety training; ability to understand safety and emergency instructions; and other essential information relevant to safety.

- Hand out forms to all new starters

- Assist them with completion of forms

- If English is poor, use a translator

- Include a section on 'safety rules'

**3. Safety rules – individuals and supervisors (4 mins)**

The site health and safety rules are specific to each facility or project. The rules should be provided in writing and explained as part of the induction.

- Hand out safety rules to all personnel

- If English is poor, use a translator

- Give help or explanation where asked or needed

- Notify all personnel that by completing and signing the induction form they are acknowledging that they have read, understand and accept all the safety rules

### 4. Safety video (10 mins)

Show a health and safety induction video if available. The video adds content and interest but is not a substitute for the full personal training covered here.

- Show all personnel the safety induction video

- Discuss any questions that personnel may have after watching the video

### 5. Risks and hazards (4 mins)

Cover all relevant risks including those from the following checklist. Be careful to include all site-specific hazards.

- Falls from height and falling objects

- Driven plant and vehicles – segregation, access routes, high-visibility vests and so on

- Eyesight risks – goggles; hearing risks – ear protection; risks from work equipment; risks from manual handling; risks from hazardous substances

- Permits to work – hot works, electricity and so on

- Slips and trips – housekeeping, trailing cables, lighting and so on

- Fire – housekeeping, smoking and so on

- Particular dangers to specific trades – target the induction where possible

### 6. Accident and emergency procedures (2 mins)
- First aiders and first aid kits – who and where

- All personal injuries must be entered in the accident book; inform supervisor about near misses and dangerous occurrences

- Fire evacuation procedure – alarms, exits, assembly points, extinguishers

### 7. Supervision and management (1 min)
- Importance of supervision – who is your supervisor?

- Site management and safety – safety is everyone's responsibility

- Notify your supervisor of any problems, risks, hazards, dangers, near misses, dangerous occurrences and so on

- Your supervisor must explain your safe system of work to you

# A  Useful health and safety tools

### 8. Hazard reporting (1 min)

- Notify your supervisor immediately of any hazard and stop work until the problem is fixed

- If the problem doesn't get fixed, see facility/site management

- You have a legal duty to report hazards and can be prosecuted if you don't and someone is subsequently hurt

- Reporting is encouraged, contributions are valued, no fear of retribution, no labelling of people as 'troublemakers'

### 9. Welfare facilities (1 min)

- Canteen, toilets, drying room, lockers, car parking, employee benefits and so on

### 10. PPE (1 min)

- Hard hats, high-visibility vests, safety boots

- Task-specific PPE – goggles, earplugs, dust masks and so on

### 11. Disciplinary procedures (1 min)

- Personal responsibility in law to take care of yourself and others

- Tampering with safety equipment – the consequences

- Instant dismissal – serious offences and repeat offenders

- Verbal warnings

### 12. Questions and discussion (1 min)

- Ask if there are any questions

- Answer all questions openly and honestly

- Each person to sign the induction register

### Personal protective equipment (PPE)

By law, PPE must:

- be used wherever there are risks to health and safety that cannot be adequately controlled in other ways

- be appropriate for the risks involved and the conditions in the workplace

- take account of ergonomic requirements and the state of health of the person who wears it

- fit the wearer correctly

- prevent or adequately control the risks involved without increasing the overall risk

- be designed and manufactured to the applicable standard

- be maintained in good serviceable condition

- be provided free to employees if the risk assessment shows that it is necessary.

In addition, people who have to wear PPE must be trained in how to use it properly.

### Head protection

By law, safety helmets must be worn where there is a foreseeable risk of head injury. The comfort of a safety helmet is greatly increased by the provision of a sweat band, at minimal extra cost.

### Eye protection

Where people are exposed to an impact hazard, the eye protection provided must be Grade I impact goggles that conform to BS EN 166B. For protection from chemical splashes, goggles must comply with BS EN 166-3. Where workers are exposed to radiation hazards that arise from welding or other similar activities, eye protection must conform to BS 1542.

Safety glasses are often used to protect the eyes from dust. These low cost glasses are useful in dusty conditions but are not a suitable substitute where high impact goggles are required.

### Ear protection

Ear protection is discussed in Chapter 6.

### Respiratory protection

Where control measures cannot contain dust, gases or vapours, respiratory protective equipment must be worn. The equipment ranges from face masks containing appropriate filters (through which the wearer breathes normally), to 'positive pressure' masks supplying air from cylinders at above atmospheric pressure (so that substances such as asbestos cannot enter the respiratory system). Choosing the correct type of respiratory protection requires specialist knowledge, so seek advice.

For protection from general nuisance dust, for example when sweeping a floor, disposable masks should be used. However, their adequacy should be assessed on a case-by-case basis.

### Foot protection

Work on construction, demolition and other industrial sites requires safety footwear to protect the feet against a variety of hazards, particularly falling objects, or sharp objects (eg nails) on the ground that could potentially penetrate the sole of the foot.

Foot protection should provide both toe and sole protection. Different grades of footwear are available that can withstand the chemical spillages or extreme heat encountered in specific industries, and may also have slip-resistant soles.

Where people have to pour wet concrete, or work in water, sewage and so on, then industrial Wellington boots must be provided. Boots of this type are heavy duty, with steel toe-caps and pierce-resistant protective mid-soles.

### Hand protection

Gloves of various designs provide protection against a range of industrial hazards, including:

- sharp or dangerously placed objects

- extremes of temperature

- vibration

- skin irritation and dermatitis

- contact with toxic or corrosive liquids.

When choosing which type to wear, consult manufacturers' catalogues or seek specialist advice, particularly where dealing with chemical hazards.

### Body protection

Body protection includes:

- overalls and aprons to protect against asbestos, chemicals and other hazardous substances

- wet weather clothing

- cold weather clothing

- clothing to protect against machinery, eg chainsaws

- high-visibility clothing for working on roads, railways and in airports

- life jackets and buoyancy aids.

### Fall protection

The only acceptable type of harness is the full body type. Belts are not designed for fall arrest but for 'work positioning' by specialist trades. Harnesses must be connected to a lanyard that is a maximum of 2m in length and incorporates a shock-absorbing device. If further movement is required, 'inertia reel' devices (which play out a wire rope that is arrested in the event of a fall) can be used.

Lanyards must be connected to a secure anchorage point above the worker and to a D-ring on the worker's harness. Normally, the D-ring should be fitted to the back of the harness, although in some cases, such as rescue, it should be fitted to the front. Never attach a D-ring to the side of a harness.

Harnesses must be visually inspected on a daily basis, for discolouration (indicating the effects of chemicals or sunlight), tears and nicks, and grit (which can cut fibres). They must also be thoroughly examined every six months and the results recorded.

Workers must be trained in how to check, wear and adjust harnesses.

### Health and safety signs

Regulations have standardised the colour and shape of health and safety signs across the European Union. The objective of these signs is to communicate essential information in a uniform way so that they can be readily understood by all, regardless of reading ability or language. The need for signs should be determined by both common sense and risk assessment, where it has not been possible to eliminate a risk.

| Colour | Purpose | Examples |
|---|---|---|
| Red and white | Prohibition/fire-fighting | No smoking; No entry; No parking; Speed limit; Stop; Slow; Fire equipment (eg extinguishers, alarm bells and fire points) |
| Yellow and black | Warning | Danger – forklift trucks; Danger – slippery surface; Caution – fragile roof; Caution – site entrance; Warning – asbestos insulation |
| Blue and white | Mandatory action | Keep out; Wash hands; Keep fire door shut; Use adjustable guard; Hearing protection must be worn; All visitors must report to reception |
| Green and white | Safe condition | Fire exit; Emergency assembly point; Emergency stop button; First aid station |

# A Useful health and safety tools

## Accident reporting and first aid

**Suggested contents of a first aid kit**

| Contents | Number |
|---|---|
| Guidance card | 1 |
| Assorted sterile plasters (not prescribed but useful) | 20 |
| Sterile eye pad with bandage | 6 |
| Triangular bandage | 6 |
| Safety pins | 12 |
| No. 8 medium unmedicated dressings | 8 |
| No. 9 large unmedicated dressings | 4 |
| Extra large unmedicated dressings | 4 |
| Hygienic resusciade kit | 2 |
| Scissors (stainless steel) | 1 |
| Primapore wound dressing (8.3cm × 6cm) | 1 pack |
| Primapore wound dressing (10cm × 8cm) | 1 pack |
| Sterile adhesive skin sutures (leukostrip) | 2 packs of 4 |
| Sterile skin-cleaning wipes | 2 packs of 10 |
| Assorted fingerstalls | 12 |
| Sterile saline solution (eyewash) 20ml (not necessary if clean water is immediately available) | 10 |
| Packet of 100 pairs of disposable polythene gloves | 1 |
| Emergency foil blanket | 1 |
| *Note: medicines and painkillers are not allowed* | |

### Reporting of injuries, diseases and dangerous occurrences

The Reporting of Injuries, Diseases and Dangerous Occurrences Regulations 1995, known as RIDDOR, require the reporting of:

- deaths

- major injuries

- accidents resulting in more than three days off work

- diseases

- dangerous occurrences.

### Major injuries

The following injuries are reportable:

- fracture other than to fingers, thumbs or toes

- amputation

- dislocation of the shoulder, hip, knee or spine

- loss of sight (temporary or permanent)

- chemical or hot metal burn to the eye, or any penetrating injury to the eye

- injury resulting from an electric shock or electrical burn that leads to unconsciousness; or requiring resuscitation; or requiring admittance to hospital for more than 24 hours

- any other injury leading to hypothermia, heat-induced illness or unconsciousness; or requiring resuscitation; or requiring admittance to hospital for more than 24 hours

- unconsciousness caused by asphyxia or exposure to a harmful substance or biological agent

- acute illness requiring medical treatment, or loss of consciousness arising from absorption of any substance by inhalation, ingestion or through the skin

- acute illness requiring medical treatment where there is reason to believe that this resulted from exposure to a biological agent, its toxins or infected material.

### Diseases

If a doctor notifies you that your employee suffers from a reportable work-related disease, you must report it to the enforcing authority.

Many diseases are reportable; the main ones include:

- certain poisonings

- some skin diseases such as occupational dermatitis, skin cancer, chrome ulcer, oil folliculitis/acne

- lung diseases, including occupational asthma, farmer's lung, pneumoconiosis, asbestosis, mesothelioma

- infections such as Weil's disease (leptospirosis), hepatitis, tuberculosis, anthrax, legionellosis, tetanus

- other conditions such as occupational cancer, certain musculoskeletal disorders, decompression illness, hand–arm vibration syndrome.

### Dangerous occurrences

The following dangerous occurrences are reportable:

- collapse, overturning or failure of load-bearing parts of lifts and lifting equipment

- explosion, collapse or bursting of any closed vessel or associated pipe work

- failure of any freight container in any of its load-bearing parts

- plant or equipment coming into contact with overhead power lines

- electrical short circuit or overload causing fire or explosion

- any unintentional explosion, misfire, failure of demolition to cause the intended collapse, projection of material beyond a site boundary; injury caused by an explosion

- accidental release of a biological agent likely to cause severe human illness

- failure of industrial radiography or irradiation equipment to de-energise or return to its safe position after the intended exposure period

- malfunction of breathing apparatus while in use or when tested prior to use

- failure or endangering of diving equipment, the trapping of a diver, an explosion near a diver, or an uncontrolled ascent

- collapse or partial collapse of a scaffold over 5m high, or erected near water where there could be a risk of drowning after a fall

- unintended collision of a train with any vehicle

- dangerous occurrence at a well (other than a water well)

- dangerous occurrence at a pipeline

- failure of any load-bearing fairground equipment, or derailment or unintended collision of cars or trains

- overturning of a road tanker carrying a dangerous substance, leading to serious damage, fire or release of the substance

- fire or release of a dangerous substance being conveyed by road

- unintended collapse of a building or structure under construction, alteration or demolition where over 5 tonnes of material falls; the collapse of a wall or floor in a place of work; the collapse of any false work (except where these are in relation to offshore workplaces)

- explosion or fire causing suspension of normal work for over 24 hours

- sudden, uncontrolled release in a building of 100kg or more of flammable liquid; 10kg of flammable liquid above its boiling point; 10kg or more of flammable gas; or 500kg of these substances if the release is in the open air

- accidental release of any substance that may damage health.

## Who do I report to?

All accidents, diseases and dangerous occurrences must be reported to the Incident Contact Centre. The Contact Centre was established in April 2001 as a single point of contact for reporting all incidents in the UK.

To report an accident or dangerous occurrence, form F2508 must be used, available from HSE Books. Occupational diseases are reported on form F2508A. The easiest way to report is to access the HSE website at www.hse.gov.uk, where both forms can be completed online and transmitted instantly. The report must be sent within 10 days – late reporting is an offence.

Alternatively, telephone 0845 300 9923, or complete a hard copy form and send it by fax to 0845 300 9924. It can also be sent by post to:

Incident Contact Centre
Caerphilly Business Park
Caerphilly, CF83 3GG

The Incident Contact Centre will forward details of incidents to the relevant enforcing authority, which is the environmental health department of your local authority if your business is:

- office based

- retail or wholesale

- warehousing

- hotel and catering

# A  Useful health and safety tools

- sports and leisure

- residential accommodation, excluding nursing homes

- concerned with places of worship

- pre-school childcare

- mobile vending.

For all other types of business, including construction, the relevant authority is the area office of the HSE.

### Accident statistics

In small organisations a single accident is a significant event that will merit a full investigation, with a view to corrective action to prevent a recurrence. By contrast, a large construction company, for example, may have lots of accidents occurring in different locations and will try to analyse trends across the organisation in order to focus on those particular activities that give rise to the most accidents.

Tools used in benchmarking performance are frequency rates and incidence rates. The frequency rate is calculated as follows:

$$\frac{\text{Number of injuries in one year} \times 100{,}000}{\text{Total number of hours worked}}$$

An approximation of the total number of hours worked is usually used in order to reduce the administrative burden of collecting 'hours worked' figures, calculated as follows:

Average workforce × number of weeks worked × average hours per week per worker

The incidence rate is often used where the hours worked are not accurately known. It is calculated as follows:

$$\frac{\text{Number of injuries in one year} \times 1{,}000}{\text{Average number employed}}$$

It should be noted that while frequency rates for differing periods can be compared, this is mathematically not the case with incidence rates. Therefore, it is always best to adopt the one-year period for comparison purposes.

An organisation with a positive health and safety programme will seek to reduce the accident frequency rate year on year. However, a precursor of such target setting is a culture of consistent and honest accident reporting.

## Toolbox talks on safe working practices

## Basic lifting

Good handling techniques are essential to prevent injury. The correct method of lifting is to use the leg and thigh muscles and to maintain a straight back throughout the lift.

### Before lifting, ask yourself...

- Where is the load to be placed? What handling aids are available? Will I need help with the load? What are the consequences if I have to drop the load? Are there any obstructions? Do I have to carry the load further than 10m? If so, where can I put the load down to get a rest and change grip?

  If you are unsure about the answer to any of these questions, ask your supervisor first before attempting the operation.

### Place the feet

- Keep the feet apart to give a balanced and stable base for lifting. The leading leg should be as far forward as is comfortable.

### Adopt a good posture

- Bend the knees so that the hands, when grasping the load, are as level with the waist as possible. Do not kneel or over-flex the knees. Keep the back straight. If necessary, to get a good grip, lean forward a little over the load. Keep shoulders level and facing in the same direction as the hips.

### Get a firm grip

- Keep the arms within the boundary formed by the legs. The grip must be secure. A hook grip is less tiring than keeping the fingers straight. If it is necessary to vary the grip as the lift proceeds, this needs to be done as smoothly as possible.

**Do not jerk**

- Carry out the lifting movements smoothly, keeping control of the load.

**Move the feet**

- When turning to the side, move the feet – do not twist the trunk.

**Keep close to the load**

- Keep the heaviest side of the load as close to the trunk as possible. If a close approach to the load is not possible, slide it towards you before lifting.

**Put down, then adjust**

- If precise positioning of the load is necessary, put it down first, then slide it to the required position.

**Stability of the load**

- Loads on trolleys must be stable to prevent tipping. Loads in boxes require securing so that they cannot shift and cause a loss of grip. Sudden movement of a liquid in a drum will affect handling, so extra people will be required to lift such a load. Extreme care is needed when handling sheet material, as the grip may be awkward, the load may be affected by the wind, and the view may be obstructed. In such circumstances, an extra person can prove essential, so do not struggle on your own.

## B Toolbox talks on safe working practices

### Noisy environments

In a noisy environment, ear protection must be worn. Where a noise assessment shows that ear protection is needed, it is essential that employees wear it. If ear protection is not worn, or is worn incorrectly or inconsistently, permanent loss of hearing can occur.

- In the task under discussion, it is likely that you will be working in noise levels that could permanently damage your hearing.

- The noise level here has been assessed as ..... dB(A) (*enter figure*). By law you must wear ear protection at 85 dB(A) and above.

- This is why we are issuing ear protection, and why you must wear it. To make it a little easier, you have a choice of earmuffs or earplugs (although in cases where the working environment is extremely noisy, either special earmuffs or a combination of both earplugs and earmuffs may be required). Whatever you choose, to ensure that ear protection is effective you must wear it properly.

- I am responsible for issuing you with ear protection. If you are unhappy about the protection, or if it is damaged or dirty, let me know and I will get it fixed.

- You have a personal duty in law to wear this ear protection, and to look after it properly. If you are found not wearing the ear protection you could be disciplined by the company, or be prosecuted by the authorities.

- In a noisy environment, you must wear the protection at all times. Taking it off for only a few minutes can cause you considerable harm. If you must remove it for any reason, first leave the noisy working environment.

- Earmuffs must fit snugly against the head (*demonstrate*). To facilitate this, tie back long hair and remove large earrings. If you wear spectacles, or have to use safety glasses, then you will be better off fitting earplugs, so that the arms of the glasses do not interfere with the seal. If you have to wear a hard hat, then we provide earmuffs that can be attached to the hat. Even the leads from a personal stereo can reduce the effectiveness of your ear protection.

- Earplugs have to be inserted into the ear canal. Putting them into the front of the ear is far less effective. This is how they are fitted (*demonstrate*).

- These earplugs and earmuffs are clean and in good condition (*show ear protection*). That is how yours should look. Check them daily. You are responsible for maintaining them in this condition, and storing them in your locker when not in use. If you have any problems, let me know and I will sort them out or get you new equipment. Earplugs in particular should be changed regularly – we want you to stay healthy and will be happy to replace them.

- Finally, you will find the areas where you must use ear protection clearly signed. These are ear protection zones, which you must not enter without wearing ear protection.

## B  Toolbox talks on safe working practices

### Vibrating equipment

- The constant use of vibrating equipment such as road breakers or chainsaws can cause an injury known as hand–arm vibration syndrome. The most common form affects the fingers and is known as vibration white finger. The first stages of it are a tingling sensation or pins and needles in the fingers, accompanied by numbness. With continued exposure, the injured person may suffer periodic attacks in which the fingers change colour when exposed to the cold. In mild cases, the whiteness and numbness only affect the tips of the fingers. As the condition becomes more severe, whole fingers, down to the knuckles, become white.

- In severe cases, the attacks are more frequent in cold weather and may last up to an hour, causing considerable pain and loss of manual dexterity. As the condition worsens, the attacks occur even in warm conditions. In very severe cases, blood circulation can be permanently impaired and the fingers look black and blue.

- Because of this I want you to tell me about any tools or work activities that you think may be causing vibration problems. I can then consider what needs to be done to reduce the risk, including supplying you with reduced-vibration equipment.

- You must co-operate with new ways of working that reduce the risk.

- Keep warm at work. Exercise your hands, and wear gloves and extra clothing. Doing so will keep your blood circulation at a normal rate and so help reduce the chance of vibration white finger developing.

- If you smoke, try to stop or cut down. Smoking reduces the blood circulation, making you more susceptible to vibration white finger.

- Use the right tool for the job. Keep it in good working order. Tell your supervisor if anything is wrong with your tool(s) or equipment.

- Work in short sessions rather than all in one go.

- Swap jobs with your work mates on a regular basis.

- Take an active role in health and safety training and any health programme.

- Don't ignore any symptoms. Tell your supervisor and your doctor.

## Fixed scaffolds

This list of dos and don'ts is designed for people who work on scaffolds provided by others.

**You must:**

- check that the platform is properly constructed, ie fully boarded with double guardrails and toe boards (if the scaffold does not have these, do not use it and report to your supervisor)

- use the ladder or the stairs when you wish to go up the scaffold

- only stack material on a scaffold if it is designed to take the load, and then only if you stack it adjacent to the standards or uprights

- report to your supervisor if there are any gaps or 'traps' in the platform or guardrails

- obey any warning signs or tags that are fixed to the scaffold.

**You must not:**

- climb up the outside of a scaffold

- overload the working platform so that it bends

- stack materials in the centre of bays or above the height of guardrails

- move ladder access points

- climb a ladder that is not tied

- remove scaffold ties

- remove cross-braces

- remove boards from the platform

- dig trenches under or near scaffolds

- interfere with any scaffold component

- make your own working platform (however low) out of planks placed on blocks, bricks or oil drums

- erect or use trestles/bandstands as substitutes for scaffolds if they are more than 600mm high, unless they have been specially designed for the purpose.

## Mobile tower scaffolds

- Tower scaffolds provide good access if used properly, but can be dangerous if incorrectly assembled or misused.

- They must be erected by trained and competent people in accordance with the manufacturer's instructions. The erection instructions must be provided by the hirer.

- All components must be checked before they are used to ensure that they are in good condition. Check wheels for effective rotation, and that brake and locking devices work properly.

- Towers must only be used on firm surfaces; where the ground is soft or sloping, adequate support must be provided.

- The platform height should not be more than three times the smallest side of the tower. For instance, if the smallest side of a tower is 1.5m, the maximum platform height is 4.5m. The maximum height can be increased by the use of outriggers.

- When working on the platform, care must be taken to ensure that pulling or pushing actions do not overturn the tower.

- Do not climb on the outside of the tower; instead, use the internal ladder.

- Do not pull heavy items up the side of the tower; instead, use lifting devices. Always check the manufacturer's information for the safe working load and do not exceed it.

- Do not place an external ladder against the tower as this can cause the tower to overturn.

- Towers must be inspected before use, and the results of the inspection must be recorded if erected for more than a week.

**Working platforms must have:**

- trap doors to enable access from inside the tower

- a minimum platform width of 600mm

- double guardrails and toe boards.

**Moving mobile towers**

- Mobile towers must not be moved when people or materials are on the platform.

- Before moving a mobile tower to its new location, ensure that the route is free from obstructions. In particular, ensure that any holes, pits, ducts or gratings are securely covered and that there are no overhead obstructions, eg electric cables or beams.

- After moving and before use, lock the wheels in position.

## B Toolbox talks on safe working practices

### Roofs

- If you fall through or from a roof, you are likely to be severely injured or killed, so take great care.

- You may only work on roofs if you have been properly trained.

- You must be briefed on a safe method of working before work starts.

- Where running lines for safety harnesses have been installed, they must be used.

- Suitable crawling boards or roof ladders must be used on sloping roofs (other than suitably battened roofs).

- Where crawling boards are used for access over fragile material or near roof edges, guardrails are required on either side of the crawling board.

- Roof-edge barriers (or scaffolds) must be erected to prevent personnel and materials from falling.

- Wherever practicable, and for all new industrial roofing, safety nets must be installed under roofing operations.

- Openings in roofs must be securely covered or guarded.

- Access ladders must rise sufficiently above the stepping-off point to provide a safe handhold, and must be secured.

- Where access ladders rise 9m or more above ground level, an intermediate platform with guardrails and toe boards must be provided.

- Where the work is of short duration and the use of guardrails and toe boards is not practicable, use safety harnesses and attach them to suitable anchorage points.

- When using bitumen boilers, use a drip tray.

- Wet, windy (gusts over 30mph) or icy weather can seriously affect your safety during roofing work. If in doubt do not work, or consult your supervisor.

## Excavations

- Before digging, make sure that the electric, water, gas, telephone and other services have been located and are clearly marked.

- All excavations more than 1.2m deep must be supported using steel trench sheets or timbering, or the sides must be sloped to a safe angle. In poor ground, it may be necessary to support shallow trenches below 1.2m in depth. If in doubt, ask your supervisor.

- All practical steps must be taken to prevent accidental collapse of the excavation.

- Ladders must be used for access to and egress from excavations; do not climb on the supports.

- Excavations must be protected to prevent people, vehicles, plant and so on from falling into them.

- Warning barriers must be placed around all shallow excavations and scaffold, or adequate timber barriers placed around excavations more than 1.2m deep.

- All excavations must be checked prior to entry at the start of each shift, and after any event likely to have affected stability, such as heavy rain.

- A competent person must carry out a weekly inspection. The results must be recorded.

- In all excavations, regardless of depth, reinforcement starter bars must be protected. This is to prevent the possibility of injury if someone falls on them.

- Keep soil heaps, materials, tools and vehicles away from edges of excavations.

- Ensure that safety helmets are worn at all times.

- When tipping into excavations, secured stop blocks are required to prevent vehicles falling in.

- Do not jump across an excavation.

- Do not alter or remove any trench supports unless you are authorised to do so.

## B Toolbox talks on safe working practices

### Metalworking

Introduce the talk by explaining the health and safety risks associated with the specific machine used by employees. If there is more than one machine, carry out a separate talk for each.

- Do not eat, drink or smoke in the working area, as harmful substances in the oil and fluids could be ingested.

- Do not wear jewellery, rings or watches under which fluids may collect and be difficult to clean, and which may get trapped in machinery.

- Do not wear loose clothing or a tie, which may get caught up in machinery. For the same reason, tie back long hair.

- Do not wear gloves when operating rotating machinery, as they increase the chance of trapping your hands.

- Do not remove guards, which are there to protect you from the moving parts, to reduce noise, and to save you from being splashed with fluids.

- Use extraction equipment, if it is provided, to protect you from breathing in harmful aerosols, mists or fumes.

- Wash with soap and water regularly to remove oil and fluids that may otherwise irritate your skin and cause dermatitis.

- Use an after-work cream after washing and drying.

- Wear clean overalls and keep oily rags out of pockets to prevent skin complaints.

- Do not clear away swarf with bare hands. Swarf can easily cut hands, increasing the risk of harm from oils and fluids.

- Cover cuts and abrasions with waterproof plasters.

## Arc welding

- Do not wear metallic jewellery, rings or watch straps, all of which can conduct electricity.

- Make sure you know how to change electrodes safely.

- Use an insulated box or hook to rest the electrode holder when welding – not the face shield, clothing or rags, or you could start a fire.

- You must use a visor when welding, chipping or grinding, as there is a danger of arc eye, or weld bead particles entering the eye. Special visors to BS 679 are required.

- You must wear overalls, a protective apron, gloves and safety boots.

- You must set up welding screens to protect other people from arc eye.

- Check your welding leads and connections prior to carrying out work to make sure that they are not damaged.

- Have a suitable fire extinguisher easily accessible near the work area.

- Check where the equipment isolation switch is – it should be easily available.

- If your equipment has fume extraction, make use of it.

- Check with your supervisor to see if the workpiece should be earthed.

- Check with your supervisor to see if you have the correct welding set transformer.

## B Toolbox talks on safe working practices

### Paint spraying

- Use overalls, gloves, an appropriate respirator and eye protection.

- Use barrier cream.

- Remove rings and watches, which can trap paint against the skin.

- Take care with solvents and brush cleaners.

- Never eat, drink or smoke while painting, and wash hands before eating.

- Keep your overalls and respirator clean by regular washing.

- Shower at the end of the day.

- Never stand between the job and the point of extraction, as you will have paint spray drawn towards you.

- Do not over-spray, as this increases the danger of inhaling paint.

- Check the extraction filters in the spray booth are working well and do not need changing.

- Read and assimilate the information contained in the data sheets and risk assessment for the paint you are using.

- Make sure that your respirator filter does not need changing. Speak to your supervisor to make sure that you know how to check it. The type of respirator and filter to use will be given in the paint data sheet.

- Make sure that a competent person checks your respirator thoroughly on a monthly basis.

- Decant paint over a tray and keep lids on paint tins when they are not in use. Have materials ready to clean up any spills.

# Woodworking

**You must:**

- position guards properly

- set all adjustable guards to their lowest position after you have used the machine

- report any defect on the machine, safety device or guard

- use available jigs, stops, guides, fences and so on

- use a push stick, block or spike

- use the correct tools for the job, and make sure that they are sharp

- use a dust mask or special respiratory protection if told to do so by your supervisor

- make sure that dust extraction, if available, is switched on

- ask your supervisor if you are unsure about anything.

**You must not:**

- operate any machine unless you have been properly trained and authorised in writing to do so

- switch on any machine if any safety device or guard is missing, damaged or incorrectly adjusted

- operate any machine if the lighting is poor or if the area around the machine is cluttered or obstructed

- operate any machine in low temperatures, as cold working conditions will make you less alert and therefore less able to work safely

- start up a machine or cut anything unless you are wearing the necessary protective clothing

- adjust guards, clamps, guides, fences and so on while the cutters are running

- remove off-cuts or waste with your hands.

## Kitchen hygiene

Food can be contaminated very easily when it is handled. It is essential that you follow these instructions so that you do not encourage the spread of bacteria, which can make customers, even yourself, very ill. Above all, you must keep your hands clean at all times.

**Keep your hands clean and yourself healthy**

- Wash your hands before starting work, before handling ready-to-eat food, after touching raw food (particularly raw meat or poultry), after using the toilet, after a break, and after blowing your nose.

- If you have diarrhoea or stomach pains, you must let your supervisor know immediately. Also, report any other illness, keep cuts and sores covered with waterproof plasters, and do not cough or sneeze over food.

- Wear clean clothes and a clean apron. Do not wipe your hands on your apron.

- Do not smoke anywhere in the kitchen or restaurant.

- Remove your watch, rings and other jewellery before starting work.

- Do not wear anything that may fall into the food, eg false nails.

- Wear the hat provided, or a hairnet, to keep your hair out of the food and away from dangerous machinery.

**Keep the kitchen clean**

- There is a cleaning checklist that outlines what must be cleaned. Most items are cleaned daily, but some (eg the ham slicer) must be cleaned between each use.

- Disinfectants and floor cleaning chemicals must always be used strictly in accordance with instructions; instructions should be clearly posted in the cleaning materials storage cupboard.

- If you find something wrong when you are cleaning, report it immediately to your supervisor.

### Prevent cross-contamination

- The most important thing to remember is that you must not let raw meat or poultry, or any other food, drip onto ready-to-eat foods such as cooked meats, cheese or salads. If this happens, the bacteria in the meat will be transferred to the ready-to-eat food.

- Different types of food should be stored in their appropriate, designated fridges. If this is impracticable, remember to store raw meat below ready-to-eat food.

- If you are involved in food preparation, you must use the different designated chopping boards and knives for raw and ready-to-eat food, and clean them between uses.

### Cooking

Thorough cooking is very important because it kills harmful bacteria. If food isn't cooked properly, bacteria will survive and whoever eats the food could fall ill.

### Chilling

- Never use any food that is past its 'use by' date.

- Food that needs to be chilled must not be left lying around but put into the fridge without delay.

- Keep chilled food out of the fridge for the shortest time possible.

- Don't overload the fridge.

## Knives and machines in kitchens

### Knives

Knife accidents are common in the catering industry. They usually involve cuts to the hands and fingers.

- Always use the right knife for the job.

- Keep knives sharp – a blunt knife will not cut well and is unsafe.

- Make sure that you have adequate room to use the knife safely.

- Choose the right chopping boards for the purpose.

- Make sure that the knife and chopping boards are clean before starting.

- Always hold the knife firmly.

- Do not cut towards your body.

- Do not leave knives on tables or in washing up water.

- Once used, clean the knife and put it away.

- When carrying a knife, point the blade downwards so that there is no likelihood of accidentally stabbing someone.

- Never try to catch a falling knife.

- Where a significant proportion of your time is spent on cutting, wear a protective gauntlet on the non-knife hand.

### Slicers

Slicers of all types have an exposed cutting edge of the blade, which can cause serious cuts and even amputation.

- Do not use the slicer, or change or sharpen the blade, unless you have been trained and authorised to do so.

- To prevent your hand slipping onto the blade, always use a modern slicer with a blade guard, thumb guard, carriage guard and a meat pusher. Never disable these guards. Check that they are all in use and clean before starting.

- Always use a sharp blade.

- Read the warning notice next to the slicer and check that you know where the emergency stop button is.

- When operating machines, you must not wear loose or frayed clothing, a watch or jewellery.

**Food processors and mixers**

- Unless you have been trained and authorised to do so, do not use a mixer or food processor, or change a blade or mixing tool.

- When the mixer is running, never try to feel the mix or scrape down the bowl.

- While the mixer is running, never reach into the mixer bowl when adding ingredients. Use a mixer bowl extension ring wherever possible.

- Do not attempt to gain access to food processor cutter blades or remove the lid before the blades have stopped and the supply is isolated.

- Unplug or isolate food processors and mixers before cleaning.

## Cooking equipment in kitchens

### Ovens and ranges

- Always use a dry oven cloth or oven gloves when handling hot dishes.

- Always stand to one side when opening an oven door, and open the door slowly.

- Make sure that all of the relevant gas burners are lit and remain alight.

- If the fan interlock does not switch off the fan when the door is opened, report it to your supervisor.

- Do not rest a heavy meat joint on the oven door, and do not leave the door open.

### Steaming oven

- Before use, check that the heating element is covered with water and that the ball float which regulates the water level is operating correctly.

- Do not use if the steam vent is obstructed or not working.

- Open the door a little at a time to let excess steam escape.

### Microwave ovens

- Do not put metal dishes in the microwave.

- Do not put food in a sealed container in the microwave, as it may burst open unexpectedly. Similarly, do not cook eggs in their shells. Pierce any clingfilm that is being used to cover food.

- Do not use the oven if there is a fault, eg a defective door seal.

### Griddles and grillers

- Check that the relevant gas burners are lit and stay alight.

- Always use an oven cloth or oven gloves to handle hot trays.

- Take special care to avoid burns to the eyes and face.

- Regularly clean and remove carbonised fat.

**Deep-fat fryers**

- Do not overfill the fryer with oil.

- Do not top up with oil from large containers.

- Never leave the fryer unattended while it is in use.

- Check that the food is dry before immersing it in oil.

- Take care when shaking food in the basket.

- Clean up spills immediately.

**Boiling pans, brat pans and urns**

- Stand to one side and lift the lid cautiously.

- Never use a brat pan for deep-fat frying.

- Never tilt an urn – it may tip over and scald you.

**First aid**

If you are injured, or if a colleague is injured, get assistance from the first aider immediately. The most common injuries are burns and scalds. To provide first aid for these, immediately immerse the affected part in cold water (or place under cold running water) for at least 10 minutes, or until the pain subsides. Remove anything that may cause constriction if there is swelling, such as rings, belts or shoes. Cover the affected area with a dry sterile dressing. If injuries are serious, the injured party should be sent to hospital.

# B Toolbox talks on safe working practices

## Battery charging

The charging of all batteries, even those that are described as maintenance-free, gives off flammable hydrogen gas. If the gas accumulates and a flame or spark is introduced, then the gas and battery will explode, resulting in acid burns to face, eyes and hands, and other injuries. Sparking most often occurs when battery leads are being connected or disconnected during charging.

### Before you start

- The public and untrained staff must not be allowed to enter the charging room.

- Charging should be carried out in a well-ventilated place, away from any source of flame or spark, and fuel such as petrol.

- Before charging remove any metallic items such as chains, rings and watches.

- Always wear protective goggles and gloves when charging batteries.

- Check that the electrical power supply, charger and battery are in good condition.

### Disconnecting the battery

- Do not rest tools or metallic objects on top of the battery.

- Isolate the battery by turning off the ignition switch and all other switches.

- Always disconnect the earth terminal first (usually, but not always, the negative terminal – check your operating manual).

### Charging

- Disconnect the power supply to the charger.

- Connect the charging leads firmly, positive to positive, negative to negative.

- Follow the manufacturer's instructions and make sure that the battery is topped up.

- Where the manufacturer's instructions indicate, adjust the vent plugs. On large batteries, raise the battery cover to aid ventilation during charging.

- Turn on the power to the charger. If the leads need further adjustment, turn off the power, make the adjustment, and turn back on.

- Do not exceed the recommended rate of charging.

### Reconnecting the battery

- Switch off the power before disconnecting the charging leads.

- Reconnect the earth terminal last.

# B  Toolbox talks on safe working practices

## Chainsaws

This toolbox talk is not intended to replace formal training in the safe use of chainsaws. All chainsaw operators must hold a certificate of training. Only specialist tree surgeons who are trained and experienced should fell or limb trees.

### Setting up and checking the chainsaw

- The saw must be checked thoroughly before use.

- Check the operation of the chain brake. If activated in a kickback situation, the brake stops the saw chain within a fraction of a second. Do not use a chainsaw if it does not have this device.

- Check that the guide bar has been correctly mounted and the chain correctly tensioned. The chain must fit snugly against the underside of the guide bar, but it must still be possible to pull the chain along the bar by hand, with the chain brake disengaged. Check that the chain is sharp.

- Check the smooth action of the throttle trigger and throttle trigger interlock. The throttle trigger must return automatically to idle position. Check that the master control switch moves easily to stop.

- Check that the spark plug boot is secure – a loose boot may cause arcing, which can ignite combustible fumes and cause a fire.

- Check that there are no fuel leaks.

- Check that the chain lubricant tank is full and that the saw chain throws off a small amount of oil, showing that it is correctly lubricated.

- Never attempt to modify the controls or safety devices.

- For safe control, keep the handles dry and clean, free from oil and pitch.

- Do not operate the saw if it is damaged in any way or if it is not properly assembled. Report any faults to your supervisor.

Using the chainsaw

- Always hold the saw firmly with both hands, right hand on the rear handle, even if you are left-handed.

- Take special care to maintain a good footing. Work calmly and carefully, in daylight and with good visibility, and stay alert at all times. Take special care in slippery conditions such as damp, snow and ice, on slopes or uneven ground, and around freshly de-barked logs.

- Run the engine at full throttle, engage the spiked bumper firmly in the wood, and start cutting. Make sure that the spiked bumper is placed securely against the tree or branch, otherwise you may be pulled forward and knocked off balance.

- Position your body clear of the line of cutting.

- Do not cut with the guide bar nose as this may cause kickback, resulting in serious or even fatal injury. Take special care with small, tough branches that may catch the chain, causing kickback. Never cut several branches at once.

- Always pull the saw out of a cut with the chain running. Use extreme caution when re-entering a previous cut.

- Be wary of the log and forces such as sagging or hogging, which may cause the cut to close and pinch the chain.

- Never work off a ladder, in a tree, or on any other insecure support.

- Do not cut above shoulder height, with one hand, or over-reach.

Personal protective equipment

Anyone using a chainsaw, even for a short period, must wear full protective clothing – safety helmet, face visor, ear defenders, close-fitting clothes, chainsaw operator's protective gloves and trousers (made of material that can stop a chainsaw cut), and chainsaw operator's safety boots.

### Forklift trucks

All forklift truck operators must hold a certificate of training and be authorised by their employer to operate the specific type of vehicle.

You must:

- report any defects immediately

- watch out for obstructions

- check that the load is not wider than the gangway or other access routes

- ensure that, when driving on an incline:

  - the fork arms face uphill when carrying a load

  - the fork arms face downhill when no load is carried

  - where fitted, the tilt is adjusted to suit the gradient and the fork arms are raised to provide ground clearance

- avoid making sudden stops

- slow down for corners and sound the horn where necessary

- travel with fork arms lowered while maintaining ground clearance

- carry out daily inspections

- lower loads as soon as they are clear of the racking or other obstructions

- lower heavy loads slowly

- leave the truck with the fork arms fully lowered

- switch off and remove the key when leaving the truck

- take note of the load capacity indicator, where fitted

- know the weight of your laden truck and observe floor loading limits.

You must not:

- lift loads that exceed a truck's rated capacity

- travel forward if the load obscures your view

- carry passengers

- block fire-fighting equipment or exits by parking or stacking in front of them

- use attachments unless you have been trained and authorised to do so

- allow people to walk under a raised mast or loads

- travel with a raised load

- allow unauthorised people to operate the truck.

## Sewers and watercourses

* When working in sewers and watercourses, there is a risk of contracting an infection known as Weil's disease or leptospirosis. It is caused by contact with rats' urine or contaminated water. The disease is serious and can prove fatal, yet it is difficult for doctors to diagnose as the symptoms are similar to flu. For this reason it is necessary for people working in sewers and watercourses to carry a card that can be shown to their doctor if they feel unwell. (Card is shown on the page opposite.)

* In addition, you should be inoculated against tetanus and poliomyelitis. Check that you have these inoculations and that they are still current.

* If you feel off colour or develop flu/jaundice-like symptoms following contact with sewage or any stretch of water to which rodents or other animals have access, consult your doctor or hospital.

* Protective clothing and footwear must be worn and be thoroughly cleaned after use.

* Lanolin-based barrier cream should be used before work. After work, the hands, face and forearms should be washed with hot water and soap. Fingernails should be scrubbed, but not the skin, as this can roughen the skin surface and increase the risk of infection.

* The smallest scratch must be washed immediately and be covered with an antiseptic waterproof dressing.

* Every accident at work, however minor, must be reported.

* You must not eat, drink or smoke until you have thoroughly washed.

* Hands should be kept away from the face while at work. If the eyes are accidentally splashed or feel irritated, you should leave the workplace and obtain first aid.

* When working near or over water, life jackets must be worn.

* Report any signs of vermin to your pest control officer, line manager, supervisor or whoever is responsible, so that the necessary remedial action can be taken.

* You must carry a card (*show card*) which states that you work in an environment in which there is a possibility of contact with sewage or rats. It will help your doctor or hospital to diagnose any symptoms correctly. Always show it if you seek medical attention.

* Now read the card.

**Example of a card (all four pages) that should be carried by people at risk from Weil's disease (leptospirosis)**

Company name

Precautions against risk of illness for those working in contact with sewage or rat-infested premises

This card is for

*your* protection

Whenever you go to your doctor or a hospital on account of illness, show this card and make sure that those attending you know your occupation

Employee's name: _____

_____

Address: _____

_____

_____

_____

Occupation: _____

_____

Doctor's name: _____

_____

Address: _____

_____

_____

_____

Telephone no: _____

The above information and any subsequent changes should be notified to your employer.

**For the attention of your medical attendant**

**Weil's disease (leptospirosis)**

The holder of this card is engaged in work that might bring him or her into contact with sewage or water that may contain leptospira.

None of the symptoms of early leptospirosis are pathognomonic, and diagnosis is based on laboratory investigations. Should you suspect that the holder has been infected, please notify your local environmental health officer, who will advise you on where these investigations can be undertaken in your area.

**Instructions to employee**
**Precautions against risk of leptospiral jaundice**
- After working in contact with sewage or anything that might have been contaminated by it, wash your hands and forearms thoroughly with soap and water. If your clothes or boots are contaminated with sewage, wash thoroughly after handling them. It is particularly important to do this before taking any food or drink. Wet protective clothing should be dried as soon as possible.
- Infection may enter through breaks in skin, so thorough first aid treatment of all wounds is important. Take particular care to wash cuts, scratches or abrasions of the skin thoroughly, as soon as possible, whether the injury was caused at work or not. Apply an antiseptic to the wound with a clean piece of cloth or cotton wool, and protect it with a strip of gauze completely covered with adhesive plaster. Keep the wound covered until it has healed. Antiseptic gauze and impermeable plaster are available at your place of work.
- If you suffer any cut, scratch or abrasion of the skin, it must be covered with a waterproof plaster before entering the place of work.
- Avoid rubbing your nose or mouth with your hands during work.
- Keep this card in a safe place and, whenever you go to your doctor or to a hospital on account of illness, show the card and make sure that those attending you know your occupation.
- Every accident at work, however trivial, must be reported.

# Legislation and further guidance

Unless otherwise stated, all of the following publications are available from HSE Books.

HSE Books
PO Box 1999
Sudbury
Suffolk, CO10 2WA
t +44 (0)1787 881165
f +44 (0)1787 313995
www.hsebooks.com

Some HSE leaflets and guidance documents are downloadable free from the website. Both free and priced publications can be ordered online.

Another useful Web address is www.hse.gov.uk. The site has links to HSE Books and to free online copies of recent legislation.

### Chapter 1 – Policy

Health and Safety at Work etc Act 1974

Successful health and safety management (HSG65)

### Chapter 2 – Risk thinking

Management of Health and Safety at Work Regulations 1999 (as amended), and approved code of practice and guidance (L21)

Successful health and safety management (HSG65)

Five steps to risk assessment (INDG163(rev1))

A guide to risk assessment requirements (INDG218)

### Chapter 3 – Management

Management of Health and Safety at Work Regulations 1999 (as amended), and approved code of practice and guidance (L21)

Successful health and safety management (HSG65)

Principles of Health and Safety at Work (available from IOSH Services Limited, t +44 (0)1787 249293)

Working Time Regulations 1998 (as amended)

Safety Representatives and Safety Committees Regulations 1977

Health and Safety (Consultation with Employees) Regulations 1996, and guidance (L95)

Health and Safety Information for Employees Regulations 1989 (modified and repealed)

### Chapter 4 – Premises

Workplace (Health, Safety and Welfare) Regulations 1992

How to deal with sick building syndrome (HSG132)

Control of Asbestos at Work Regulations 2002

### Chapter 5 – Fire

Regulatory Reform (Fire Safety) Order 2005

Management of Health and Safety at Work Regulations 1999 (as amended), and approved code of practice and guidance (L21)

Fire Precautions Act 1971*

Fire Certificates (Special Premises) Regulations 1976*

Fire Safety and Safety of Places of Sport Act 1987

Fire Precautions (Factories, Offices, Shops and Railway Premises) Order 1989*

Fire Precautions (Workplace) Regulations 1997*

Fire Precautions (Workplace) (Amendment) Regulations 1999*

Fire safety – an employer's guide

Fire safety in construction work (HSG168)

Building Regulations Approved Document B – Fire safety
(available at
www.odpm.gov.uk/stellent/groups/odpm_buildreg/documents/divisionhomepage/br0043.hcsp)

Dangerous Substances and Explosive Atmospheres Regulations 2002

### Chapter 6 – Health

Manual Handling Operations Regulations 1992 (as amended), and guidance (L23)

Backs for the future – safe manual handling in construction (HSG149)

Getting to grips with manual handling (INDG143(rev2))

Upper limb disorders in the workplace (HSG60(rev))

Aching arms (or RSI) in small businesses (INDG171(rev1))

Noise at Work Regulations 2005, and guidance (L108)

Noise at work – advice for employers (INDG362)

* Will be repealed by the Regulatory Reform (Fire Safety) Order 2005, due to come into force in 2006

Control of Vibration at Work Regulations 2005

Hand-arm vibration (HSG88)

Vibration solutions (HSG170)

Hand arm vibration syndrome in the workplace (available from Offshore Contractors' Association, 58 Queens Road, Aberdeen, AB15 4YE, or from http://step.steel-sci.org)

Control of Substances Hazardous to Health Regulations 2002 (as amended), and approved code of practice (L5)

COSHH: a brief guide to the regulations (INDG136(rev3))

Respiratory sensitisers and COSHH (INDG95(rev2))

The selection, use and maintenance of respiratory protective equipment – a practical guide (HSG53) (see www.tsoshop.co.uk/bookstore.asp)

Preventing dermatitis at work (INDG233)

Health risks management: a guide to working with solvents (HSG188)

Working safely with solvents: a guide to safe working practices (INDG273)

Ionising Radiations Regulations 1999

Control of Lead at Work Regulations 2002, and approved code of practice and guidance (L132)

### Chapter 7 – Construction and demolition
Many regulations have a bearing on construction and demolition activities, including most of the above. The following are of particular relevance to construction.

Construction (Design and Management) Regulations 1994 (as amended)

Managing health and safety in construction (HSG224)

Construction (Health, Safety and Welfare) Regulations 1996

Construction (Head Protection) Regulations 1989

Working at Height Regulations 2005

Safe use of lifting equipment: Lifting Operations and Lifting Equipment Regulations 1998, and approved code of practice and guidance (L113)

Safe use of work equipment: Provision and Use of Work Equipment Regulations 1998, and approved code of practice and guidance (L22)

## C Legislation and further guidance

Protecting the public – your next move (HSG151)

The safe use of vehicles on construction sites (HSG144)

Health and safety in excavations – be safe and shore (HSG185)

Backs for the future – safe manual handling in construction (HSG149)

Health and safety in roof work (HSG33)

### Chapter 8 – Workshops and factories

Safe use of work equipment: Provision and Use of Work Equipment Regulations 1998, and approved code of practice and guidance (L22)

Safe use of woodworking machinery (L114)

Health and safety in engineering workshops (HSG129)

Safety in the use of abrasive wheels (HSG17)

HSE woodworking information sheets (see www.hse.gov.uk/pubns/woodindx.htm)

### Chapter 9 – Hotels, restaurants and catering

Food Safety Act 1990

Food Premises (Registration) Regulations 1991 (as amended)

Food Safety (General Food Hygiene) Regulations 1995 (as amended)

Food Safety (Temperature Control) Regulations 1995

HSE catering information sheets (see www.hse.gov.uk/pubns/caterdex.htm)

The Food Standards Agency (see www.food.gov.uk)

Manual handling in laundries: Canadian Centre for Occupational Health and Safety (see www.ccohs.ca/oshanswers/occup_workplace/laundry.html)

### Chapter 10 – Events and exhibitions

Managing crowds safely (HSG154)

The event safety guide: a guide to health, safety and welfare at music and similar events (HSG195)

Temporary demountable structures: guidance on procurement, design and use (available from the Institution of Structural Engineers, t +44 (0)207 235 4535)

### Chapter 11 – Grounds maintenance, parks and golf courses

Health and safety in golf course management and maintenance (HSG79)

Control of Pesticides Regulations 1986 (as amended)

### Chapter 12 – Offices, shops and warehousing
Health and Safety (Display Screen Equipment) Regulations 1992 (as amended)

Safety in working with lift trucks (HSG6)

Rider-operated lift trucks: operator training (L117)

### Chapter 13 – Maintenance and facilities management
Improving maintenance – a guide to reducing human error

Electricity at Work Regulations 1989

Gas Safety (Installation and Use) Regulations 1998

Lighting at work (HSG38)

Legionnaires' disease – the control of legionella bacteria in water systems (L8)

Control of Asbestos at Work Regulations 2002

Work with asbestos which does not normally require a licence (L27)

Work with asbestos insulation, asbestos coating and asbestos insulating board (L28)

Asbestos essentials task manual (HSG210)

Hazardous Waste (England and Wales) Regulations 2005

Confined Spaces Regulations 1997

### Chapter 14 – Contractors
Successful health and safety management (HSG65)

Construction (Design and Management) Regulations 1994 (as amended)

Managing health and safety in construction (HSG224)

### Appendix A – Useful health and safety tools
Reporting of Injuries, Diseases and Dangerous Occurrences Regulations 1995

Personal Protective Equipment at Work Regulations 1992

Health and Safety (Safety Signs and Signals) Regulations 1996

Health and Safety (First Aid) Regulations 1981

*Remember that all legislation is subject to revision and the documents referred to in this section and the information provided throughout the book may be updated from time to time.*